ST. THOMAS AQUINAS

ST. FRANCIS OF ASSISI

G.K. CHESTERTON

# ST. THOMAS AQUINAS

*with an introduction by Ralph McInerny*

# ST. FRANCIS OF ASSISI

*with an introduction by Joseph Pearce*

IN ONE VOLUME

IGNATIUS PRESS SAN FRANCISCO

Original editions:

*St. Thomas Aquinas*
Sheed and Ward, Inc., New York, © 1933

*St. Francis of Assisi*
Sheed and Ward, Inc., New York, © 1923

Cover art:

*Portrait of Saint Thomas Aquinas*
School of Fra Bartolomeo (1472–1517)
Museo di San Marco, Florence, Italy
Copyright Nicolo Orsi Battaglini/Art Resource, New York

*Saint Francis*
Margaritone d'Arezzo (13th c.)
Museo d'Arte Medioevale e Moderna
Copyright Scala/Art Resource, New York

Cover design by Roxanne Mei Lum


ISBN 978-0-89870-945-2
Library of Congress control number 2002105237
Printed in the United States of America ♾

CONTENTS

## ST. THOMAS AQUINAS



## ST. FRANCIS OF ASSISI

# ST. THOMAS AQUINAS

# ST. THOMAS AQUINAS

## AN INTRODUCTION

by Ralph McInerny

Chesterton was a genius in that he knew things he had not learned and learned things the rest of us miss. But how in the world he knew enough about Thomas Aquinas to write this remarkable little book is still something of a mystery—or perhaps only a proof of his genius.

Maisie Ward's account of the composition of the book, given in her 1943 biography of Chesterton—still, I think, the best—seems scarcely credible. As Ward got the story from Chesterton's secretary Dorothy Collins, Chesterton, flush from the success of his book on St. Francis, gladly took on the task of writing about Thomas Aquinas. Now there is nothing in Chesterton's background that suggests that he studied Aquinas. Nonetheless, according to Collins, he first dictated half the book and then asked if she would not run up to London and bring him back some works on St. Thomas. She did; he leafed through them briefly, and then he dictated the rest of the book. How in the world could he have done this? One thing is clear: those who have spent a lifetime studying St. Thomas read this little work of Chesterton with awe. Étienne Gilson, the great historian of medieval thought and ferocious Thomist, regarded it as one of the best books on Thomas.

There are two major themes that run through this book and which I think explain at least in part the mystery of its composition. First, there is the way that Chesterton goes unerringly to the central teaching of Thomas, namely, that faith and reason are compatible, and that there cannot be a conflict between them. Latin Averroism, the more or less chuckle-headed way in which young masters of arts in thirteenth-century Paris thought they could think one thing and believe its opposite, holding one thing by faith and its contradictory by reason, elicited the wrath of Aquinas, something not easy to do. But he saw in Latin Averroism the height, or depth, of impiety. The Latin Averroist was saying in effect that God asks us to believe what we know to be false.

The complementarity of faith and reason is in many ways the centerpiece of Chesterton's account of Thomas, and it is as relevant now as it ever was. Believers have a woeful tendency to speak of the faith as unrelated to reason, as if it were not reasonable to believe in the God of Revelation. The technical name for this distrust of reason is Fideism. Chesterton's little book will inoculate the reader against any tendency to fideism.

The second great theme of the book explains I think how Chesterton found himself so immediately on Thomas' wavelength. Like Thomas, Chesterton was a champion of the common man, that is, of the ordinary human being's capacity to know things for sure. Not only are there questions no one can fail to ask, there are answers to these questions that are common to the race. John Paul II made this point in *Fides et Ratio* with the concept of "implicit philosophy". For Thomas such common sense knowledge provided the starting point of philosophy. And it was never a matter of "Hang on to the brush, I'm taking away the ladder." However sophisticated philosophical discussions might become, if they did not retain an umbilical relation to what everyone knows, they become fantastic and false. After Aquinas, it became usual for philosophers to imagine that their task was to replace the knowledge we had prior to the study of philosophy, to show that it was all deception and error, to erase it from our minds. Thomas has long been seen as an antidote to such nonsense. That was the sense of the Thomistic revival inaugurated by Leo XIII in *Aeterni Patris*. We can be sure that it was Chesterton's own deep sense of the capacity of the human mind in every person that provided an affinity with the thought of Thomas Aquinas.

And of course the book is a delight to read. Chesterton has a rollicking style. He was an author in love with the English language. Belloc wrote a little book called *The Place of Gilbert Chesterton in English Letters*. That a man who thought of himself a journalist, who wrote for the evanescent pages of periodicals, should have dashed off so many immortal pages is one of those marks of genius impossible to ignore. Chesterton wrote of Dickens and Chaucer; he composed verse that is disciplined, lyrical, elevating—and often extremely funny. Chesterton once said that there is a divine attribute we are too prone to forget, God's sense of humor, his laughter. You cannot read a paragraph of Chesterton without having to smile, or a page without laughing aloud. It would have been one of his paradoxes to note that anything worth taking seriously is worth laughing about. "Wherever the Catholic sun doth shine, there's plenty of laughter and good red wine." There is a lot of wine in Chesterton, and we can wonder what became of beer. But wine predominates in Austen and Dickens and Trollope too. In Chesterton's case, as in Belloc's, the preference for wine might have something to do with a dislike of the beer barons who bought their way into the peerage.

*Orthodoxy* was written before Chesterton became a Catholic. *The Everlasting Man*, which is even better, came after his conversion. But there is perhaps no more Catholic work in the Chestertonian canon than *St. Thomas Aquinas*, sometimes titled *The Dumb Ox*. In it a great and simple mind speaks to us of another great and simple mind. We are the better for having read it.

TO

DOROTHY COLLINS

WITHOUT WHOSE HELP THE AUTHOR
WOULD HAVE BEEN MORE
THAN NORMALLY HELPLESS

# INTRODUCTORY NOTE

This book makes no pretence to be anything but a popular sketch of a great historical character who ought to be more popular. Its aim will be achieved, if it leads those who have hardly even heard of St. Thomas Aquinas to read about him in better books. But from this necessary limitation certain consequences follow, which should perhaps be allowed for from the start.

First, it follows that the tale is told very largely to those who are not of the communion of St. Thomas; and who may be interested in him as I might be in Confucius or Mahomet. Yet, on the other hand, the very need of presenting a clean-cut outline involved its cutting into other outlines of thought, among those who may think differently. If I write a sketch of Nelson mainly for foreigners, I may have to explain elaborately many things that all Englishmen know, and possibly cut out, for brevity, many details that many Englishmen would like to know. But, on the other side, it would be difficult to write a very vivid and moving narrative of Nelson, while entirely concealing the fact that he fought with the French. It would be futile to make a sketch of St. Thomas and conceal the fact that he fought with heretics; and yet the fact itself may embarrass the very purpose for which it is employed. I can only express the hope, and indeed the confidence, that those who regard me as the heretic will hardly blame me for expressing my own convictions, and certainly not for expressing my hero's convictions. There is only one point upon which such a question concerns this very simple narrative. It is the conviction, which I have expressed once or twice in the course of it, that the sixteenth-century schism was really a belated revolt of the thirteenth-century pessimists. It was a back-wash of the old

Augustinian Puritanism against the Aristotelian liberality. Without that, I could not place my historical figure in history. But the whole is meant only for a rough sketch of a figure in a landscape; and not of a landscape with figures.

Second, it follows that in any such simplification I can hardly say much of the philosopher beyond showing that he had a philosophy. I have only, so to speak, given samples of that philosophy. Lastly, it follows that it is practically impossible to deal adequately with the theology. A lady I know picked up a book of selections from St. Thomas, with a commentary; and began hopefully to read a section with the innocent heading, "The Simplicity of God." She then laid down the book with a sigh and said, "Well, if that's His simplicity, I wonder what His complexity is like." With all respect to that excellent Thomistic commentary, I have no desire to have this book laid down, at the very first glance, with a similar sigh. I have taken the view that the biography is an introduction to the philosophy, and that the philosophy is an introduction to the theology; and that I can only carry the reader just beyond the first stage of the story.

Third, I have not thought it necessary to notice those critics who, from time to time, desperately play to the gallery by reprinting paragraphs of medieval demonology in the hope of horrifying the modern public merely by an unfamiliar language. I have taken it for granted that educated men know that Aquinas and all his contemporaries, and all his opponents for centuries after, did believe in demons, and similar facts, but I have not thought them worth mentioning here, for the simple reason that they do not help to detach or distinguish the portrait. In all that, there was no disagreement between Protestant or Catholic theologians, for all the hundreds of years during which there was any theology; and St. Thomas is not notable as holding such views, except in holding them rather mildly. I have not discussed such matters, not because I have any reason to conceal them, but because they do not in any way personally concern the one person whom it is here my business to reveal. There is hardly room, even as it is, for such a figure in such a frame.

# I

# ON TWO FRIARS

Let me at once anticipate comment by answering to the name of that notorious character, who rushes in where even the Angels of the Angelic Doctor might fear to tread. Some time ago I wrote a little book of this type and shape on St. Francis of Assisi; and some time after (I know not when or how, as the song says, and certainly not why) I promised to write a book of the same size, or the same smallness on St. Thomas Aquinas. The promise was Franciscan only in its rashness; and the parallel was very far from being Thomistic in its logic. You can make a sketch of St. Francis: you could only make a plan of St. Thomas, like the plan of a labyrinthine city. And yet in a sense he would fit into a much larger or a much smaller book. What we really know of his life might be pretty fairly dealt with in a few pages; for he did not, like St. Francis, disappear in a shower of personal anecdotes and popular legends. What we know, or could know, or may eventually have the luck to learn, of his work, will probably fill even more libraries in the future than it has filled in the past. It was allowable to sketch St. Francis in an outline; but with St. Thomas everything depends on the filling up of the outline. It was even medieval in a manner to illuminate a miniature of the Poverello, whose very title is a diminutive. But to make a digest, in the tabloid manner, of the Dumb Ox of Sicily passes all digestive experiments in the matter of an ox in a tea-cup. But we must hope it is possible to make an outline of biography, now that anybody seems capable of writing an outline of history or an outline of anything. Only in the present case the outline is rather an outsize. The gown that could contain the colossal friar is not kept in stock.

I have said that these can only be portraits in outline. But the concrete contrast is here so striking, that even if we actually saw the two human figures in outline, coming over the hill in their friar's gowns, we should find that contrast even comic. It would be like seeing, even afar off, the silhouettes of Don Quixote and Sancho Panza, or of Falstaff and Master Slender. St. Francis was a lean and lively little man; thin as a thread and vibrant as a bowstring; and in his motions like an arrow from the bow. All his life was a series of plunges and scampers; darting after the beggar, dashing naked into the woods, tossing himself into the strange ship, hurling himself into the Sultan's tent and offering to hurl himself into the fire. In appearance he must have been like a thin brown skeleton autumn leaf dancing eternally before the wind; but in truth it was he that was the wind.

St. Thomas was a huge heavy bull of a man, fat and slow and quiet; very mild and magnanimous but not very sociable; shy, even apart from the humility of holiness; and abstracted, even apart from his occasional and carefully concealed experiences of trance or ecstasy. St. Francis was so fiery and even fidgety that the ecclesiastics, before whom he appeared quite suddenly, thought he was a madman. St. Thomas was so stolid that the scholars, in the schools which he attended regularly, thought he was a dunce. Indeed, he was the sort of schoolboy, not unknown, who would much rather be thought a dunce than have his own dreams invaded, by more active or animated dunces. This external contrast extends to almost every point in the two personalities. It was the paradox of St. Francis that while he was passionately fond of poems, he was rather distrustful of books. It was the outstanding fact about St. Thomas that he loved books and lived on books; that he lived the very life of the clerk or scholar in *The Canterbury Tales*, who would rather have a hundred books of Aristotle and his philosophy than any wealth the world could give him. When asked for what he thanked God most, he answered simply, "I have understood every page I ever read." St. Francis was very vivid in his poems and rather vague in his documents; St. Thomas devoted his whole life to documenting whole systems of Pagan and Christian literature; and occasionally wrote a hymn like a man taking a holiday. They saw the same problem from different angles, of simplicity and subtlety; St. Francis thought it would be enough to pour out his heart to the Mohammedans, to persuade them not to worship Mahound. St. Thomas bothered his head with every hair-splitting distinction and deduction, about the Absolute or the Accident, merely to prevent them from misunderstanding Aristotle. St. Francis was the son of a shopkeeper, or middle class trader; and while his whole life was a revolt against the mercantile life of his father, he retained none the less, something of the quickness and social adaptability which makes the market hum like a hive. In the common phrase, fond as he was of green fields, he did not let the grass grow under his feet. He was what American millionaires and gangsters call a live wire. It is typical of the mechanistic moderns that, even when they try to imagine a live thing, they can only think of a mechanical metaphor from a dead thing. There is such a thing as a live worm; but there is no such thing as a live wire. St. Francis would have heartily agreed that he was a worm; but he was a very live worm. Greatest of all foes to the go-getting ideal, he had certainly abandoned getting, but he was still going. St. Thomas, on the other hand, came out of a world where he might have enjoyed leisure, and he remained one of those men whose labour has something of the placidity of leisure. He was a hard worker, but nobody could possibly mistake him for a hustler. He had something indefinable about him, which marks those who work when they need not work. For he was by birth a gentleman of a great house, and such repose can remain as a habit, when it is no longer a motive. But in him it was expressed only in its most amiable elements; for instance, there was possibly something of it in his effortless courtesy and patience. Every saint is a man before he is a saint; and a saint may be made of every sort or kind of man; and most of us will choose between these different types according to our different tastes. But I will confess that, while the romantic glory of St. Francis has lost nothing of its glamour for me, I have in later years grown to feel almost as much affection, or in some aspects even more, for this man who unconsciously inhabited a large heart and a large head, like one inheriting a large house, and exercised there an equally generous if rather more absent-minded hospitality. There are moments when St. Francis, the most unworldly man who ever walked the world, is almost too efficient for me.

St. Thomas Aquinas has recently reappeared, in the current culture of the colleges and the salons, in a way that would have been quite startling even ten years ago. And the mood that has concentrated on him is doubtless very different from that which popularised St. Francis quite twenty years ago.

The Saint is a medicine because he is an antidote. Indeed that is why the saint is often a martyr; he is mistaken for a poison because he is an antidote. He will generally be found restoring the world to sanity by exaggerating whatever the world neglects, which is by no means always the same element in every age. Yet each generation seeks its saint by instinct; and he is not what the people want, but rather what the people need. This is surely the very much mistaken meaning of those words to the first saints, "Ye are the salt of the earth," which caused the Ex-Kaiser to remark with all solemnity that his beefy Germans were the salt of the earth; meaning thereby merely that they were the earth's beefiest and therefore best. But salt seasons and preserves beef, not because it is like beef; but because it is very unlike it. Christ did not tell his apostles that they were only the excellent people, or the only excellent people, but that they were the exceptional people; the permanently incongruous and incompatible people; and the text about the salt of the earth is really as sharp and shrewd and tart as the taste of salt. It is because they were the exceptional people, that they must not lose their exceptional quality. "If salt lose its savour, wherewith shall it be salted?" is a much more pointed question than any mere lament over the price of the best beef. If the world grows too worldly, it can be rebuked by the Church; but if the Church grows too worldly, it cannot be adequately rebuked for worldliness by the world.

Therefore it is the paradox of history that each generation is converted by the saint who contradicts it most. St. Francis had a curious and almost uncanny attraction for the Victorians; for the nineteenth century English who seemed superficially to be most complacent about their commerce and their common sense. Not only a rather complacent Englishman like Matthew Arnold, but even the English Liberals whom he criticised for their complacency, began slowly to discover the mystery of the Middle Ages through the strange story told in feathers and flames in the hagiographical pictures of Giotto. There was something in the story of St. Francis that pierced through all those English qualities which are most famous and fatuous, to all those English qualities which are most hidden and human: the secret softness of heart; the poetical vagueness of mind; the love of landscape and of animals. St. Francis of Assisi was the only medieval Catholic who really became popular in England on his own merits. It was largely because of a subconscious feeling that the modern world had neglected those particular merits. The English middle classes found their only missionary in the figure, which of all types in the world they most despised; an Italian beggar.

So, as the nineteenth century clutched at the Franciscan romance, precisely because it had neglected romance, so the twentieth century is already clutching at the Thomist rational theology, because it has neglected reason. In a world that was too stolid, Christianity returned in the form of a vagabond; in a world that has grown a great deal too wild, Christianity has returned in the form of a teacher of logic. In the world of Herbert Spencer men wanted a cure for indigestion; in the world of Einstein they want a cure for vertigo. In the first case, they dimly perceived the fact that it was after a long fast that St. Francis sang the Song of the Sun and the praise of the fruitful earth. In the second case, they already dimly perceived that, even if they only want to understand Einstein, it is necessary first to understand the use of the understanding. They begin to see that, as the eighteenth century thought itself the age of reason, and the nineteenth century thought itself the age of common sense, the twentieth century cannot as yet even manage to think itself anything but the age of uncommon nonsense. In those conditions the world needs a saint; but above all, it needs a philosopher. And these two cases do show that the world, to do it justice, has an instinct for what it needs. The earth was really very flat, for those Victorians who most vigorously repeated that it was round, and Alverno of the Stigmata stood up as a single mountain in the plain. But the earth is an earthquake, a ceaseless and apparently endless earthquake, for the moderns for whom Newton has been scrapped along with Ptolemy. And for them there is something more steep and even incredible than a mountain; a piece of really solid ground; the level of the level-headed man. Thus in our time the two saints have appealed to two generations, an age of romantics and an age of sceptics; yet in their own age they were doing the same work; a work that has changed the world.

Again, it may be said truly that the comparison is idle, and does not fit in well even as a fancy; since the men were not properly even of the same generation or the same historic moment. If two friars are to be presented as a pair of Heavenly Twins, the obvious comparison is between St. Francis and St. Dominic. The relations of St. Francis and St. Thomas were, at nearest, those of uncle and nephew; and my fanciful excursus may appear only a highly profane version of "Tommy make room for your uncle"[1]. For if St. Francis and St. Dominic were the great twin brethren, Thomas was obviously the first great son of St. Dominic, as was his friend Bonaventure of St. Francis. Nevertheless, I have a reason (indeed two reasons) for taking as a text the accident of two title-pages; and putting St. Thomas beside St. Francis, instead of pairing him off with Bonaventure the Franciscan. It is because the comparison, remote and perverse as it may seem, is really a sort of short cut to the heart of history; and brings us by the most rapid route to the real question of the life and work of St. Thomas Aquinas. For most people now have a rough but picturesque picture in their minds of the life and work of St. Francis of Assisi. And the shortest way of telling the other story is to say that, while the two men were thus a contrast in almost every feature, they were really doing the same thing. One of them was doing it in the world of the mind and the other in the world of the worldly. But it was the same great medieval movement; still but little understood. In a constructive sense, it was more important than the Reformation. Nay, in a constructive sense, it was the Reformation.

About this medieval movement there are two facts that must first be emphasised. They are not, of course, contrary

[1] "Tommy Make Room for Your Uncle" is a song written by T. S. Lansdale in 1875.

facts, but they are perhaps answers to contrary fallacies. First, in spite of all that was once said about superstition, the Dark Ages and the sterility of Scholasticism, it was in every sense a movement of enlargement, always moving towards greater light and even greater liberty. Second, in spite of all that was said later on about progress and the Renaissance and forerunners of modern thought, it was almost entirely a movement of orthodox theological enthusiasm, unfolded from within. It was *not* a compromise with the world, or a surrender to heathens or heretics, or even a mere borrowing of external aids, even when it did borrow them. In so far as it did reach out to the light of common day, it was like the action of a plant which by its own force thrusts out its leaves into the sun; not like the action of one who merely lets daylight into a prison.

In short, it was what is technically called a Development in doctrine. But there seems to be a queer ignorance, not only about the technical, but the natural meaning of the word Development. The critics of Catholic theology seem to suppose that it is not so much an evolution as an evasion; that it is at best an adaptation. They fancy that its very success is the success of surrender. But that is not the natural meaning of the word Development. When we talk of a child being well-developed, we mean that he has grown bigger and stronger with his own strength; not that he is padded with borrowed pillows or walks on stilts to make him look taller. When we say that a puppy develops into a dog, we do not mean that his growth is a gradual compromise with a cat; we mean that he becomes more doggy and not less. Development is the expansion of all the possibilities and implications of a doctrine, as there is time to distinguish them and draw them out; and the point here is that the enlargement of medieval theology was simply the full comprehension of that theology. And it is of primary importance to realise this fact first, about the time of the great Dominican and the first Franciscan, because their tendency, humanistic and naturalistic in a hundred ways, was truly the development of the supreme doctrine, which was also the dogma of all dogmas. It is in this that the popular poetry of St. Francis and the almost rationalistic prose of St. Thomas appear most vividly as part of the same movement. There are both great growths of Catholic development, depending upon external things only as every living and growing thing depends on them; that is, it digests and transforms them, but continues in its own image and not in theirs. A Buddhist or a Communist might dream of two things which simultaneously eat each other, as the perfect form of unification. But it is not so with living things. St. Francis was content to call himself the Troubadour of God; but not content with the God of the Troubadours. St. Thomas did not reconcile Christ to Aristotle; he reconciled Aristotle to Christ.

Yes; in spite of the contrasts that are as conspicuous and even comic as the comparison between the fat man and the thin man, the tall man and the short; in spite of the contrast between the vagabond and the student, between the apprentice and the aristocrat, between the book-hater and the book-lover, between the wildest of all missionaries and the mildest of all professors, the great fact of medieval history is that these two great men were doing the same great work; one in the study and the other in the street. They were not bringing something new into Christianity; in the sense of something heathen or heretical into Christianity; on the contrary, they were bringing Christianity into Christendom. But they were bringing it back against the pressure of certain historic tendencies, which had hardened into habits in many great schools and authorities in the Christian Church; and they were using tools and weapons which seemed to many people to be associated with heresy or heathenry. St. Francis used Nature much as St. Thomas used Aristotle; and to some they seemed to be using a Pagan goddess and a Pagan sage. What they were really doing, and especially what St. Thomas was really doing, will form the main matter of these pages; but it is convenient to be able to compare him from the first with a more popular saint; because we may thus sum up the substance of it in the most popular way. Perhaps it would sound too paradoxical to say that these two saints saved us from Spirituality; a dreadful doom. Perhaps it may be misunderstood if I say that St. Francis, for all his love of animals, saved us from being Buddhists; and that St. Thomas, for all his love of Greek philosophy, saved us from being Platonists. But it is best to say the truth in its simplest form; that they both reaffirmed the Incarnation, by bringing God back to earth.

This analogy, which may seem rather remote, is really perhaps the best practical preface to the philosophy of St. Thomas. As we shall have to consider more closely later on, the purely spiritual or mystical side of Catholicism had very much got the upper hand in the first Catholic centuries; through the genius of Augustine, who had been a Platonist, and perhaps never ceased to be a Platonist; through the transcendentalism of the supposed work of the Areopagite; through the Oriental trend of the later Empire and something Asiatic about the almost pontifical kinghood of Byzantium; all these things weighed down what we should now roughly call the Western element; though it has as good a right to be called the Christian element; since its common sense is but the holy familiarity of the word made flesh. Anyhow, it must suffice for the moment to say that theologians had somewhat stiffened into a sort of Platonic pride in the possession of intangible and untranslatable truths within; as if no part of their wisdom had any root anywhere in the real world. Now the first thing that Aquinas did, though by no means the last, was to say to these pure transcendentalists something substantially like this.

"Far be it from a poor friar to deny that you have these dazzling diamonds in your head, all designed in the most perfect mathematical shapes and shining with a purely celestial light; all there, almost before you begin to think, let alone to see or hear or feel. But I am not ashamed to say that I find my reason fed by my senses; that I owe a great deal of what I think to what I see and smell and taste and handle; and that so far as my reason is concerned, I feel obliged to treat all this reality as real. To be brief, in all humility, I do not believe that God meant Man to exercise only that peculiar, uplifted and abstracted sort of intellect which you are so fortunate as to possess: but I believe that there is a middle field of facts which are given by the senses to be the subject matter of the reason; and that in that field the reason has a right to rule, as the representative of God in Man. It is true that all this is lower than the angels; but it is higher than the animals, and all the actual material objects Man finds around him. True, man also can be an object; and even a deplorable object. But what man has done man may do; and if an antiquated old heathen called Aristotle can help me to do it I will thank him in all humility."

Thus began what is commonly called the appeal to Aquinas and Aristotle. It might be called the appeal to Reason and the Authority of the Senses. And it will be obvious that there is a sort of popular parallel to it in the fact that St. Francis did not only listen for the angels, but also listened to the birds. And before we come to those aspects of St. Thomas that were very severely intellectual, we may note that in him as in St. Francis there is a preliminary practical element which is rather moral; a sort of good and straightforward humility; and a readiness in the man to regard even himself in some ways as an animal; as St. Francis compared his body to a donkey. It may be said that the contrast holds everywhere, even in zoological metaphor, and that if St. Francis was like that common or garden donkey who carried Christ into Jerusalem, St. Thomas, who was actually compared to an ox, rather resembled that Apocalyptic monster of almost Assyrian mystery; the winged bull. But again, we must not let all that can be contrasted eclipse what was common; or forget that neither of them would have been too proud to wait as patiently as the ox and ass in the stable of Bethlehem.

There were of course, as we shall soon see, many other much more curious and complicated ideas in the philosophy of St. Thomas; besides this primary idea of a central common sense that is nourished by the five senses. But at this stage, the point of the story is not only that this was a Thomist doctrine, but that it is a truly and eminently Christian doctrine. For upon this point modern writers write a great deal of nonsense; and show more than their normal ingenuity in missing the point. Having assumed without argument, at the start, that all emancipation must lead men away from religion and towards irreligion, they have just blankly and blindly forgotten what is the outstanding feature of the religion itself.

It will not be possible to conceal much longer from anybody the fact that St. Thomas Aquinas was one of the great liberators of the human intellect. The sectarians of the seventeenth and eighteenth centuries were essentially obscurantists, and they guarded an obscurantist legend that the Schoolman was an obscurantist. This was wearing thin even in the nineteenth century; it will be impossible in the twentieth. It has nothing to do with the truth of their theology or his; but only with the truth of historical proportion, which begins to reappear as quarrels begin to die down. Simply as one of the facts that bulk big in history, it is true to say that Thomas was a very great man who reconciled religion with reason, who expanded it towards experimental science, who insisted that the senses were the windows of the soul and that the reason had a divine right to feed upon facts, and that it was the business of the Faith to digest the strong meat of the toughest and most practical of pagan philosophies. It is a fact, like the military strategy of Napoleon, that Aquinas was thus fighting for all that is liberal and enlightened, as compared with his rivals, or for that matter his successors and supplanters. Those who, for other reasons, honestly accept the final effect of the Reformation will none the less face the fact, that it was the Schoolman who was the Reformer; and that the later Reformers were by comparison reactionaries. I use the word not as a reproach from my own standpoint, but as a fact from the ordinary modern progressive standpoint. For instance, they riveted the mind back to the literal sufficiency of the Hebrew Scriptures; when St. Thomas had already spoken of the Spirit giving grace to the Greek philosophies. He insisted on the social duty of works; they only on the spiritual duty of faith. It was the very life of the Thomist teaching that Reason can be trusted: it was the very life of the Lutheran teaching that Reason is utterly untrustworthy.

Now when this fact is found to be a fact, the danger is that all the unstable opposition will suddenly slide to the opposite extreme. Those who up to that moment have been abusing the Schoolman as a dogmatist will begin to admire the Schoolman as a Modernist who diluted dogma. They will hastily begin to adorn his statue with all the faded garlands of progress, to present him as a man in advance of his age, which is always supposed to mean in agreement with our age; and to load him with the unprovoked imputation of having produced the modern mind. They will discover his attraction, and somewhat hastily assume that he was like themselves, because he was attractive. Up to a point this is pardonable enough; up to a point it has already happened in the case of St. Francis. But it would not go beyond a certain point in the case of St. Francis. Nobody, not even a Freethinker like Renan or Matthew Arnold, would pretend that St. Francis was anything but a devout Christian, or had any other original motive except the imitation of Christ. Yet St. Francis also had that liberating and humanising effect upon religion; though perhaps rather on the imagination than the intellect. But nobody says that St. Francis was loosening the Christian code, when he was obviously tightening it; like the rope round his friar's frock. Nobody says he merely opened the gates to sceptical science, or sold the pass to heathen humanism, or looked forward only to the Renaissance or met the Rationalists half way. No biographer pretends that St. Francis, when he is reported to have opened the Gospels at random and read the great texts about Poverty, really only opened the *Aeneid* and practised the *Sors Virgiliana* out of respect for heathen letters and learning. No historian will pretend that St. Francis wrote *The Canticle of the Sun* in close imitation of a Homeric Hymn to Apollo or loved birds because he had carefully learned all the trick of the Roman Augurs.

In short, most people, Christian or heathen, would now agree that the Franciscan sentiment was primarily a Christian sentiment, unfolded from within, out of an innocent (or, if you will, ignorant) faith in the Christian religion itself. Nobody, as I have said, says that St. Francis drew his primary inspiration from Ovid. It would be every bit as false to say that Aquinas drew his primary inspiration from Aristotle. The whole lesson of his life, especially of his early life, the whole story of his childhood and choice of a career, shows that he was supremely and directly devotional; and that he passionately loved the Catholic worship long before he found he had to fight for it. But there is also a special and clinching instance of this, which once more connects St. Thomas with St. Francis. It seems to be strangely forgotten that both these saints were in actual fact imitating a Master, who was not Aristotle let alone Ovid, when they sanctified the senses or the simple things of nature; when St. Francis walked humbly among the beasts or St. Thomas debated courteously among the Gentiles.

Those who miss this, miss the point of the religion, even if it be a superstition; nay, they miss the very point they would call most superstitious. I mean the whole staggering story of the God-Man in the Gospels. A few even miss it touching St. Francis and his unmixed and unlearned appeal to the Gospels. They will talk of the readiness of St. Francis to learn from the flowers or the birds as something that can only point onward to the Pagan Renaissance. Whereas the fact stares them in the face; first, that it points backwards to the New Testament, and second that it points forward, if it points to anything, to the Aristotelian realism of the *Summa* of St. Thomas Aquinas. They vaguely imagine that anybody who is humanising divinity must be paganising divinity; without seeing that the humanising of divinity is actually the strongest and starkest and most incredible dogma in the Creed. St. Francis was becoming more like Christ, and not merely more like Buddha, when he considered the lilies of the field or the fowls of the air; and St. Thomas was becoming more of a Christian, and not merely more of an Aristotelian, when he insisted that God and the image of God had come in contact through matter with a material world. These saints were, in the most exact sense of the term, Humanists; because they were insisting on the immense importance of the human being in the theological scheme of things. But they were not Humanists marching along a path of progress that leads to Modernism and general scepticism; for in their very Humanism they were affirming a dogma now often regarded as the most superstitious Superhumanism. They were strengthening that staggering doctrine of Incarnation, which the sceptics find it hardest to believe. There cannot be a stiffer piece of Christian divinity than the divinity of Christ.

This is a point that is here very much to the point; that these men became more orthodox, when they became more rational or natural. Only by being thus orthodox could they be thus rational and natural. In other words, what may really be called a liberal theology was unfolded from within, from out of the original mysteries of Catholicism. But that liberality had nothing to do with liberalism; in fact it cannot even now coexist with liberalism.* The matter is so cogent, that I will take one or two special ideas of St. Thomas to illustrate what I mean. Without anticipating the elementary sketch of Thomism that must be made later, the following points may be noted here.

For instance, it was a very special idea of St. Thomas that Man is to be studied in his whole manhood; that a man is not a man without his body, just as he is not a man without his soul. A corpse is not a man; but also a ghost is not a man. The earlier school of Augustine and even of Anselm had rather neglected this, treating the soul as the only necessary treasure, wrapped for a time in a negligible napkin. Even here they were less orthodox in being more spiritual. They sometimes hovered on the edge of those Eastern deserts that stretch away to the land of transmigration; where the essential soul may pass through a hundred unessential bodies; reincarnated even in the bodies of beasts or birds. St. Thomas stood up stoutly for the fact that a man's body is his body as

* I use the word liberalism here in the strictly limited theological sense, in which Newman and other theologians use it. In its popular political sense, as I point out later, St. Thomas rather tended to be a Liberal, especially for his time [GKC].

his mind is his mind; and that *he* can only be a balance and union of the two. Now this is in some ways a naturalistic notion, very near to the modern respect for material things; a praise of the body that might be sung by Walt Whitman or justified by D. H. Lawrence: a thing that might be called Humanism or even claimed by Modernism. In fact, it may be Materialism; but it is the flat contrary of Modernism. It is bound up, in the modern view, with the most monstrous, the most material, and therefore the most miraculous of miracles. It is specially connected with the most startling sort of dogma, which the Modernist can least accept; the Resurrection of the Body.

Or again, his argument for Revelation is quite rationalistic; and on the other side, decidedly democratic and popular. His argument for Revelation is not in the least an argument against Reason. On the contrary, he seems inclined to admit that truth could be reached by a rational process, if only it were rational enough; and also long enough. Indeed, something in his character, which I have called elsewhere optimism, and for which I know no other approximate term, led him rather to exaggerate the extent to which all men would ultimately listen to reason. In his controversies, he always assumes that they will listen to reason. That is, he does emphatically believe that men can be convinced by argument; when they reach the end of the argument. Only his common sense also told him that the argument never ends. I might convince a man that matter as the origin of Mind is quite meaningless, if he and I were very fond of each other and fought each other every night for forty years. But long before he was convinced on his deathbed, a thousand other materialists would have been born, and nobody can explain everything to everybody. St. Thomas takes the view that the souls of all the ordinary hard-working and simple-minded people are quite as important as the souls of thinkers and truth-seekers; and he asks how all these people are possibly to find time for the amount of reasoning that is needed to find truth. The whole tone of the passage shows both a respect for scientific enquiry and a strong sympathy with the average man. His argument for Revelation is not an argument against Reason; but it is an argument for Revelation. The *conclusion* he draws from it is that men must receive the highest moral truths in a miraculous manner; or most men would not receive them at all. His arguments are rational and natural; but his own deduction is all for the supernatural; and, as is common in the case of his argument, it is not easy to find any deduction except his own deduction. And when we come to that, we find it is something as simple as St. Francis himself could desire; the message from heaven; the story that is told out of the sky; the fairytale that is really true.

It is plainer still in more popular problems like Free Will. If St. Thomas stands for one thing more than another, it is what may be called subordinate sovereignties or autonomies. He was, if the flippancy may be used, a strong Home Ruler. We might even say he was always defending the independence of dependent things. He insisted that such a thing could have its own rights in its own region. It was his attitude to the Home Rule of the reason and even the senses; "Daughter am I in my father's house; but mistress in my own." And in exactly this sense he emphasised a certain dignity in Man, which was sometimes rather swallowed up in the purely theistic generalisations about God. Nobody would say he wanted to divide Man from God; but he did want to distinguish Man from God. In this strong sense of human dignity and liberty there is much that can be and is appreciated now as a noble humanistic liberality. But let us not forget that its upshot was that very Free Will, or moral responsibility of Man, which so many modern liberals would deny. Upon this sublime and perilous liberty hang heaven and hell, and all the mysterious drama of the soul. It is distinction and not division; but a man *can* divide himself from God, which, in a certain aspect, is the greatest distinction of all.

Again, though it is a more metaphysical matter, which must be mentioned later, and then only too slightly, it is the same with the old philosophical dispute about the Many and the One. Are things so different that they can never be classified; or so unified that they can never be distinguished? Without pretending to answer such questions here, we may say broadly that St. Thomas comes down definitely on the side of Variety, as a thing that is real as well as Unity. In this, and questions akin to this, he often departs from the great Greek philosophers who were sometimes his models; and entirely departs from the great Oriental philosophers who are in some sense his rivals. He seems fairly certain that the difference between chalk and cheese, or pigs and pelicans, is not a mere illusion, or dazzle of our bewildered mind blinded by a single light; but is pretty much what we all feel it to be. It may be said that this is mere common sense; the common sense that pigs are pigs; to that extent related to the earth-bound Aristotelian common sense; to a human and even a heathen common sense. But note that here again the extremes of earth and heaven meet. It is also connected with the dogmatic Christian idea of the Creation; of a Creator who created pigs, as distinct from a Cosmos that merely evolved them.

In all these cases we see repeated the point stated at the start. The Thomist movement in metaphysics, like the Franciscan movement in morals and manners, was an enlargement and a liberation, it was emphatically a growth of Christian theology from within; it was emphatically *not* a shrinking of Christian theology under heathen or even human influences. The Franciscan was free to be a friar, instead of being bound to be a monk. But he was more of a Christian, more of a Catholic, even more of an ascetic. So the

Thomist was free to be an Aristotelian, instead of being bound to be an Augustinian. But he was even more of a theologian; more of an orthodox theologian; more of a dogmatist, in having recovered through Aristotle the most defiant of all dogmas, the wedding of God with Man and therefore with Matter. Nobody can understand the greatness of the thirteenth century, who does not realise that it was a great growth of new things produced by a living thing. In that sense it was really bolder and freer than what we call the Renaissance, which was a resurrection of old things discovered in a dead thing. In that sense medievalism was not a Renascence, but rather a Nascence. It did not model its temples upon the tombs, or call up dead gods from Hades. It made an architecture as new as modern engineering: indeed it still remains the most modern architecture. Only it was followed at the Renaissance by a more antiquated architecture. In that sense the Renaissance might be called the Relapse. Whatever may be said of the Gothic and the Gospel according to St. Thomas, they were not a Relapse. It was a new thrust like the titanic thrust of Gothic engineering; and its strength was in a God who makes all things new.

In a word, St. Thomas was making Christendom more Christian in making it more Aristotelian. This is not a paradox but a plain truism, which can only be missed by those who may know what is meant by an Aristotelian, but have simply forgotten what is meant by a Christian. As compared with a Jew, a Moslem, a Buddhist, a Deist, or most obvious alternatives, a Christian *means* a man who believes that deity or sanctity has attached to matter or entered the world of the senses. Some modern writers, missing this simple point, have even talked as if the acceptance of Aristotle was a sort of concession to the Arabs; like a Modernist vicar making a concession to the Agnostics. They might as well say that the Crusades were a concession to the Arabs as say that Aquinas rescuing Aristotle from Averrhoes was a concessions to the Arabs. The Crusaders wanted to recover the place where the body of Christ had been, because they believed, rightly or wrongly, that it was a Christian place. St. Thomas wanted to recover what was in essence the body of Christ itself; the sanctified body of the Son of Man which had become a miraculous medium between heaven and earth. And he wanted the body, and all its senses, because he believed, rightly or wrongly, that it was a Christian thing. It might be a humbler or homelier thing than the Platonic mind; that is why it was Christian. St. Thomas was, if you will, taking the lower road when he walked in the steps of Aristotle. So was God, when He worked in the workshop of Joseph.

Lastly, these two great men were not only united to each other but separated from most of their comrades and contemporaries by the very revolutionary character of their own revolution. In 1215, Dominic Guzman, the Castilian, founded an Order very similar to that of Francis; and, by a most curious coincidence of history, at almost exactly the same moment as Francis. It was directed primarily to preaching the Catholic philosophy to the Albigensian heretics; whose own philosophy was one of the many forms of that Manicheanism with which this story is much concerned. It had its roots in the remote mysticism and moral detachment of the East; and it was therefore inevitable that the Dominicans should be rather more a brotherhood of philosophers, where the Franciscans were by comparison a brotherhood of poets. For this and other reasons, St. Dominic and his followers are little known or understood in modern England; they were involved eventually in a religious war, which followed on a theological argument; and there was something in the atmosphere of our country, during the last century or so, which made the theological argument even more incomprehensible than the religious war. The ultimate effect is in some ways curious;

because St. Dominic, even more than St. Francis, was marked by that intellectual independence, and strict standard of virtue and veracity, which Protestant cultures are wont to regard as specially Protestant. It was of him that the tale was told, and would certainly have been told more widely among us if it had been told of a Puritan, that the Pope pointed to his gorgeous Papal Palace and said, "Peter can no longer say 'Silver and gold have I none'"; and the Spanish friar answered, "No, and neither can he now say, 'Rise and walk.'"

Thus there is another way in which the popular story of St. Francis can be a sort of bridge between the modern and medieval world. And it is based on that very fact already mentioned: that St. Francis and St. Dominic stand together in history as having done the same work, and yet are divided in English popular tradition in the most strange and startling way. In their own lands they are like Heavenly Twins, irradiating the same light from heaven, seeming sometimes to be two saints in one halo, as another order depicted Holy Poverty as two knights on one horse. In the legends of our own land, they are about as much united as St. George and the Dragon. Dominic is still conceived as an Inquisitor devising thumbscrews; while Francis is already accepted as a humanitarian deploring mousetraps. It seems, for instance, quite natural to us, and full of the same associations of flowers and starry fancies, that the name of Francis should belong to Francis Thompson. But I fancy it would seem less natural to call him Dominic Thompson; or find that a man, with a long record of popular sympathies and practical tenderness to the poor, could bear such a name as Dominic Plater.[2] It would sound as if he had been called Torquemada Thompson.

[2] Charles Dominic Plater, S. J. (1875–1921) was a leader in the British Catholic social movement during the early twentieth century. Best known for his role in founding and directing the work of the Catholic Social Guild.

Now there must be something wrong behind this contradiction; turning those who were allies at home into antagonists abroad. On any other question, the fact would be apparent to common sense. Suppose English Liberals or Free-Traders found that, in remote parts of China, it was generally held that Cobden[3] was a cruel monster but Bright[4] a stainless saint. They would think there was a mistake somewhere. Suppose that American Evangelicals learned that in France or Italy, or other civilizations impenetrable by Moody[5] and Sankey, there was a popular belief that Moody was an angel but Sankey a devil; they would guess that there must be a muddle somewhere. Some other later accidental distinction must have cut across the main course of a historical tendency. These parallels are not so fantastic as they may sound. Cobden and Bright have actually been called 'child-torturers', in anger at their alleged callousness about the evils amended by the Factory Acts; and some would call the Moody and Sankey sermon on Hell a hellish exhibition. All that is a matter of opinion; but both men held the same sort of opinion, and there must be a blunder in an opinion that separates them so completely. And of course there is a complete blunder in the legend about St. Dominic. Those who know anything about St. Dominic know that he was a missionary and not a militant persecutor; that his contribution to religion was the Rosary and not the Rack; that his whole career is meaningless, unless we understand that his famous victories were victories of persuasion and not persecution. He did believe in

[3] Richard Cobden (1804–1854) was a British politician of the Anti-Corn Law League.

[4] John Bright (1811–1889), an orator and British statesman, was the co-founder of that League. Both Cobden and Bright were leading spokesmen for the Manchester School of Economics.

[5] Dwight Lyman Moody (1837–1899) was an American evanelist who met Ira Sankey in 1870 and joined him in evangelistic campaigns.

the justification of persecution; in the sense that the secular arm could repress religious disorders. So did everybody else believe in persecution; and none more than the elegant blasphemer, Frederick II who believed in nothing else. Some say he was the first to burn heretics; but anyhow, he thought it was one of his imperial privileges and duties to persecute heretics. But to talk as if Dominic did nothing but persecute heretics, is like blaming Father Matthew,[6] who persuaded millions of drunkards to take a temperance pledge, because the accepted law sometimes allowed a drunkard to be arrested by a policeman. It is to miss the whole point; which is that this particular man had a genius for conversion, quite apart from compulsion. The real difference between Francis and Dominic, which is no discredit to either of them, is that Dominic did happen to be confronted with a huge campaign for the conversion of heretics, while Francis had only the more subtle task of the conversion of human beings. It is an old story that, while we may need somebody like Dominic to convert the heathen to Christianity, we are in even greater need of somebody like Francis, to convert the Christians to Christianity. Still, we must not lose sight of St. Dominic's special problem, which was that of dealing with a whole population, kingdoms and cities and countrysides, that had drifted from the Faith and solidified into strange and abnormal new religions. That he did win back masses of men so deceived, merely by talking and preaching, remains an enormous triumph worthy of a colossal trophy. St. Francis is called humane because he tried to convert Saracens and failed; St. Dominic is called bigoted and besotted because he tried to convert Albigensians and succeeded. But we happen

[6] Theobald Matthew (1796–1856) was an Irish priest better known as the Apostle of Temperance. He was remarkably successful in the promotion of total abstinence.

to be in a curious nook or corner of the hills of history, from which we can see Assisi and the Umbrian hills, but are out of sight of the vast battle-field of the Southern Crusade; the miracle of Muret and the greater miracle of Dominic, when the roots of the Pyrenees and the shores of the Mediterranean saw defeated the Asiatic despair.

But there is an earlier and more essential link between Dominic and Francis, which is more to the immediate purpose of this book. They were in later times bracketed in glory because they were in their own time bracketed in infamy; or at least in unpopularity. For they did the most unpopular thing that men can do; they started a popular movement. A man who dares to make a direct appeal to the populace always makes a long series of enemies—beginning with the populace. In proportion as the poor begin to understand that he means to help and not hurt them, the solid classes above begin to close in, resolved to hinder and not help. The rich, and even the learned, sometimes feel not unreasonably that the thing will change the world, not only in its worldliness or its worldly wisdom, but to some extent perhaps in its real wisdom. Such a feeling was not unnatural in this case; when we consider, for instance, St. Francis's really reckless attitude about rejecting books and scholarship; or the tendency that the Friars afterwards showed to appeal to the Pope in contempt of local bishops and ecclesiastical officers. In short, St. Dominic and St. Francis created a Revolution, quite as popular and unpopular as the French Revolution. But it is very hard today to feel that even the French Revolution was as fresh as it really was. The Marseillaise once sounded like the human voice of the volcano or the dance-tune of the earthquake, and the kings of the earth trembled, some fearing that the heavens might fall; some fearing far more that justice might be done. The Marseillaise is played today at diplomatic dinner-parties, where smiling monarchs meet beaming millionaires, and is rather less revolutionary than "Home, Sweet Home". Also, it is highly pertinent to recall, the modern revolutionists would now call the revolt of the French Jacobins insufficient, just as they would call the revolt of the Friars insufficient. They would say that neither went far enough; but many, in their own day, thought they went very much too far. In the case of the Friars, the higher orders of the State, and to some extent even of the Church, were profoundly shocked at such a loosening of wild popular preachers among the people. It is not at all easy for us to feel that distant events were thus disconcerting and even disreputable. Revolutions turn into institutions; revolts that renew the youth of old societies in their turn grow old; and the past, which was full of new things, of splits and innovations and insurrections, seems to us a single texture of tradition.

But if we wish for one fact that will make vivid this shock of change and challenge, and show how raw and ragged, how almost rowdy in its reckless novelty, how much of the gutter and how remote from refined life, this experiment of the Friars did really seem to many in its own day, there is here a very relevant fact to reveal it. It shows how much a settled and already ancient Christendom did feel it as something like the end of an age; and how the very roads of the earth seem to shake under the feet of the new and nameless army; the march of the Beggars. A mystic nursery rhyme suggests the atmosphere of such a crisis: "Hark, hark, the dogs do bark; the Beggars are coming to town". There were many towns that almost fortified themselves against them and many watchdogs of property and rank did really bark, and bark loudly, when those Beggars went by; but louder was the singing of the Beggars who sang their Canticle to the Sun, and louder the baying of the Hounds of Heaven; the *Domini canes* of the medieval pun; the Dogs of God. And if we would measure how real and rending seemed that revolution, what a break with the past, we can see it in the first and most extraordinary event in the life of St. Thomas Aquinas.

# II

# THE RUNAWAY ABBOT

Thomas Aquinas, in a strange and rather symbolic manner, sprang out of the very centre of the civilised world of his time; the central knot or coil of the powers then controlling Christendom. He was closely connected with all of them; even with some of them that might well be described as destroying Christendom. The whole religious quarrel, the whole international quarrel, was for him, a family quarrel. He was born in the purple; almost literally on the hem of the imperial purple; for his own cousin was the Holy Roman Emperor. He could have quartered half the kingdoms of Europe on his shield—if he had not thrown away the shield. He was Italian and French and German and in every way European. On one side, he inherited from the energy that made the episode of the Normans, whose strange organising raids rang and rattled like flights of arrows in the corners of Europe and the ends of the earth; one flight of them following Duke William far northward through the blinding snows to Chester; another treading in Greek and Punic footsteps through the island of Sicily to the gates of Syracuse. Another bond of blood bound him to the great Emperors of the Rhine and Danube who claimed to wear the crown of Charlemagne; Red Barbarossa, who sleeps under the rushing river, was his great uncle, and Frederick II, the Wonder of the World, his second cousin, and yet he held by a hundred more intimate ties to the lively inner life, the local vivacity, the little walled nations and the thousand shrines of Italy. While inheriting this physical kinship with the Emperor, he maintained far more firmly his spiritual kinship with the Pope. He understood the meaning of Rome, and in what sense it was still ruling the world; and was not likely to think that the German Emperors of his time, any more than the Greek Emperors of a previous time, would be able to be really Roman in defiance of Rome. To this cosmopolitan comprehensiveness in his inherited position, he afterwards added many things of his own, that made for mutual understanding among the peoples, and gave him something of the character of an ambassador and interpreter. He travelled a great deal; he was not only well known in Paris and the German universities, but he almost certainly visited England; probably he went to Oxford and London; and it has been said that we may be treading in the footsteps of him and his Dominican companions, whenever we go down by the river to the railway-station that still bears the name of Black-friars. But the truth applies to the travels of his mind as well as his body. He studied the literature even of the opponents of Christianity much more carefully and impartially than was then the fashion; he really tried to understand the Arabian Aristotelianism of the Moslems; and wrote a highly humane and reasonable treatise on the problem of the treatment of the Jews. He always attempted to look at everything from the inside; but he was certainly lucky in having been born in the inside of the state system and the high politics of his day. What he thought of them may perhaps be inferred from the next passage in his history.

St. Thomas might thus stand very well for the International Man, to borrow the title of a modern book. But it is only fair to remember that he lived in the International Age; in a world that was international in a sense not to be suggested in any modern book, or by any modern man. If I remember right, the modern candidate for the post of International Man was Cobden, who was an almost abnormally national man; a narrowly national man; a very fine type, but one which can hardly be imagined except as moving between Midhurst and Manchester. He had an international policy and he indulged in international travel; but if he always remained a national person, it was because he remained a normal person; that is normal to the nineteenth century. But it was not so in the thirteenth century. There a man of international influence, like Cobden, could be also almost a man of international nationality. The names of nations and cities and places of origin did not connote that deep division that is the mark of the modern world. Aquinas as a student was nicknamed the ox of Sicily, though his birthplace was near Naples; but this did not prevent the city of Paris regarding him as simply and solidly as a Parisian, because he had been a glory of the Sorbonne, that it proposed to bury his bones when he was dead. Or take a more obvious contrast with modern times. Consider what is meant in most modern talk by a German Professor. And then realise that the greatest of all German Professors, Albertus Magnus, was himself one of the glories of the University of Paris; and it was in Paris that Aquinas supported him. Think of the modern German Professor being famous throughout Europe for his popularity when lecturing in Paris.

Thus, if there was war in Christendom, it was international war in the special sense in which we speak of international peace. It was not the war of two nations; but the war of two internationalisms: of two World States: the Catholic Church and the Holy Roman Empire. The political crisis in Christendom affected the life of Aquinas at the start in one sharp disaster, and afterwards in many indirect ways. It had many elements; the Crusades; the embers of the Albigensian pessimism, over which St. Dominic had triumphed in argument and Simon de Montfort in arms; the dubious experiment of an Inquisition which started from it; and many other things. But, broadly speaking, it is the period of the great duel between the Popes and the Emperors, that is the German Emperors who called themselves Holy Roman

Emperors, the House of Hohenstaufen. The particular period of the life of Aquinas, however, is entirely overshadowed by the particular Emperor who was himself more an Italian than a German; the brilliant Frederick II who was called the Wonder of the World. It may be remarked, in passing, that Latin was the most living of languages at this time, and we often feel a certain weakness in the necessary translation. For I seem to have read somewhere that the word used was stronger than the Wonder of the World; that his medieval title was *Stupor Mundi*, which is more exactly the Stupefaction of the World. Something of the sort may be noted later of philosophical language, and the weakness of translating a word like *Ens* by a word like Being. But for the moment the parenthesis has another application; for it might well be said that Frederick did indeed stupefy the world; that there was something stunning and blinding about the blows he struck at religion, as in that blow which almost begins the biography of Thomas Aquinas. He may also be called stupefying in another sense; in that his very brilliancy has made some of his modern admirers very stupid.

For Frederick II is the first figure, and that a rather fierce and ominous figure, who rides across the scene of his cousin's birth and boyhood: a scene of wild fighting and of fire. And it may be allowable to pause for a parenthesis upon his name, for two particular reasons: first that his romantic reputation, even among modern historians, covers and partly conceals the true background of the time; and second that the tradition in question directly involves the whole status of St. Thomas Aquinas. The nineteenth century view, still so strangely called the modern view by many moderns, touching such a man as Frederick II, was well summed up by some solid Victorian, I think by Macaulay; Frederick was "a statesman in an age of Crusaders; a philosopher in an age of monks." It may be noted that the antithesis involves the assumption that a Crusader cannot easily be a statesman; and that a monk cannot easily be a philosopher. Yet, to take only that special instance, it would be easy to point out that the cases of two famous men in the age of Frederick II would alone be strong enough to upset both the assumption and the antithesis. St. Louis, though a Crusader and even an unsuccessful Crusader, was really a far more successful statesman than Frederick II. By the test of practical politics, he popularised, solidified and sanctified the most powerful government in Europe, the order and concentration of the French Monarchy; the single dynasty that steadily increased its strength for five hundred years up to the glories of the Grand Siècle whereas Frederick went down in ruin before the Papacy and the Republics and a vast combination of priests and peoples. The Holy Roman Empire he wished to found was an ideal rather in the sense of a dream; it was certainly never a fact like the square and solid State which the French statesman did found. Or, to take another example from the next generation, one of the most strictly practical statesmen in history, our own Edward I, was also a Crusader.

The other half of the antithesis is even more false and here even more relevant. Frederick II was not a philosopher in the age of monks. He was a gentleman dabbling in philosophy in the age of the monk Thomas Aquinas. He was doubtless an intelligent and even brilliant gentleman; but if he did leave any notes on the nature of Being and Becoming, or the precise sense in which realities can be relative to Reality, I do not imagine those notes are now exciting undergraduates at Oxford or literary men in Paris, let alone the little groups of Thomists who have already sprung up even in New York and Chicago. It is no disrespect to the Emperor to say that he certainly was not a philosopher in the sense in which Thomas Aquinas was a philosopher, let alone so great or so universal or so permanent a philosopher. And Thomas

Aquinas lived in that very age of monks, and in that very world of monks, which Macaulay talks of as if it were incapable of producing philosophy.

We need not dwell on the causes of this Victorian prejudice, which some still think so very advanced. It arose mainly from one narrow or insular notion; that no man could possibly be building up the best of the modern world, if he went with the main movement of the medieval world. These Victorians thought that only the heretic had ever helped humanity; only the man who nearly wrecked medieval civilisation could be of any use in constructing modern civilisation. Hence came a score of comic fables; as that the cathedrals must have been built by a secret society of Freemasons; or that the epic of Dante must be a cryptogram referring to the political hopes of Garibaldi. But the generalisation is not in its nature probable and it is not in fact true. This medieval period was rather specially the period of communal or corporate thinking, and in some matters it was really rather larger than the individualistic modern thinking. This could be proved in a flash from the mere fact of the use of the word 'statesman'. To a man of Macaulay's period, a statesman *always* meant a man who maintained the more narrow national interests of his own state against other states, as Richelieu maintained those of France, or Chatham of England, or Bismarck of Prussia. But if a man actually wanted to defend all these states, to combine all these states, to make a living brotherhood of all these states, to resist some outer peril as from the Mongolian millions—then that poor devil, of course, could not really be called a statesman. He was only a Crusader.

In this way it is but fair to Frederick II to say that he was a Crusader; if he was also rather like an Anti-Crusader. Certainly he was an international statesman. Indeed he was a particular type, which may be called an international soldier. The international soldier is always very much disliked by internationalists. They dislike Charlemagne and Charles V and Napoleon; and everybody who tried to create the World State for which they cry aloud day and night. But Frederick is more dubious and less doubted; he was supposed to be the head of the Holy Roman Empire; and accused of wanting to be the head of a very Unholy Roman Empire. But even if he were Antichrist, he would still be a witness to the unity of Christendom.

Nevertheless, there is a queer quality in that time; which, while it was international was also internal and intimate. War, in the wide modern sense, is possible, not because more men disagree, but because more men agree. Under the peculiarly modern coercions, such as Compulsory Education and Conscription, there are such very large *peaceful* areas, that they can all agree upon War. In that age men disagreed even about war; and peace might break out anywhere. Peace was interrupted by feuds and feuds by pardons. Individuality wound in and out of a maze; spiritual extremes were walled up with one another in one little walled town; and we see the great soul of Dante divided, a cloven flame; loving and hating his own city. This individual complexity is intensely vivid in the particular story we have here to tell, in a very rough outline. If anyone wishes to know what is meant by saying that action was more individual, and indeed incalculable, he may well note some of the stages in the story of the great feudal house of Aquino, which had its castle not far from Naples. In the mere hasty anecdote we have now to tell, we shall note in succession five or six stages of this sort. Landulf of Aquino, a heavy feudal fighter typical of the times, rode in armour behind the imperial banners, and attacked a monastery, because the Emperor regarded the monastery as a fortress held for his enemy the Pope. Later, we shall see, the same feudal lord sent his own son to the same monastery; probably on the friendly advice of the same Pope. Later still, another of his sons, entirely on his own, rebelled against the Emperor, and went over to the armies of the Pope. For this he was executed by the Emperor, with promptitude and despatch. I wish we knew more about that brother of Thomas Aquinas who risked and lost his life to support the cause of the Pope; which was in all human essentials the cause of the People. He may not have been a saint; but he must have had some qualities of a martyr. Meanwhile, two other brothers, still ardent and active apparently, in the service of the Emperor who killed the third brother, themselves proceeded to kidnap another brother, because they did not approve of his sympathy with the new social movements in religion. That is the sort of tangle in which this one distinguished medieval family found itself. It was not a war of nations, but it was a rather widespread family quarrel.

The reason for dwelling here, however, upon the position of the Emperor Frederick, as a type of his time, in his culture and his violence, in his concern for philosophy and his quarrel with religion, is not merely concerned with these things. He may here be the first figure that crosses the stage, because one of his very typical actions precipitated the first action, or obstinate inaction, which began the personal adventures of Thomas Aquinas in this world. The story also illustrates the extraordinary tangle in which a family like that of the Count of Aquino found itself; being at once so close to the Church and so much at odds with it. For Frederick II, in the course of these remarkable manoeuvres, military and political, which ranged from burning heretics to allying himself with Saracens, made a swoop as of a predatory eagle (and the Imperial eagle was rather predatory) upon a very large and wealthy monastery; the Benedictine Abbey of Monte Cassino; and stormed and sacked the place.

Some miles from the monastery of Monte Cassino stood a great crag or cliff, standing up like a pillar of the Apennines. It was crowned with a castle that bore the name of The Dry Rock, and was the eyrie in which the eaglets of the Aquino branch of the Imperial family were nursed to fly. Here lived Count Landulf of Aquino, who was the father of Thomas Aquinas and some seven other sons. In military affairs he doubtless rode with his family, in the feudal manner; and apparently had something to do with the destruction of the monastery. But it was typical of the tangle of the time, that Count Landulf seems afterwards to have thought that it would be a tactful and delicate act to put in his son Thomas as Abbot of the monastery. This would be of the nature of a graceful apology to the Church, and also, it would appear, the solution of a family difficulty.

For it had been long apparent to Count Landulf that nothing could be done with his seventh son Thomas, except to make him an Abbot or something of that kind. Born in 1226, he had from childhood a mysterious objection to becoming a predatory eagle, or even to taking an ordinary interest in falconry or tilting or any other gentlemanly pursuits. He was a large and heavy and quiet boy, and phenomenally silent, scarcely opening his mouth except to say suddenly to his schoolmaster in an explosive manner, "What is God?" The answer is not recorded but it is probable that the asker went on worrying out answers for himself. The only place for a person of this kind was the Church and presumably the cloister; and so far as that went, there was no particular difficulty. It was easy enough for a man in Count Landulf's position to arrange with some monastery for his son to be received there; and in this particular case he thought it would be a good idea if he were received in some official capacity, that would be worthy of his worldly rank. So everything was smoothly arranged for Thomas Aquinas becoming a monk, which would seem to be what he himself wanted; and sooner or later becoming

Abbot of Monte Cassino. And then the curious thing happened.

In so far as we may follow rather dim and disputed events, it would seem that the young Thomas Aquinas walked into his father's castle one day and calmly announced that he had become one of the Begging Friars, of the new order founded by Dominic the Spaniard; much as the eldest son of the squire might go home and airily inform the family that he had married a gypsy; or the heir of a Tory Duke state that he was walking tomorrow with the Hunger Marchers organised by alleged Communists. By this, as has been noted already, we may pretty well measure the abyss between the old monasticism and the new, and the earthquake of the Dominican and Franciscan revolution. Thomas had appeared to wish to be a Monk; and the gates were silently opened to him and the long avenues of the abbey, the very carpet, so to speak, laid for him up to the throne of the mitred abbot. He said he wished to be a Friar, and his family flew at him like wild beasts; his brothers pursued him along the public roads, half-rent his friar's frock from his back and finally locked him up in a tower like a lunatic.

It is not very easy to trace the course of this furious family quarrel, and how it eventually spent itself against the tenacity of the young Friar; according to some stories, his mother's disapproval was short-lived and she went over to his side; but it was not only his relatives that were embroiled. We might say that the central governing class of Europe, which partly consisted of his family, were in a turmoil over the deplorable youth; even the Pope was asked for tactful intervention, and it was at one time proposed that Thomas should be allowed to wear the Dominican habit while acting as Abbot in the Benedictine Abbey. To many this would seem a tactful compromise; but it did not commend itself to the narrow medieval mind of Thomas Aquinas. He indicated sharply that he wished to be a Dominican in the Dominican Order, and not at a fancy-dress ball; and the diplomatic proposal appears to have been dropped.

Thomas of Aquino wanted to be a Friar. It was a staggering fact to his contemporaries; and it is rather an intriguing fact even to us; for this desire, limited literally and strictly to this statement, was the one practical thing to which his will was clamped with adamantine obstinacy till his death. He would not be an Abbot; he would not be a Monk; he would not even be a Prior or ruler in his own fraternity; he would not be a prominent or important Friar; he would be a Friar. It is as if Napoleon had insisted on remaining a private soldier all his life. Something in this heavy, quiet, cultivated, rather academic gentleman would not be satisfied till he was, by fixed authoritative proclamation and official pronouncement, established and appointed to be a Beggar. It is all the more interesting because, while he did more than his duty a thousand times over, he was not at all like a Beggar; nor at all likely to be a good Beggar. He had nothing of the native vagabond about him, as had his great precursors; he was not born with something of the wandering minstrel, like St. Francis; or something of the tramping missionary, like St. Dominic. But he insisted upon putting himself under military orders, to do these things at the will of another, if required. He may be compared with some of the more magnanimous aristocrats who have enrolled themselves in revolutionary armies; or some of the best of the poets and scholars who volunteered as private soldiers in the Great War. Something in the courage and consistency of Dominic and Francis had challenged his deep sense of justice; and while remaining a very reasonable person, and even a diplomatic one, he never let anything shake the iron immobility of this one decision of his youth; nor was he to be turned from his tall and towering ambition to take the lowest place.

The first effect of his decision, as we have seen, was much more stimulating and even startling. The General of the Dominicans, under whom Thomas had enrolled himself, was probably well aware of the diplomatic attempts to dislodge him and the worldly difficulties of resisting them. His expedient was to take his young follower out of Italy altogether; bidding him proceed with a few other friars to Paris. There was something prophetic even about this first progress of the travelling teacher of the nations; for Paris was indeed destined to be in some sense the goal of his spiritual journey; since it was there that he was to deliver both his great defence of the Friars and his great defiance to the antagonists of Aristotle. But this his first journey to Paris was destined to be broken off very short indeed. The friars had reached a turn of the road by a wayside fountain, a little way north of Rome, when they were overtaken by a wild cavalcade of captors, who seized on Thomas like brigands, but who were in fact only rather needlessly agitated brothers. He had a large number of brothers: perhaps only two were here involved. Indeed he was the seventh; and friends of Birth Control may lament that this philosopher was needlessly added to the noble line of ruffians who kidnapped him. It was an odd affair altogether. There is something quaint and picturesque in the idea of kidnapping a begging friar, who might in a sense be called a runaway abbot. There is a comic and tragic tangle in the motives and purposes of such a trio of strange kinsmen. There is a sort of Christian cross-purposes in the contrast between the feverish illusion of the importance of things, always marking men who are called practical; and the much more practical pertinacity of the man who is called theoretical.

Thus at least did those three strange brethren stagger or trail along their tragic road, tied together, as it were, like criminal and constable; only that the criminals were making the arrest. So their figures are seen for an instant against the horizon of history; brothers as sinister as any since Cain and Abel. For this queer outrage in the great family of Aquino does really stand out symbolically, as representing something that will forever make the Middle Ages a mystery and a bewilderment; capable of sharply contrasted interpretations like darkness and light. For in two of those men there raged, we might say screamed, a savage pride of blood and blazonry of arms, though they were princes of the most refined world of their time, which would seem more suitable to a tribe dancing round a totem. For the moment they had forgotten everything except the name of a family, that is narrower than a tribe, and far narrower than a nation. And the third figure of that trio, born of the same mother and perhaps visibly one with the others in face or form, had a conception of brotherhood broader than most modern democracy, for it was not national but international; a faith in mercy and modesty far deeper than any mere mildness of manners in the modern world; and a drastic oath of poverty, which would now be counted quite a mad exaggeration of the revolt against plutocracy and pride. Out of the same Italian castle came two savages and one sage; or one saint more pacific than most modern sages. That is the double aspect confusing a hundred controversies. That is what makes the riddle of the medieval age; that it was not one age but two ages. We look into the moods of some men, and it might be the Stone Age; we look into the minds of other men, and they might be living in the Golden Age; in the most modern sort of Utopia. There were always good men and bad men; but in this time good men who were subtle lived with bad men who were simple. They lived in the same family; they were brought up in the same nursery; and they came out to struggle, as the brothers of Aquino struggled by the wayside, when they dragged the new friar along the road and shut him up in the castle on the hill.

When his relations tried to despoil him of his friar's frock he seems to have laid about them in the fighting manner of his fathers, and it would seem successfully, since this attempt was abandoned. He accepted the imprisonment itself with his customary composure, and probably did not mind very much whether he was left to philosophise in a dungeon or in a cell. Indeed there is something in the way the whole tale is told, which suggests that through a great part of that strange abduction, he had been carried about like a lumbering stone statue. Only one tale told of his captivity shows him merely in anger; and that shows him angrier than he ever was before or after. It struck the imagination of his own time for more important reasons; but it has an interest that is psychological as well as moral. For once in his life, for the first time and the last, Thomas of Aquino was really *hors de lui*; riding a storm outside that tower of intellect and contemplation in which he commonly lived. And that was when his brothers introduced into his room some specially gorgeous and painted courtesan, with the idea of surprising him by a sudden temptation, or at least involving him in a scandal. His anger was justified, even by less strict moral standards than his own; for the meanness was even worse than the foulness of the expedient. Even on the lowest grounds, he knew his brothers knew, and they knew that he knew, that it was an insult to him as a gentleman to suppose that he would break his pledge upon so base a provocation; and he had behind him a far more terrible sensibility; all that huge ambition of humility which was to him the voice of God out of heaven. In this one flash alone we see that huge unwieldy figure in an attitude of activity, or even animation; and he was very animated indeed. He sprang from his seat and snatched a brand out of the fire, and stood brandishing it like a flaming sword. The woman not unnaturally shrieked and fled, which was all that he wanted; but it is quaint to think of what she must have thought of that madman of monstrous stature juggling with flames and apparently threatening to burn down the house. All he did, however, was to stride after her to the door and bang and bar it behind her; and then, with a sort of impulse of violent ritual, he rammed the burning brand into the door, blackening and blistering it with one big black sign of the cross. Then he returned, and dropped it again into the fire; and sat down on that seat of sedentary scholarship, that chair of philosophy, that secret throne of contemplation, from which he never rose again.

# III

# THE ARISTOTELIAN REVOLUTION

Albert, the Swabian, rightly called the Great, was the founder of modern science. He did more than any other man to prepare that process, which has turned the alchemist into the chemist, and the astrologer into the astronomer. It is odd that, having been in his time, in this sense almost the first astronomer, he now lingers in legend almost as the last astrologer. Serious historians are abandoning the absurd notion that the medieval Church persecuted all scientists as wizards. It is very nearly the opposite of the truth. The world sometimes persecuted them as wizards, and sometimes ran after them as wizards; the sort of pursuing that is the reverse of persecuting. The Church alone regarded them really and solely as scientists. Many an enquiring cleric was charged with mere magic in making his lenses and mirrors; he was charged by his rude and rustic neighbours; and would probably have been charged in exactly the same way if they had been Pagan neighbours or Puritan neighbours or Seventh-Day Adventist neighbours. But even then he stood a better chance when judged by the Papacy, than if he had been merely lynched by the laity. The Catholic Pontiff did not denounce Albertus Magnus as a magician. It was the half-heathen tribes of the north who admired him as a magician. It is the half-heathen tribes of the industrial towns today, the readers of cheap dream-books, and quack pamphlets, and newspaper prophets, who still admire him as an astrologer. It is admitted that the range of his recorded knowledge, of strictly material and mechanical facts, was amazing in a man of his time. It is true that, in most other cases, there was a certain limitation to the data of medieval science; but this certainly had nothing to do with medieval religion. For the data of Aristotle, and the great Greek civilisation, were in many ways more limited still. But it is not really so much a question of access to the facts, as of attitude to the facts. Most of the Schoolmen, if informed by the only informants they had that a unicorn has one horn or a salamander lives in the fire, still used it more as an illustration of logic than an incident of life. What they really said was, "If a unicorn has one horn, two unicorns have as many horns as one cow." And that has not one inch the less a fact because the unicorn is a fable. But with Albertus in medieval times, as with Aristotle in ancient times, there did begin something like the idea of emphasising the question: "But *does* the unicorn only have one horn or the salamander a fire instead of a fireside?" Doubtless when the social and geographical limits of medieval life began to allow them to search the fire for salamanders or the desert for unicorns, they had to modify many of their scientific ideas. A fact which will expose them to the very proper scorn of a generation of scientists which has just discovered that Newton is nonsense, that space is limited, and that there is no such thing as an atom.

This great German, known in his most famous period as a professor in Paris, was previously for some time professor at Cologne. In that beautiful Roman city, there gathered round him in thousands the lovers of that extraordinary life; the student life of the Middle Ages. They came together in great groups called Nations; and the fact illustrates very well the difference between medieval nationalism and modern nationalism. For although there might any morning be a brawl between the Spanish students and the Scottish students, or between the Flemish and the French, and swords flash or stones fly on the most purely patriotic principles, the fact remains that they had all come to the same school to learn the same philosophy. And though that might not prevent the starting of a quarrel, it might have a great deal to do with the ending of it. Before these motley groups of men from the ends of the earth, the father of science unrolled his scroll of strange wisdom; of sun and comet, of fish and bird. He was an Aristotelian developing, as it were, the one experimental hint of Aristotle; and in this he was entirely original. He cared less to be original about the deeper matters of men and morals; about which he was content to hand on a decent and Christianised Aristotelianism; he was even in a sense ready to compromise upon the merely metaphysical issue of the Nominalists[1] and the Realists. He would never have maintained alone the great war that was coming, for a balanced and humanised Christianity; but when it came, he was entirely on its side. He was called the Universal Doctor, because of the range of his scientific studies; yet he was in truth a specialist. The popular legend is never quite wrong; if a man of science is a magician, he was a magician. And the man of science has always been much *more* of a magician than the priest; since he would "control the elements" rather than submit to the Spirit who is more elementary than the elements.

Among the students thronging into the lecture-rooms there was one student, conspicuous by his tall and bulky figure, and completely failing or refusing to be conspicuous for anything else. He was so dumb in the debates that his fellows began to assume an American significance in the word dumbness; for in that land it is a synonym for dullness. It is clear that, before long, even his imposing stature began to have only the ignominious immensity of the big boy left behind in the lowest form. He was called the Dumb Ox. He was the

[1] Nominalism denies that universals (represented by such common nouns as cow, dog, etc.) exist in the mind or in things. A universal is thus only a word (a nomen). Realism, on the other hand, insists on the existence of universals in both the mind and reality.

object, not merely of mockery, but of pity. One good-natured student pitied him so much as to try to help him with his lessons, going over the elements of logic like an alphabet in a horn-book. The dunce thanked him with pathetic politeness; and the philanthropist went on swimmingly, till he came to a passage about which he was himself a little doubtful; about which, in point of fact, he was wrong. Whereupon the dunce, with every appearance of embarrassment and disturbance, pointed out a possible solution which happened to be right. The benevolent student was left staring, as at a monster, at this mysterious lump of ignorance and intelligence; and strange whispers began to run round the schools.

A regular religious biographer of Thomas Aquinas (who, needless to say, was the dunce in question) has said that by the end of this interview "his love of truth overcame his humility"; which, properly understood, is precisely true. But it does not, in the secondary psychological and social sense, describe all the welter of elements that went on within that massive head. All the relatively few anecdotes about Aquinas have a very peculiar vividness if we visualise the type of man; and this is an excellent example. Amid those elements was something of the difficulty which the generalising intellect has in adapting itself suddenly to a tiny detail of daily life; there was something of the shyness of really well-bred people about showing off; there was something even, perhaps, of that queer paralysis, and temptation to prefer even misunderstandings to long explanations, which led Sir James Barrie,[2] in his amusing sketch, to allow himself to be saddled with a Brother Henry he never possessed, rather than exert himself to put in a word of warning. These other elements

[2] Sir James Barrie (1860–1937) was a novelist and a playwright.

doubtless worked with the very extraordinary humility of this very extraordinary man; but another element worked with his equally unquestionable "love of truth" in bringing the misunderstanding to an end. It is an element that must never be left out of the make-up of St. Thomas. However dreamy or distracted or immersed in theories he might be, he had any amount of Common Sense; and by the time it came, not only to being taught, but to being taught wrong, there was something in him that said sharply, "Oh, this has got to stop!"

It seems probable that it was Albertus Magnus himself, the lecturer and learned teacher of all these youths, who first suspected something of the kind. He gave Thomas small jobs to do, of annotation or exposition; he persuaded him to banish his bashfulness so as to take part in at least one debate. He was a very shrewd old man and had studied the habits of other animals besides the salamander and the unicorn. He had studied many specimens of the most monstrous of all monstrosities; that is called Man. He knew the signs and marks of the sort of man, who is in an innocent way something of a monster among men. He was too good a schoolmaster not to know that the dunce is not always a dunce. He learned with amusement that this dunce had been nicknamed the Dumb Ox by his schoolfellows. All that is natural enough; but it does not take away the savour of something rather strange and symbolic, about the extraordinary emphasis with which he spoke at last. For Aquinas was still generally known only as one obscure and obstinately unresponsive pupil, among many more brilliant and promising pupils, when the great Albert broke silence with his famous cry and prophecy; "You call him a Dumb Ox; I tell you this Dumb Ox shall bellow so loud that his bellowings will fill the world".

To Albertus Magnus, as to Aristotle or Augustine or any number of other and older teachers, St. Thomas was always ready, with the hearty sort of humility, to give thanks for all his thinking. None the less, his own thinking was an advance on Albertus and the other Aristotelians, just as it was an advance on Augustine and the Augustinians. Albert had drawn attention to the direct study of natural facts, if only through fables like the unicorn and the salamander but the monster called Man awaited a much more subtle and flexible vivi-section. The two men, however, became close friends and their friendship counts for a great deal in this central fight of the Middle Ages. For, as we shall see, the rehabilitation of Aristotle was a revolution almost as revolutionary as the exaltation of Dominic and Francis; and St. Thomas was destined to play a striking part in both.

It will be realised that the Aquino family had ultimately abandoned its avenging pursuit of its ugly duckling; who, as a black friar, should perhaps be called its black sheep. Of that escape some picturesque stories are told. The black sheep generally profits at last by quarrels among the white sheep of a family. They begin by quarrelling with him, but they end by quarrelling with each other. There is a rather confusing account concerning which members of his family came over to his side, while he was still imprisoned in the tower. But it is a fact that he was very fond of his sisters, and therefore probably not a fable that it was they who engineered his escape. According to the story, they rigged up a rope to the top of the tower, attached to a big basket, and it must have been rather a big basket if he was indeed lowered in this fashion from his prison, and escaped into the world. Anyhow, he did escape by energy, external or internal. But it was only an individual energy. The world was still pursuing and persecuting the Friars, quite as much as when they fled along the road to Rome. Thomas Aquinas had the good fortune to gather under the shadow of the one great outstanding Friar, whose respectability it was difficult to dispute, the learned and orthodox Albertus; but even he and his were soon troubled by the growing storm that threatened the new popular movements in the Church. Albertus was summoned to Paris, to receive the degree of a Doctor; but everyone knew that every move in that game had the character of a challenge. He made only the request, which probably looked like an eccentric request, that he should take his Dumb Ox along with him. They set out, like ordinary Friars or religious vagabonds; they slept in such monasteries as they could find; and finally in the monastery of St. James in Paris, where Thomas met another Friar who was also another friend.

Perhaps under the shadow of the storm that menaced all Friars, Bonaventure, the Franciscan, grew into so great a friendship with Thomas the Dominican, that their contemporaries compared them to David and Jonathan. The point is of some interest; because it would be quite easy to represent the Franciscan and the Dominican as flatly contradicting each other. The Franciscan may be represented as the Father of all the Mystics; and the Mystics can be represented as men who maintain that the final fruition or joy of the soul is rather a sensation than a thought. The motto of the Mystics has always been, "Taste and see". Now St. Thomas also began by saving, "Taste and see"; but he said it of the first rudimentary impressions of the human animal. It might well be maintained that the Franciscan puts Taste last and the Dominican puts it first. It might be said that the Thomist begins with something solid like the taste of an apple, and afterwards deduces a divine life for the intellect; while the Mystic exhausts the intellect first, and says finally that the sense of God is something like the taste of an apple. A common enemy might claim that St. Thomas begins with the taste of fruit and St. Bonaventure ends with the taste of fruit. But they are both right; if I may say so, it is a privilege of people who contradict each other in their cosmos to be both right. The Mystic is right in saying that the relation of God and Man is essentially a love-story; the pattern and type of all love-stories. The Dominican rationalist is equally right in saying that the intellect is at home in the topmost heavens; and that the appetite for truth may outlast and even devour all the duller appetites of man.

At the moment Aquinas and Bonaventure were encouraged in the possibility that they were both right; by the almost universal agreement that they were both wrong. It was in any case a time of wild disturbance, and, as is common in such times, those who were trying to put things right were most vigorously accused of putting things wrong. Nobody knew who would win in that welter; Islam, or the Manichees of the Midi; or the two-faced and mocking Emperor; or the Crusades; or the old Orders of Christendom. But some men had a very vivid feeling that everything was breaking up; and that all the recent experiments or excesses were part of the same social dissolution; and there were two things that such men regarded as signs of ruin; one was the awful apparition of Aristotle out of the East, a sort of Greek god supported by Arabian worshippers; and the other was the new freedom of the Friars. It was the opening of the monastery and the scattering of the monks to wander over the world. The general feeling that they wandered like sparks from a furnace hitherto contained; the furnace of the abnormal love of God: the sense that they would utterly unbalance the common people with the counsels of perfection; that they would drift into being demagogues; all this finally burst out in a famous book called *The Perils of the Latter Times*, by a furious reactionary, William de St. Amour. It challenged the French King and the Pope, so that they established an enquiry. And Aquinas and Bonaventure, the two incongruous friends, with their respectively topsy-turvy universes, went up to Rome together, to defend the freedom of the Friars.

Thomas Aquinas defended the great vow of his youth, for freedom and for the poor; and it was probably the topmost moment of his generally triumphant career; for he turned back the whole backward movement of his time. Responsible authorities have said that, but for him, the whole great popular movement of the Friars might have been destroyed. With this popular victory the shy and awkward student finally becomes a historical character and a public man. After that, he was identified with the Mendicant Orders. But while St. Thomas may be said to have made his name in the defence of the Mendicant Orders against the reactionaries, who took the same view of them as his own family had taken, there is generally a difference between a man making his name and a man really doing his work. The work of Thomas Aquinas was yet to come; but less shrewd observers than he could already see that it was coming. Broadly speaking, the danger was the danger of the orthodox, or those who too easily identify the old order with the orthodox, forcing a final and conclusive condemnation of Aristotle. There had already been rash and random condemnations to that effect, issued here and there, and the pressure of the narrower Augustinians upon the Pope and the principal judges became daily more pressing. The peril had appeared, not unnaturally, because of the historical and geographical accident of the Moslem proximity to the culture of Byzantium. The Arabs had got hold of the Greek manuscripts before the Latins who were the true heirs of the Greeks. And Moslems, though not very orthodox Moslems, were turning Aristotle into a pantheist philosophy still less acceptable to orthodox Christians. This second controversy, however, requires more explanation than the first. As is remarked on an introductory page, most modern people do know that St. Francis at least was a liberator of large sympathies; that, whatever their positive view of medievalism, the Friars were in a relative sense a popular movement, pointing to greater fraternity and freedom; and a very little further information would inform them that this was every bit as true of the Dominican as of the Franciscan Friars. Nobody now is particularly likely to start up in defence of feudal abbots or fixed and stationary monks, against such impudent innovators as St. Francis and St. Thomas. We may therefore be allowed to summarise briefly the great debate about the Friars, though it shook all Christendom in its day. But the greater debate about Aristotle presents a greater difficulty; because there are modern misconceptions about it which can only be approached with a little more elaboration.

Perhaps there is really no such thing as a Revolution recorded in history. What happened was always a Counter-Revolution. Men were always rebelling against the last rebels; or even repenting of the last rebellion. This could be seen in the most casual contemporary fashions, if the fashionable mind had not fallen into the habit of seeing the very latest rebel as rebelling against all ages at once. The Modern Girl with the lipstick and the cocktail is as much a rebel against the Woman's Rights Woman of the '80's, with her stiff stick-up collars and strict teetotalism, as the latter was a rebel against the Early Victorian lady of the languid waltz tunes and the album full of quotations from Byron; or as the last, again, was a rebel against a Puritan mother to whom the waltz was a wild orgy and Byron the Bolshevist of his age. Trace even the Puritan mother back through history and she represents a rebellion against the Cavalier laxity of the English Church, which was at first a rebel against the Catholic civilisation, which had been a rebel against the Pagan civilisation. Nobody but a lunatic could pretend that these things were a progress; for they obviously go first one way and then the other. But whichever is right, one thing is certainly wrong; and that is the modern habit of looking at them only from the modern end. For that is only to see the end of the tale; they rebel against they know not what, because it arose they know not when; intent only on its ending, they are ignorant of its beginning; and therefore of its very being. The difference between the smaller cases and the larger, is that in the latter there is really so huge a human upheaval that men start from it like men in a new world; and that very novelty enables them to go on very long; and generally to go on too long. It is *because* these things start with a vigorous revolt that the intellectual impetus lasts long enough to make them seem like a survival. An excellent example of this is the real story of the revival and the neglect of Aristotle. By the end of the medieval time, Aristotelianism did eventually grow stale. Only a very fresh and successful novelty ever gets quite so stale as that.

When the moderns, drawing the blackest curtain of obscurantism that ever obscured history, decided that nothing mattered much before the Renaissance and the Reformation, they instantly began their modern career by falling into a big blunder. It was the blunder about Platonism. They found, hanging about the courts of the swaggering princes of the sixteenth century (which was as far back in history as they were allowed to go) certain anti-clerical artists and scholars who said they were bored with Aristotle and were supposed to be secretly indulging in Plato. The moderns, utterly ignorant of the whole story of the medievals, instantly fell into the trap. They assumed that Aristotle was some crabbed antiquity and tyranny from the black back of the Dark Ages, and that Plato was an entirely new Pagan pleasure never yet tasted by Christian men. Father Knox has shown in what a startling state of innocence is the mind of Mr. H. L. Mencken, for instance, upon this point. In fact, of course, the story is exactly the other way round. If anything, it was Platonism that was the old orthodoxy. It was Aristotelianism that was the very modern revolution. And the leader of that modern revolution was the man who is the subject of this book.

The truth is that the historical Catholic Church began by being Platonist; by being rather too Platonist. Platonism was in that very golden Greek air that was breathed by the first great Greek theologians. The Christian Fathers were much more like the Neo-Platonists than were the scholars of the Renaissance; who were only Neo-Neo-Platonists. For Chrysostom or Basil it was as ordinary and normal to think in terms of the Logos, or the Wisdom which is the aim of philosophers, as it is to any men of any religion today to talk about social problems or progress or the economic crisis throughout the world. St. Augustine followed a natural mental evolution when he was a Platonist before he was a Manichean, and a Manichean before he was a Christian. And it was exactly in that last association that the first faint hint, of the danger of being *too* Platonist, may be seen.

From the Renaissance to the nineteenth century, the Moderns have had an almost monstrous love of the Ancients. In considering medieval life, they could never regard the Christians as anything but the pupils of the Pagans; of Plato in ideas, or Aristotle in reason and science. It was not so. On some points, even from the most monotonously modern standpoint, Catholicism was centuries ahead of Platonism or Aristotelianism. We can see it still, for instance, in the tiresome tenacity of Astrology. On that matter the philosophers were all in favour of superstition; and the saints and all such superstitious people were against superstition. But even the great saints found it difficult to get disentangled from this superstition. Two points were always put by those suspicious of the Aristotelianism of Aquinas; and they sound to us now very quaint and comic, taken together. One was the view that the stars are personal beings, governing our lives; the other the great general theory that men have one mind between them; a view obviously opposed to immortality; that is, to individuality. Both linger among the Moderns; so strong is still the tyranny of the Ancients. Astrology sprawls over the Sunday papers, and the other doctrine has its hundredth form in what is called Communism; or the Soul of the Hive.

For on one preliminary point, this position must not be misunderstood. When we praise the practical value of the Aristotelian Revolution, and the originality of Aquinas in leading it, we do not mean that the Scholastic philosophers before him had not been philosophers, or had not been highly philosophical, or had not been in touch with ancient philosophy. In so far as there was ever a bad break in philosophical history, it was not before St. Thomas, or at the beginning of medieval history; it was after St. Thomas and at the beginning of modern history. The great intellectual tradition that comes down to us from Pythagoras and Plato was never interrupted or lost through such trifles as the sack of Rome, the triumph of Attila or all the barbarian invasions of the Dark Ages. It was only lost after the introduction of printing, the discovery of America, the founding of the Royal Society and all the enlightenment of the Renaissance and the modern world. It was there, if anywhere, that there was lost or impatiently snapped the long thin delicate thread that had descended from distant antiquity; the thread of that unusual human hobby; the habit of thinking. This is proved by the fact that the printed books of this later period largely had to wait for the eighteenth century, or the end of the seventeenth century, to find even the names of the new philosophers; who were at the best a new kind of philosophers. But the decline of the Empire, the Dark Ages and the early Middle Ages, though too much tempted to neglect what was opposed to Platonic philosophy, had never neglected philosophy. In that sense St. Thomas, like most other very original men, has a long and clear pedigree. He himself is constantly referring back to the authorities from St. Augustine to St. Anselm, and from St. Anselm to St. Albert, and even when he differs, he also defers.

A very learned Anglican once said to me, not perhaps without a touch of tartness, "I can't understand why everybody talks as if Thomas Aquinas were the beginning of the Scholastic philosophy. I could understand their saying he was the end of it." Whether or no the comment was meant to be tart, we may be sure that the reply of St. Thomas would have been perfectly urbane. And indeed it would be easy to answer, with a certain placidity, that in his Thomist language, the end of a thing does not mean its destruction, but its fulfilment. No Thomist will complain, if Thomism is the end of our philosophy, in the sense in which God is the end of our existence. For that does not mean that we cease to exist, but that we become as perennial as the *philosophia perennis*. Putting this claim on one side, however, it is important to remember that my distinguished interlocutor was perfectly right, in that there had been whole dynasties of doctrinal philosophers before Aquinas, leading up to the day of the great revolt of the Aristotelians. Nor was even that revolt a thing entirely abrupt and unforeseen. An able writer in the *Dublin Review* not long ago pointed out that in some respects the whole nature of metaphysics had advanced a long way since Aristotle, by the time it came to Aquinas. And that it is no disrespect to the primitive and gigantic genius of the Stagirite to say that in some respects he was really but a rude and rough founder of philosophy, compared with some of the subsequent subtleties of medievalism; that the Greek gave a few grand hints which the Scholastics developed into the most delicate fine shades. This may be an overstatement, but there is a truth in it. Anyhow, it is certain that even in Aristotelian philosophy, let alone Platonic philosophy, there was already a tradition of highly intelligent interpretation. If that delicacy afterwards degenerated into hair-splitting, it was none the less delicate hair-splitting; and work requiring very scientific tools.

What made the Aristotelian Revolution really revolutionary was the fact that it was really religious. It is the fact, so fundamental that I thought it well to lay it down in the first few pages of this book; that the revolt was largely a revolt of the most Christian elements in Christendom. St. Thomas, every bit as much as St. Francis, felt subconsciously that the hold of his people was slipping on the solid Catholic doctrine and discipline, worn smooth by more than a thousand years of routine; and that the Faith needed to be shown under a new light and dealt with from another angle. But he had no motive except the desire to make it popular for the salvation of the people. It was true, broadly speaking, that for some time past it had been too Platonist to be popular. It needed something like the shrewd and homely touch of Aristotle to turn it again into a religion of common sense. Both the motive and the method are illustrated in the war of Aquinas against the Augustinians.

First, it must be remembered that the Greek influence continued to flow from the Greek Empire; or at least from the centre of the Roman Empire which was in the Greek city of Byzantium, and no longer in Rome. That influence was Byzantine in every good and bad sense; like Byzantine art, it was severe and mathematical and a little terrible; like Byzantine etiquette, it was Oriental and faintly decadent. We owe to the learning of Mr. Christopher Dawson much enlightenment upon the way in which Byzantium slowly stiffened into a sort of Asiatic theocracy, more like that which served the Sacred Emperor in China. But even the unlearned can see the difference, in the way in which Eastern Christianity flattened everything, as it flattened the faces of the images into icons. It became a thing of patterns rather than pictures; and it made definite and destructive war upon statues. Thus we see, strangely enough, that the East was the land of the Cross and the West was the land of the Crucifix. The Greeks were being dehumanised by a radiant symbol, while the Goths were being humanised by an instrument of torture. Only the West made realistic pictures of the greatest of all the tales out of the East. Hence the Greek element in Christian theology tended more and more to be a sort of dried up Platonism; a thing of diagrams and abstractions; to the last indeed noble abstractions, but not sufficiently touched by that great thing that is by definition almost the opposite of abstraction: Incarnation. Their Logos was the Word; but not the Word made Flesh. In a thousand very subtle ways, often escaping doctrinal definition, this spirit spread over the world of Christendom from the place where the Sacred Emperor sat under his golden mosaics; and the flat pavement of the Roman Empire was at last a sort of smooth pathway for Mahomet. For Islam was the ultimate fulfilment of the Iconoclasts. Long before that, however, there was this tendency to make the Cross merely decorative like the Crescent; to make it a pattern like the Greek key or the Wheel of Buddha. But there is something passive about such a world of patterns, and the Greek Key does not open any door, while the Wheel of Buddha always moves round and never moves on.

Partly through these negative influences, partly through a necessary and noble asceticism which sought to emulate the awful standard of the martyrs, the earlier Christian ages had been excessively anti-corporeal and too near the danger-line of Manichean mysticism. But there was far less danger in the fact that the saints macerated the body than in the fact that the sages neglected it. Granted all the grandeur of Augustine's contribution to Christianity, there was in a sense a more subtle danger in Augustine the Platonist than even in Augustine the Manichee. There came from it a mood which unconsciously committed the heresy of dividing the substance of the Trinity. It thought of God too exclusively as a Spirit who purifies or a Saviour who redeems; and too little as a Creator who creates. That is why men like Aquinas thought it right to correct Plato by an appeal to Aristotle; Aristotle who took things as he found them, just as Aquinas accepted things as God created them. In all the work of St. Thomas the world of positive creation is perpetually present. Humanly speaking, it was he who saved the human element in Christian theology, if he used for convenience certain elements in heathen philosophy. Only, as has already been urged, the human element is also the Christian one.

The panic upon the Aristotelian peril, that had passed across the high places of the Church, was probably a dry wind from the desert. It was really filled rather with fear of Mahomet than fear of Aristotle. And this was ironic, because there was really much more difficulty in reconciling Aristotle with Mahomet than in reconciling him with Christ. Islam is essentially a simple creed for simple men; and nobody can ever really turn pantheism into a simple creed. It is at once too abstract and too complicated. There are simple believers in a personal God; and there are atheists more simple-minded than any believers in a personal God. But few can, in mere simplicity, accept a godless universe as a god. And while the Moslem, as compared with the Christian, had perhaps a less human God, he had if possible a more personal God. The will of Allah was very much of a will, and could not be turned into a stream of tendency. On all that cosmic and abstract side the Catholic was more accommodating than the Moslem—up to a point. The Catholic could admit at least that Aristotle was right about the impersonal elements of a personal God. Hence, we may say broadly of the Moslem philosophers, that those who became good philosophers became bad Moslems. It is not altogether unnatural that many bishops and doctors feared that the Thomists might become good philosophers and bad Christians. But there were also many, of the strict school of Plato and Augustine, who stoutly denied that they were even good philosophers. Between those rather incongruous passions, the love of Plato and the fear of Mahomet, there was a moment when the prospects of any Aristotelian culture in Christendom looked very dark indeed. Anathema after anathema was thundered from high places; and under the shadow of the persecution, as so often happens, it seemed for a moment that barely one or two figures stood alone in the storm-swept area. They were both in the black and white of the Dominicans; for Albertus and Aquinas stood firm.

In that sort of combat there is always confusion; and majorities change into minorities and back again, as if by magic. It is always difficult to date the turn of the tide, which seems to be a welter of eddies; the very dates seeming to overlap and confuse the crisis. But the change, from the moment when the two Dominicans stood alone to the moment when the whole Church at last wheeled into line with them, may perhaps be found at about the moment when they were practically brought before a hostile but a not unjust judge. Stephen Tempier, the Bishop of Paris, was apparently a rather fine specimen of the old fanatical Churchman, who thought that admiring Aristotle was a weakness likely to be followed by adoring Apollo. He was also, by a piece of bad luck, one of the old social conservatives, who had intensely resented the popular revolution of the Preaching Friars. But he was an honest man; and Thomas Aquinas never asked for anything but permission to address honest men. All around him there were other Aristotelian revolutionaries of a much more dubious sort. There was Siger, the sophist from Brabant, who learned all his Aristotelianism from the Arabs; and had an ingenious theory about how an Arabian agnostic could also be a Christian. There were a thousand young men of the sort that had shouted for Abelard; full of the youth of the thirteenth century and drunken with the Greek wine of Stagira. Over against them, lowering and implacable, was the old Puritan party of the Augustinians; only too delighted to class the rationalistic Albert and Thomas with equivocal Moslem meta-physicians.

It would seem that the triumph of Thomas was really a personal triumph. He withdrew not a single one of his propositions; though it is said that the reactionary Bishop did condemn some of them after his death. On the whole, however, Aquinas convinced most of his critics that he was quite as good a Catholic as they were. There was a sequel of squabbles between the Religious Orders, following upon this controversial crisis. But it is probably true to say that the fact, that a man like Aquinas had managed even partially to satisfy a man like Tempier, was the end of the essential quarrel. What was already familiar to the few became familiar to the many; that an Aristotelian could really be a Christian. Another fact assisted in the common conversion. It rather curiously resembles the story of the translation of the Bible; and the alleged Catholic suppression of the Bible. Behind the scenes, where the Pope was much more tolerant than the Paris Bishop, the friends of Aquinas had been hard at work producing a new translation of Aristotle. It demonstrated that in many ways the heretical translation had been a very heretical translation. With the final consummation of this work, we may say that the great Greek philosophy entered finally into the system of Christendom. The process has been half humourously described as the Baptism of Aristotle.

We have all heard of the humility of the man of science; of many who were very genuinely humble; and of some who were very proud of their humility. It will be the somewhat too recurrent burden of this brief study that Thomas Aquinas really did have the humility of the man of science; as a special variant of the humility of the saint. It is true that he did not himself contribute anything concrete in the experiment or detail of physical science; in this, it may be said, he even lagged behind the last generation, and was far less of an experimental scientist than his tutor Albertus Magnus. But for all that, he was historically a great friend to the freedom of science. The principles he laid down, properly understood, are perhaps the best that can be produced for protecting science from mere obscurantist persecution. For instance, in the matter of the inspiration of Scripture, he fixed first on the obvious fact, which was forgotten by four furious centuries of sectarian battle, that the meaning of Scripture is very far from self-evident; and that we must often interpret it in the light of other truths. If a literal interpretation is really and flatly contradicted by an obvious fact, why then we can only say that the literal interpretation must be a false interpretation. But the fact must really be an obvious fact. And unfortunately, nineteenth-century scientists were just as ready to jump to the conclusion that any guess about nature was an obvious fact, as were seventeenth-century sectarians to jump to the conclusion that any guess about Scripture was the obvious explanation. Thus, private theories about what the Bible ought to mean, and premature theories about what the world ought to mean, have met in loud and widely advertised controversy, especially in the Victorian time; and this clumsy collision of two very impatient forms of ignorance was known as the quarrel of Science and Religion.

But St. Thomas had the scientific humility in this very vivid and special sense; that he was ready to take the lowest place; for the examination of the lowest things. He did not, like a modern specialist, study the worm as if it were the world; but he was willing to begin to study the reality of the world in the reality of the worm. His Aristotelianism simply meant that the study of the humblest fact will lead to the study of the highest truth. That for him the process was logical and not biological, was concerned with philosophy rather than science, does not alter the essential idea that he believed in beginning at the bottom of the ladder. But he also gave, by his view of Scripture and Science, and other questions, a sort of charter for pioneers more purely practical than himself. He practically said that if they could really prove their practical discoveries, the traditional interpretation of Scripture must give way before those discoveries. He could hardly, as the common phrase goes, say fairer than that. If the matter had been left to him, and men like him, there never would have been any quarrel between Science and Religion. He did his very best to map out two provinces for them, and to trace a just frontier between them.

It is often cheerfully remarked that Christianity has failed, by which is meant that it has never had that sweeping, imperial and imposed supremacy, which has belonged to each of the great revolutions, every one of which has subsequently failed. There was never a moment when men could say that every man was a Christian; as they might say for several months that every man was a Royalist or a Republican or a Communist. But if sane historians want to understand the sense in which the Christian character has succeeded, they could not find a better case than the massive moral pressure of a man like St. Thomas, in support of the buried rationalism of the heathens, which had as yet only been dug up for the amusement of the heretics. It was, quite strictly and exactly, because a new kind of man was conducting rational enquiry in a new kind of way, that men forgot the curse that had fallen on the temples of the dead demons and the palaces of the dead despots; forgot even the new fury out of Arabia against which they were fighting for their lives; because the man who was asking them to return to sense, or to return to their senses, was not a sophist but a saint. Aristotle had described the magnanimous man, who is great and knows that he is great. But Aristotle would never have recovered his own greatness, but for the miracle that created the more magnanimous man; who is great and knows that he is small.

There is a certain historical importance in what some would call the heaviness of the style employed. It carries a curious impression of candour, which really did have, I think, a considerable effect upon contemporaries. The saint has sometimes been called a sceptic. The truth is that he was very largely tolerated as a sceptic because he was obviously a saint. When he seemed to stand up as a stubborn Aristotelian, hardly distinguishable from the Arabian heretics, I do seriously believe that what protected him was very largely the prodigious power of his simplicity and his obvious goodness and love of truth. Those who went out against the haughty confidence of the heretics were stopped and brought up all standing, against a sort of huge humility which was like a mountain; or perhaps like that immense valley that is the mould of a mountain. Allowing for all medieval conventions, we can feel that with the other innovators, this was not always so. The others, from Abelard down to Siger of Brabant, have never quite lost, in the long process of history, a faint air of showing off. Nobody could feel for a moment that Thomas Aquinas was showing off. The very dullness of diction, of which some complain, was enormously convincing. He could have given wit as well as wisdom; but he was so prodigiously in earnest that he gave his wisdom without his wit.

After the hour of triumph came the moment of peril. It is always so with alliances, and especially because Aquinas was fighting on two fronts. His main business was to defend the Faith against the abuse of Aristotle; and he boldly did it by supporting the use of Aristotle. He knew perfectly well that armies of atheists and anarchists were roaring applause in the background at his Aristotelian victory over all he held most dear. Nevertheless, it was never the existence of atheists, any more than Arabs or Aristotelian pagans, that disturbed the extraordinary controversial composure of Thomas Aquinas. The real peril that followed on the victory he had won for Aristotle was vividly presented in the curious case of Siger of Brabant; and it is well worth study, for anyone who would begin to comprehend the strange history of Christendom. It is marked by one rather queer quality; which has always been the unique note of the Faith, though it is not noticed by its modern enemies, and rarely by its modern friends. It is the fact symbolised in the legend of Antichrist, who was the double of Christ; in the profound proverb that the Devil is the ape of God. It is the fact that falsehood is never so false as when it is very nearly true. It is when the stab comes near the nerve of truth, that the Christian conscience cries out in pain. And Siger of Brabant, following on some of the Arabian Aristotelians, advanced a theory which most modern newspaper readers would instantly have declared to be the same as the theory of St. Thomas. That was what finally roused St. Thomas to his last and most emphatic protest. He had won his battle for a wider scope of philosophy and science; he had cleared the ground for a general understanding about faith and enquiry; an understanding that has generally been observed among Catholics, and certainly never deserted without disaster. It was the idea that the scientist should go on exploring and experimenting freely, so long as he did not claim an infallibility and finality which it was against his own principles to claim. Meanwhile the Church should go on developing and defining, about supernatural things, so long as she did not claim a right to alter the deposit of faith, which it was against her own principles to claim. And when he had said this, Siger of Brabant got up and said something so horribly like it, and so horribly unlike, that (like Antichrist) he might have deceived the very elect.

Siger of Brabant said this: the Church must be right theologically, but she can be wrong scientifically. There are two truths; the truth of the supernatural world, and the truth of the natural world, which contradicts the supernatural world. While we are being naturalists, we can suppose that Christianity is all nonsense; but then, when we remember that we are Christians, we must admit that Christianity is true even if it is nonsense. In other words, Siger of Brabant split the human head in two, like the blow in an old legend of battle; and declared that a man has two minds, with one of which he must entirely believe and with the other may utterly disbelieve. To many this would at least seem like a parody of Thomism. As a fact, it was the assassination of Thomism. It was not two ways of finding the same truth; it was an untruthful way of pretending that there are two truths. And it is extraordinarily interesting to note that this is the one occasion when the Dumb Ox really came out like a wild bull. When he stood up to answer Siger of Brabant, he was altogether transfigured, and the very style of his sentences, which is a thing like the tone of a man's voice, is suddenly altered. He had never been angry with any of the enemies who disagreed with him. But these enemies had attempted the worst treachery: they had made him agree with them.

Those who complain that theologians draw fine distinctions could hardly find a better example of their own folly. In fact, a fine distinction can be a flat contradiction. It was notably so in this case. St. Thomas was willing to allow the one truth to be approached by two paths, precisely *because* he was sure there was only one truth. Because the Faith was the one truth, nothing discovered in nature could ultimately contradict the Faith. Because the Faith was the one truth, nothing really deduced from the Faith could ultimately contradict the facts. It was in truth a curiously daring confidence in the reality of his religion; and though some may linger to dispute it, it has been justified. The scientific facts, which were supposed to contradict the Faith in the nineteenth century, are nearly all of them regarded as unscientific fictions in the twentieth century. Even the materialists have fled from materialism; and those who lectured us about determinism in psychology are already talking about indeterminism in matter. But whether his confidence was right or wrong, it was specially and supremely a confidence that there is one truth which cannot contradict itself. And this last group of enemies suddenly sprang up, to tell him they entirely agreed with him in saying that there are two contradictory truths. Truth, in the medieval phrase, carried two faces under one hood; and these double-faced sophists practically dared to suggest that it was the Dominican hood.

So, in his last battle and for the first time, he fought as with a battle-axe. There is a ring in the words altogether beyond the almost impersonal patience he maintained in debate with so many enemies. "Behold our refutation of the error. It is not based on documents of faith, but on the reasons and statements of the philosophers themselves. If then anyone there be who, boastfully taking pride in his supposed wisdom, wishes to challenge what we have written, let him not do it in some corner nor before children who are powerless to decide on such difficult matters. Let him reply openly if he dare. He shall find me then confronting him, and not only my negligible self, but many another whose study is truth. We shall do battle with his errors or bring a cure to his ignorance."

The Dumb Ox is bellowing now; like one at bay and yet terrible and towering over all the baying pack. We have already noted why, in this one quarrel with Siger of Brabant, Thomas Aquinas let loose such thunders of purely moral passion; it was because the whole work of his life was being betrayed behind his back, by those who had used his victories over the reactionaries. The point at the moment is that this is perhaps his one moment of personal passion, save for a single flash in the troubles of his youth; and he is once more fighting his enemies with a firebrand. And yet, even in this isolated apocalypse of anger, there is one phrase that may be commended for all time to men who are angry with much less cause. If there is one sentence that could be carved in marble, as representing the calmest and most enduring rationality of his unique intelligence, it is a sentence which came pouring out with all the rest of this molten lava. If there is one phrase that stands before history as typical of Thomas Aquinas, it is that phrase about his own argument: "It is not based on documents of faith, but on the reasons and statements of the philosophers themselves." Would that all Orthodox doctors in deliberation were as reasonable as Aquinas in anger! Would that all Christian apologists would remember that maxim; and write it up in large letters on the wall, before they nail any theses there. At the top of his fury, Thomas Aquinas understands, what so many defenders of orthodoxy will not understand. It is no good to tell an atheist that he is an atheist; or to charge a denier of immortality with the infamy of denying it; or to imagine that one can force an opponent to admit he is wrong, by proving that he is wrong on somebody else's principles, but not on his own. After the great example of St. Thomas, the principle stands, or ought always to have stood established; that we must either not argue with a man at all, or we must argue on his grounds and not ours. We may do other things *instead* of arguing, according to our views of what actions are morally permissible; but if we argue we must argue 'on the reasons and statements of the philosophers themselves.' This is the common sense in a saying attributed to a friend of St. Thomas, the great St. Louis, King of France, which shallow people quote as a sample of fanaticism; the sense of which is, that I must either argue with an infidel as a real philosopher can argue, or else 'thrust a sword through his body as far as it will go.' A real philosopher (even of the opposite school) will be the first to agree that St. Louis was entirely philosophical.

So, in the last great controversial crisis of his theological campaign, Thomas Aquinas contrived to give his friends and enemies not only a lesson in theology, but a lesson in controversy. But it was in fact his last controversy. He had been a man with a huge controversial appetite, a thing that exists in some men and not others, in saints and in sinners. But after this great and victorious duel with Siger of Brabant, he was suddenly overwhelmed with a desire for silence and repose. He said one strange thing about this mood of his to a friend, which will fall into its more appropriate place elsewhere. He fell back on the extreme simplicities of his monastic round and seemed to desire nothing but a sort of permanent retreat. A request came to him from the Pope that he should set out upon some further mission of diplomacy or disputation; and he made ready to obey. But before he had gone many miles on the journey, he was dead.

## IV

# A MEDITATION ON THE MANICHEES

There is one casual anecdote about St. Thomas Aquinas which illuminates him like a lightning-flash, not only without but within. For it not only shows him as a character, and even as a comedy character, and shows the colours of his period and social background; but also, as if for an instant, makes a transparency of his mind. It is a trivial incident which occurred one day, when he was reluctantly dragged from his work, and we might almost say from his play. For both were for him found in the unusual hobby of thinking, which is for some men a thing much more intoxicating than mere drinking. He had declined any number of society invitations, to the courts of kings and princes, not because he was unfriendly, for he was not; but because he was always glowing within with the really gigantic plans of exposition and argument which filled his life. On one occasion, however, he was invited to the court of King Louis IX of France, more famous as the great St. Louis; and for some reason or other, the Dominican authorities of his Order told him to accept; so he immediately did so, being an obedient friar even in his sleep; or rather in his permanent trance of reflection.

It is a real case against conventional hagiography that it sometimes tends to make all saints seem to be the same. Whereas in fact no men are more different than saints; not even murderers. And there could hardly be a more complete contrast, given the essentials of holiness, than between St. Thomas and St. Louis. St. Louis was born a knight and a king; but he was one of those men in whom a certain simplicity, combined with courage and activity, makes it natural, and in a sense easy, to fulfil directly and promptly any duty or office, however official. He was a man in whom holiness and healthiness had no quarrel; and their issue was in action. He did not go in for thinking much, in the sense of theorising much. But, even in theory, he had that sort of presence of mind, which belongs to the rare and really practical man when he has to think. He never said the wrong thing; and he was orthodox by instinct. In the old pagan proverb about kings being philosophers or philosophers kings, there was a certain miscalculation, connected with a mystery that only Christianity could reveal. For while it is possible for a king to wish very much to be a saint, it is not possible for a saint to wish very much to be a king. A good man will hardly be always dreaming of being a great monarch; but, such is the liberality of the Church, that she cannot forbid even a great monarch to dream of being a good man. But Louis was a straight-forward soldierly sort of person who did not particularly mind being a king, any more than he would have minded being a captain or a sergeant or any other rank in his army. Now a man like St. Thomas would definitely dislike being a king, or being entangled with the pomp and politics of kings; not only his humility, but a sort of subconscious fastidiousness and fine dislike of futility, often found in leisurely and learned men with large minds, would really have prevented him making contact with the complexity of court life. Also, he was anxious all his life to keep out of politics; and there was no political symbol more striking, or in a sense more challenging, at that moment, than the power of the King in Paris.

Paris was truly at that time an *aurora borealis*; a Sunrise in the North. We must realise that lands much nearer to Rome had rotted with paganism and pessimism and Oriental influences of which the most respectable was that of Mahound. Provence and all the South had been full of a fever of nihilism or negative mysticism, and from Northern France had come the spears and swords that swept away the unchristian thing. In Northern France also sprang up that splendour of building that shine like swords and spears: the first spires of the Gothic. We talk now of grey Gothic buildings; but they must have been very different when they went up white and gleaming into the northern skies, partly picked out with gold and bright colours; a new flight of architecture, as startling as flying-ships. The new Paris ultimately left behind by St. Louis must have been a thing white like lilies and splendid as the oriflamme. It was the beginning of the great new thing: the nation of France, which was to pierce and overpower the old quarrel of Pope and Emperor in the lands from which Thomas came. But Thomas came very unwillingly, and, if we may say it of so kindly a man, rather sulkily. As he entered Paris, they showed him from the hill that splendour of new spires beginning, and somebody said something like, "How grand it must be to own all this." And Thomas Aquinas only muttered, "I would rather have that Chrysostom MS. I can't get hold of."

Somehow they steered that reluctant bulk of reflection to a seat in the royal banquet hall; and all that we know of Thomas tells us that he was perfectly courteous to those who spoke to him, but spoke little, and was soon forgotten in the most brilliant and noisy clatter in the world: the noise of French talking. What the Frenchmen were talking about we do not know; but they forgot all about the large fat Italian in their midst, and it seems only too possible that he forgot all about them. Sudden silences will occur even in French conversation; and in one of these the interruption came. There had long been no word or motion in that huge heap of black and white weeds, like motley in mourning, which marked him as a mendicant friar out of the streets, and contrasted with all the colours and patterns and quarterings of that first and freshest dawn of chivalry and heraldry.

The triangular shields and pennons and pointed spears, the triangular swords of the Crusade, the pointed windows and the conical hoods, repeated everywhere that fresh French medieval spirit that did, in every sense, come to the point. But the colours of the coats were gay and varied, with little to rebuke their richness; for St. Louis, who had himself a special quality of coming to the point, had said to his courtiers, "Vanity should be avoided; but every man should dress well, in the manner of his rank, that his wife may the more easily love him."

And then suddenly the goblets leapt and rattled on the board and the great table shook, for the friar had brought down his huge fist like a club of stone, with a crash that startled everyone like an explosion; and had cried out in a strong voice, but like a man in the grip of a dream, "And *that* will settle the Manichees!"

The palace of a king, even when it is the palace of a saint, has it conventions. A shock thrilled through the court, and every one felt as if the fat friar from Italy had thrown a plate at King Louis, or knocked his crown sideways. They all looked timidly at the terrible seat, that was for a thousand years the throne of the Capets; and many there were presumably prepared to pitch the big black-robed beggarman out of the window. But St. Louis, simple as he seemed, was no mere medieval fountain of honour or even fountain of mercy; but also the fountain of two eternal rivers; the irony and the courtesy of France. And he turned to his secretaries, asking them in a low voice to take their tablets round to the seat of the absent-minded controversialist, and take a note of the argument that had just occurred to him; because it must be a very good one and he might forget it. I have paused upon this anecdote, first, as has been said, because it is the one which gives us the most vivid snapshot of a great medieval character; indeed of two great medieval characters. But it also specially fitted to be taken as a type or a turning-point, because of the glimpse it gives of the man's main preoccupation; and the sort of thing that might have been found in his thoughts, if they had been thus surprised at any moment by a philosophical eavesdropper or through a psychological keyhole. It was not for nothing that he was still brooding, even in the white court of St. Louis, upon the dark cloud of the Manichees.

This book is meant only to be the sketch of a man; but it must at least lightly touch, later on, upon a method and a meaning; or what our journalism has an annoying way of calling a message. A few very inadequate pages must be given to the man in relation to his theology and his philosophy; but the thing of which I mean to speak here is something at once more general and more personal even than his philosophy. I have therefore introduced it here, before we come to anything like technical talk about his philosophy. It was something that might alternatively be called his moral attitude, or his temperamental predisposition, or the purpose of his life so far as social and human effects were concerned: for he knew better than most of us that there is but one purpose in this life, and it is one that is beyond this life. But if we wanted to put in a picturesque and simplified form what he wanted for the world, and what was his work in history, apart from theoretical and theological definitions, we might well say that it really was to strike a blow and settle the Manichees.

The full meaning of this may not be apparent to those who do not study theological history; and perhaps even less apparent to those who do. Indeed it may seem equally irrelevant to the history and the theology. In history St. Dominic and Simon de Montfort between them had already pretty well settled the Manichees. And in theology, of course, an encyclopaedic doctor like Aquinas dealt with a thousand other heresies besides the Manichean heresy. Nevertheless, it does represent his main position and the turn he gave to the whole history of Christendom.

I think it well to interpose this chapter, though its scope may seem more vague than the rest; because there is a sort of big blunder about St. Thomas and his creed, which is an obstacle for most modern people in even beginning to understand them. It arises roughly thus. St. Thomas, like other monks, and especially other saints, lived a life of renunciation and austerity; his fasts, for instance, being in marked contrast to the luxury in which he might have lived if he chose. This element stands high in his religion, as a manner of asserting the will against the power of nature, of thanking the Redeemer by partially sharing his sufferings, of making a man ready for anything as a missionary or martyr, and similar ideals. These happen to be rare in the modern industrial society of the West, outside his communion; and it is therefore assumed that they are the whole meaning of that communion. Because it is uncommon for an alderman to fast forty days, or a politician to take a Trappist vow of silence, or a man about town to live a life of strict celibacy, the average outsider is convinced, not only that Catholicism is nothing except asceticism, but that asceticism is nothing except pessimism. He is so obliging as to explain to Catholics why they hold this heroic virtue in respect; and is ever ready to point out that the philosophy behind it is an Oriental hatred of anything connected with Nature, and a purely Schopenhauerian disgust with the Will to Live. I read in a "high-class" review of Miss Rebecca West's book on St. Augustine, the astounding statement that the Catholic Church regards sex as having the nature of sin. How marriage can be a sacrament if sex is a sin, or why it is the Catholics who are in favour of birth and their foes who are in favour of birth-control, I will leave the critic to worry out for himself. My concern is not with that part of the argument; but with another.

The ordinary modern critic, seeing this ascetic ideal in an authoritative Church, and not seeing it in most other inhabitants of Brixton or Brighton, is apt to say, "This is the result of Authority; it would be better to have Religion without Authority." But in truth, a wider experience outside Brixton or Brighton would reveal the mistake. It is rare to find a fasting alderman or a Trappist politician, but it is still more rare to see nuns suspended in the air on hooks or spikes; it is unusual for a Catholic Evidence Guild orator in Hyde Park to begin his speech by gashing himself all over with knives; a stranger calling at an ordinary presbytery will seldom find the parish priest lying on the floor with a fire lighted on his chest and scorching him while he utters spiritual ejaculations. Yet all these things are done all over Asia, for instance, by voluntary enthusiasts acting solely on the great impulse of Religion; of Religion, in their case, not commonly imposed by any immediate Authority; and certainly not imposed by this particular Authority. In short, a real knowledge of mankind will tell anybody that Religion is a very terrible thing; that it is truly a raging fire, and that Authority is often quite as much needed to restrain it as to impose it. Asceticism, or the war with the appetites, is itself an appetite. It can never be eliminated from among the strange ambitions of Man. But it can be kept in some reasonable control; and it is indulged in much saner proportion under Catholic Authority than in Pagan or Puritan anarchy. Meanwhile, the whole of this ideal, though an essential part of Catholic idealism when it is understood, is in some ways entirely a side issue. It is not the primary principle of Catholic philosophy; it is only a particular deduction from Catholic ethics. And when we begin to talk about primary philosophy, we realise the full and flat contradiction between the monk fasting and the fakir hanging himself on hooks.

Now nobody will begin to understand the Thomist philosophy, or indeed the Catholic philosophy, who does not realise that the primary and fundamental part of it is entirely the praise of Life, the praise of Being, the praise of God as the Creator of the World. Everything else follows a long way after that, being conditioned by various complications like the Fall or the vocation of heroes. The trouble occurs because the Catholic mind moves upon two planes; that of the Creation and that of the Fall. The nearest parallel is, for instance, that of England invaded; there might be strict martial law in Kent because the enemy had landed in Kent, and relative liberty in Hereford; but this would not affect the affection of an English patriot for Hereford or Kent, and strategic caution in Kent would not affect the love of Kent. For the love of England would remain, both of the parts to be redeemed by discipline and the parts to be enjoyed in liberty. Any extreme of Catholic asceticism is a wise, or unwise, precaution against the evil of the Fall; it is *never* a doubt about the good of the Creation. And *that* is where it really does differ, nor only from the rather excessive eccentricity of the gentleman who hangs himself on hooks, but from the whole cosmic theory which is the hook on which he hangs. In the case of many Oriental religions, it really is true that the asceticism is pessimism; that the ascetic tortures himself to death out of an abstract hatred of life; that he does not merely mean to control Nature as he should, but to contradict Nature as much as he can. And though it takes a milder form than hooks in millions of the religious populations of Asia, it is a fact far too little realised, that the dogma of the denial of life does really rule as a first principal on so vast a scale. One historic form it took was that great enemy of Christianity from its beginnings: the Manichees.

What is called the Manichean philosophy has had many forms; indeed it has attacked what is immortal and immutable with a very curious kind of immortal mutability. It is like the legend of the magician who turns himself into a snake or a cloud; and the whole has that nameless note of irresponsibility, which belongs to much of the metaphysics and morals of Asia, from which the Manichean mystery came. But it is always in one way or another a notion that nature is evil; or that evil is at least rooted in nature. The essential point is that as evil has roots in nature, so it has rights in nature. Wrong has as much right to exist as right. As already stated this notion took many forms. Sometimes it was a dualism, which made evil an equal partner with good; so that neither could be called an usurper. More often it was a general idea that demons had made the material world, and if there were any good spirits, they were concerned only with the spiritual world. Later, again, it took the form of Calvinism, which held that God had indeed made the world, but in a special sense, made the evil as well as the good: had made an evil will as well as an evil world. On this view, if a man chooses to damn his soul alive, he is nor thwarting God's will but rather fulfilling it. In these two forms, of the early Gnosticism and the later Calvinism, we see the superficial variety and fundamental unity of Manicheanism. The old Manicheans taught that Satan originated the whole work of creation commonly attributed to God. The new Calvinists taught that God originates the whole work of damnation commonly attributed to Satan. One looked back to the first day when a devil acted like a god, the other looked forward to a last day when a god acted like a devil. But both had the idea that the creator of the earth was primarily the creator of the evil, whether we call him a devil or a god.

Since there are a good many Manicheans among the Moderns, as we may remark in a moment, some may agree with this view, some may be puzzled about it, some may only be puzzled about why we should object to it. To understand the medieval controversy, a word must be said of the Catholic doctrine, which is as modern as it is medieval. That 'God looked on all things and saw that they were good' contains a subtlety which the popular pessimist cannot follow, or is too hasty to notice. It is the thesis that there are no bad things, but only bad uses of things. If you will, there are no bad things but only bad thoughts; and especially bad intentions. Only Calvinists can really believe that hell is paved with good intentions. That is exactly the one thing it cannot be paved with. But it is possible to have bad intentions about good things; and good things, like the world and the flesh have been twisted by a bad intention called the devil. But he cannot make *things* bad; they remain as on the first day of creation. The work of heaven alone was material; the making of a material world. The work of hell is entirely spiritual.

This error then had many forms; but especially, like nearly every error, it had two forms, a fiercer one which was outside the Church and attacking the Church, and a subtler one, which was inside the Church and corrupting the Church. There has never been a time when the Church was not torn between that invasion and that treason. It was so, for instance, in the Victorian time. Darwinian "competition", in commerce or race conflict, was every bit as brazen an atheist assault, in the nineteenth century, as the Bolshevist No-God movement in the twentieth century. To brag of brute prosperity, to admire the most muddy millionaires who had cornered wheat by a trick, to talk about the "unfit" (in imitation of the scientific thinker who would finish them off because he cannot even finish his own sentence—unfit for what?)—all that is as simply and openly Anti-Christian as the Black Mass. Yet some weak and worldly Catholics did use this cant in defence of Capitalism, in their first rather feeble resistance to Socialism. At least they did until the great Encyclical of the Pope on the Rights of Labour put a stop to all their nonsense. The evil is always both within and without the Church; but in a wilder form outside and a milder form inside. So it was, again, in the seventeenth century, when there was Calvinism outside and Jansenism inside. And so it was in the thirteenth century, when the obvious danger outside was in the revolution of the Albigensians; but the potential danger inside was in the very traditionalism of the Augustinians. For the Augustinians derived only from Augustine, and Augustine derived partly from Plato, and Plato was right, but not quite right. It is a mathematical fact that if a line be not perfectly directed towards a point, it will actually go further away from it as it comes nearer to it. After a thousand years of extension, the miscalculation of Platonism had come very near to Manicheanism.

Popular errors are nearly always right. They nearly always refer to some ultimate reality, about which those who correct them are themselves incorrect. It is a very queer thing that "Platonic Love" has come to mean for the un-lettered something rather purer and cleaner than it means for the learned. Yet even those who realise the great Greek evil may well realise that perversity often comes out of the wrong sort of purity. Now it was the inmost lie of the Manichees that they identified purity with sterility. It is singularly contrasted with the language of St. Thomas, which always connects purity with fruitfulness; whether it be natural or supernatural. And, queerly enough, as I have said, there does remain a sort of reality in the vulgar colloquialism that the affair between Sam and Susan is "quite Platonic." It is true that, quite apart from the local perversion, there was in Plato a sort of idea that people would be better without their bodies; that their heads might fly off and meet in the sky in merely intellectual marriage, like cherubs in a picture. The ultimate phase of this "Platonic" philosophy was what inflamed poor D. H. Lawrence into talking nonsense, and he was probably unaware that the Catholic doctrine of marriage would say much of what he said, without talking nonsense. Anyhow, it is historically important to see that Platonic love did somewhat distort both human and divine love, in the theory of the early theologians. Many medieval men, who would indignantly deny the Albigensian doctrine of sterility, were yet in an emotional mood to abandon the body in despair; and some of them to abandon everything in despair.

In truth, this vividly illuminates the provincial stupidity of those who object to what they call "creeds and dogmas." It was precisely the creed and dogma that saved the sanity of the world. These people generally propose an alternative religion of intuition and feeling. If, in the really Dark Ages, there had been a religion of feeling, it would have been a religion of black and suicidal feeling. It was the rigid creed that resisted the rush of suicidal feeling. The critics of asceticism are probably right in supposing that many a Western hermit did *feel* rather like an Eastern fakir. But he could not really *think* like an Eastern fakir; because he was an orthodox Catholic. And what kept his thought in touch with healthier and more humanistic thought was simply and solely the Dogma. He could not deny that a good God had created the normal and natural world; he could not say that the devil had made the world; because he was not a Manichee. A thousand enthusiasts for celibacy, in the day of the great rush to the desert or the cloister, might have called marriage a sin, if they had only considered their individual ideals, in the modern manner, and their own immediate feelings about marriage. Fortunately, they had to accept the Authority of the Church, which had definitely said that marriage was not a sin. A modern emotional religion might at any moment have turned Catholicism into Manichaeism. But when Religion would have maddened men, Theology kept them sane.

In this sense St. Thomas stands up simply as the great orthodox theologian, who reminded men of the creed of Creation, when many of them were still in the mood of mere destruction. It is futile for the critics of medievalism to quote a hundred medieval phrases that may be supposed to sound like mere pessimism, if they will not understand the central fact; that medieval men did not care about being medieval and did not accept the authority of a mood, because it was melancholy, but did care very much about orthodoxy, which is not a mood. It was because St. Thomas could *prove* that his glorification of the Creator and His creative joy was more orthodox than any atmospheric pessimism, that he dominated the Church and the world, which accepted that truth as a test. But when this immense and impersonal importance is allowed for, we may agree that there was a personal element as well. Like most of the great religious teachers, he was fitted individually for the task that God had given him to do. We can if we like call that talent instinctive; we can even descend to calling it temperamental.

Anybody trying to popularise a medieval philosopher must use language that is very modern and very unphilosophical. Nor is this a sneer at modernity; it arises from the moderns having dealt so much in moods and emotions, especially in the arts, that they have developed a large but loose vocabulary, which deals more with atmosphere than with actual attitude or position. As noted elsewhere, even the modern philosophers are more like the modern poets; in giving an individual tinge even to truth, and often looking at all life through different coloured spectacles. To say that Schopenhauer had the blues, or that William James had a rather rosier outlook, would often convey more than calling the one a Pessimist or the other a Pragmatist. This modern moodiness has its value, though the moderns overrate it; just as medieval logic had its value, though it was overrated in the later Middle Ages. But the point is that to explain the medievals to the moderns, we must often use this modern language of mood. Otherwise the character will be missed, through certain prejudices and ignorances about all such medieval characters. Now there is something that lies all over the work of St. Thomas Aquinas like a great light; which is something quite primary and perhaps unconscious with him, which he would perhaps have passed over as an irrelevant personal quality; and which can now only be expressed by a rather cheap journalistic term, which he would probably have thought quite senseless.

Nevertheless, the only working word for that atmosphere is Optimism. I know that the word is now even more degraded in the twentieth century than it was in the nineteenth century. Men talked lately of being Optimists about the issue of War; they talk now of being Optimists about the revival of Trade; they may talk tomorrow of being Optimists about the International Ping-pong Tournament. But men in the Victorian time did mean a little more than that, when they used the word Optimist of Browning or Stevenson or Walt Whitman. And in a rather larger and more luminous sense than in the case of these men, the term was basically true of Thomas Aquinas. He did, with a most solid and colossal conviction, believe in Life; and in something like what Stevenson called the great theorem of the livableness of life. It breathes somehow in his very first phrases about the reality of Being. If the morbid Renaissance intellectual is supposed to say, "To be or not to be—that is the question," then the massive medieval doctor does most certainly reply in a voice of thunder, "To be—that is the answer." The point is important; many not unnaturally talk of the Renaissance as the time when certain men began to believe in Life. The truth is that it was the time when a few men, for the first time, began to disbelieve in Life. The medievals had put many restrictions, and some excessive restrictions, upon the universal human hunger and even fury for Life. Those restrictions had often been expressed in fanatical and rabid terms;

the terms of those resisting a great natural force; the force of men who desired to live. Never until modern thought began, did they really have to fight with men who desired to die. That horror had threatened them in Asiatic Albigensianism, but it never became normal to them—until now.

But this fact becomes very vivid indeed, when we compare the greatest of Christian philosophers with the only men who were anything like his equals, or capable of being his rivals. They were people with whom he did not directly dispute; most of them he had never seen; some of them he had never heard of. Plato and Augustine were the only two with whom he could confer as he did with Bonaventure or even Averrhoes. But we must look elsewhere for his real rivals, and the only real rivals of the Catholic theory. They are the heads of great heathen systems; some of them very ancient, some very modern, like Buddha on the one hand or Nietzsche on the other. It is when we see his gigantic figure against this vast and cosmic background, that we realise, first, that he was the only optimist theologian, and second, that Catholicism is the only optimist theology. Something milder and more amiable may be made out of the deliquescence of theology, and the mixture of the creed with everything that contradicts it; but among consistent cosmic creeds, this is the only one that is entirely on the side of Life.

Comparative religion has indeed allowed us to compare religions—and to contrast them. Fifty years ago, it set out to prove that all religions were much the same; generally proving, alternately, that they were all equally worthy and that they were all equally worthless. Since then this scientific process has suddenly begun to be scientific, and discovered the depths of the chasms as well as the heights of the hills. It is indeed an excellent improvement that sincerely religious people should respect each other. But respect has discovered difference, where contempt knew only indifference. The more we really appreciate the noble revulsion and renunciation of Buddha, the more we see that intellectually it was the converse and almost the contrary of the salvation of the world by Christ. The Christian would escape from the world into the universe: the Buddhist wishes to escape from the universe even more than from the world. One would uncreate himself; the other would return to his Creation: to his Creator. Indeed it was so genuinely the converse of the idea of the Cross as the Tree of Life, that there is some excuse for setting up the two things side by side, as if they were of equal significance. They are in one sense parallel and equal; as a mound and a hollow, as a valley and a hill. There is a sense in which that sublime despair is the only alternative to that divine audacity. It is even true that the truly spiritual and intellectual man sees it as a sort of dilemma; a very hard and terrible choice. There is little else on earth that can compare with these for completeness. And he who will not climb the mountain of Christ does indeed fall into the abyss of Buddha.

The same is true, in a less lucid and dignified fashion, of most other alternatives of heathen humanity; nearly all are sucked back into that whirlpool of recurrence which all the ancients knew. Nearly all return to the one idea of returning. That is what Buddha described so darkly as the Sorrowful Wheel. It is true that the sort of recurrence which Buddha described as the Sorrowful Wheel, poor Nietzsche actually managed to describe as the Joyful Wisdom. I can only say that if bare repetition was his idea of Joyful Wisdom, I should be curious to know what was his idea of Sorrowful Wisdom. But as a fact, in the case of Nietzsche, this did not belong to the moment of his breaking out, but to the moment of his breaking down. It came at the end of his life, when he was near to mental collapse; and it is really quite contrary to his earlier and finer inspirations of wild freedom or fresh and creative innovation. Once at least he had tried to break out; but he also was only broken—on the wheel.

Alone upon the earth, and lifted and liberated from all the wheels and whirlpools of the earth, stands up the faith of St. Thomas; weighted and balanced indeed with more than Oriental metaphysics and more than Pagan pomp and pageantry; but vitally and vividly alone in declaring that life is a living story, with a great beginning and a great close; rooted in the primeval joy of God and finding its fruition in the final happiness of humanity; opening with the colossal chorus in which the sons of God shouted for joy, and ending in that mystical comradeship, shown in a shadowy fashion in those ancient words that move like an archaic dance; "For His delight is with the sons of men."

It is the fate of this sketch to be sketchy about philosophy, scanty or rather empty about theology, and to achieve little more than a decent silence on the subject of sanctity. And yet it must none the less be the recurrent burden of this little book, to which it must return with some monotony, that in this story the philosophy did depend on the theology, and the theology did depend on the sanctity. In other words, it must repeat the first fact, which was emphasised in the first chapter: that this great intellectual creation was a Christian and Catholic creation and cannot be understood as anything else. It was Aquinas who baptised Aristotle, when Aristotle could not have baptised Aquinas; it was a purely Christian miracle which raised the great Pagan from the dead. And this is proved in three ways (as St. Thomas himself might say), which it will be well to summarise as a sort of summary of this book.

First, in the life of St. Thomas, it is proved in the fact that only his huge and solid orthodoxy could have supported so many things which then seemed to be unorthodox. Charity covers a multitude of sins; and in that sense orthodoxy covers a multitude of heresies; or things which are hastily mistaken for heresies. It was precisely because his personal Catholicism was so convincing, that his impersonal Aristotelianism was given the benefit of the doubt. He did not smell of the faggot because he did smell of the firebrand; of the firebrand he had so instantly and instinctively snatched up, under a real assault on essential Catholic ethics. A typically cynical modern phrase refers to the man who is so good that he is good for nothing. St. Thomas was so good that he was good for everything; that his warrant held good for what others considered the most wild and daring speculations, ending in the worship of nothing. Whether or no he baptised Aristotle, he was truly the godfather of Aristotle; he was his sponsor; he swore that the old Greek would do no harm; and the whole world trusted his word.

Second, in the philosophy of St. Thomas, it is proved by the fact that everything depended on the new Christian *motive* for the study of facts, as distinct from truths. The Thomist philosophy began with the lowest roots of thought, the senses and the truisms of the reason; and a Pagan sage might have scorned such things, as he scorned the servile arts. But the materialism, which is merely cynicism in a Pagan, can be Christian humility in a Christian. St. Thomas was willing to begin by recording the facts and sensations of the material world, just as he would have been willing to begin by washing up the plates and dishes in the monastery. The point of his Aristotelianism was that even if common sense about concrete things really was a sort of servile labour, he must not be ashamed to be *servus servorum Dei*. Among heathens the mere sceptic might become the mere cynic; Diogenes in his tub had always a touch of the tub-thumper; but even the dirt of the cynics was dignified into dust and ashes among the saints. If we miss that, we miss the whole meaning of the greatest revolution in history. There was a new *motive* for beginning with the most material, and even with the meanest things.

Third, in the theology of St. Thomas, it is proved by the tremendous truth that supports all that theology; or any other Christian theology. There really was a new reason for regarding the senses, and the sensations of the body, and the experiences of the common man, with a reverence at which great Aristotle would have stared, and no man in the ancient world could have begun to understand. The Body was no longer what it was when Plato and Porphyry and the old mystics had left it for dead. It had hung upon a gibbet. It had risen from a tomb. It was no longer possible for the soul to despise the senses, which had been the organs of something that was more than man. Plato might despise the flesh; but God had not despised it. The senses had truly become sanctified; as they are blessed one by one at a Catholic baptism. "Seeing is believing" was no longer the platitude of a mere idiot, or common individual, as in Plato's world; it was mixed up with real conditions of real belief. Those revolving mirrors that send messages to the brain of man, that light that breaks upon the brain, these had truly revealed to God himself the path to Bethany or the light on the high rock of Jerusalem. These ears that resound with common noises had reported also to the secret knowledge of God the noise of the crowd that strewed palms and the crowd that cried for Crucifixion. After the Incarnation had become the idea that is central in our civilisation, it was inevitable that there should be a return to materialism, in the sense of the serious value of matter and the making of the body. When once Christ had risen, it was inevitable that Aristotle should rise again.

Those are three real reasons, and very sufficient reasons, for the general support given by the saint to a solid and objective philosophy. And yet there was something else, very vast and vague, to which I have tried to give a faint expression by the interposition of this chapter. It is difficult to express it fully, without the awful peril of being popular, or what the Modernists quite wrongly imagine to be popular; in short, passing from religion to religiosity. But there is a general tone and temper of Aquinas, which it is as difficult to avoid as daylight in a great house of windows. It is that *positive* position of his mind, which is filled and soaked as with sunshine with the warmth of the wonder of created things. There is a certain private audacity, in his communion, by which men add to their private names the tremendous titles of the Trinity and the Redemption; so that some nun may be called "of the Holy Ghost"; or a man bear such a burden as the title of St. John of the Cross. In this sense, the man we study may specially be called St. Thomas of the Creator. The Arabs have a phrase about the hundred names of God; but they also inherit the tradition of a tremendous name unspeakable because it expresses Being itself, dumb and yet dreadful as an instant inaudible shout; the proclamation of the Absolute. And perhaps no other man ever came so near to calling the Creator by His own name, which can only be written I Am.

## V

## THE REAL LIFE OF ST. THOMAS

At this point, even so crude and external a sketch of a great saint involves the necessity of writing something that cannot fit in with the rest; the one thing which it is important to write and impossible to write. A saint may be any kind of man, with an additional quality that is at once unique and universal. We might even say that the one thing which separates a saint from ordinary men is his readiness to be one with ordinary men. In this sense the word ordinary must be understood in its native and noble meaning; which is connected with the word order. A saint is long past any desire for distinction; he is the only sort of superior man who has never been a superior person. But all this arises from a great central fact, which he does not condescend to call a privilege, but which is in its very nature a sort of privacy; and in that sense almost a form of private property. As with all sound private property, it is enough for him that he has it, he does not desire to limit the number of people who have it. He is always trying to hide it, out of a sort of celestial good manners; and Thomas Aquinas tried to hide it more than most. To reach it, in so far as we can reach it, it will be best to begin with the upper strata; and reach what was in the inside from what was most conspicuous on the outside.

The appearance or bodily presence of St. Thomas Aquinas is really easier to resurrect than that of many who lived before the age of portrait painting. It has been said that in his bodily being or bearing there was little of the Italian; but this is at the best, I fancy, an unconscious comparison between St. Thomas and St. Francis; and at worst, only a comparison between him and the hasty legend of vivacious organ-grinders and incendiary ice-cream men. Not all Italians are vivacious organ-grinders, and very few Italians are like St. Francis. A nation is never a type, but it is nearly always a tangle of two or three roughly recognizable types. St. Thomas was of a certain type, which is not so much common in Italy, as common to uncommon Italians. His bulk made it easy to regard him humorously as the sort of walking wine-barrel, common in the comedies of many nations; he joked about it himself. It may be that he, and not some irritated partisan of the Augustinian or Arabian parties, was responsible for the sublime exaggeration that a crescent was cut out of the dinner-table to allow him to sit down. It is quite certain that it was an exaggeration; and that his stature was more remarked than his stoutness; but, above all, that his head was quite powerful enough to dominate his body. And his head was of a very real and recognisable type, to judge by the traditional portraits and the personal descriptions. It was that sort of head with the heavy chin and jaws, the Roman nose and the big rather bald brow, which, in spite of its fullness, gives also a curious concave impression of hollows here and there, like caverns of thought. Napoleon carried that head upon a short body. Mussolini carries it today, upon a rather taller but equally active one. It can be seen in the busts of several Roman Emperors, and occasionally above the shabby shirt-front of an Italian waiter; but he is generally a head waiter. So unmistakable is the type, that I cannot but think that the most vivid villain of light fiction, in the Victorian shocker called *The Woman in White*, was really sketched by Wilkie Collins from an actual Italian Count; he is so complete a contrast to the conventional skinny, swarthy and gesticulating villain whom the Victorians commonly presented as an Italian Count. Count Fosco,[1] it may be remembered (I hope) by some, was a calm, corpulent, colossal gentleman, whose head was ex-

[1] Count Fosco was the first fat villain in English literature. He appears in Wilke Collins' novel *The Woman in White* (1860).

actly like a bust of Napoleon of heroic size. He may have been a melodramatic villain; but he was a tolerably convincing Italian—of that kind. If we recall his tranquil manner, and the excellent common sense of his everyday external words and actions, we shall probably have a merely material image of the type of Thomas Aquinas; given only the slight effort of faith required to imagine Count Fosco turned suddenly into a saint.

The pictures of St. Thomas, though many of them painted long after his death, are all obviously pictures of the same man. He rears himself defiantly, with the Napoleonic head and the dark bulk of body, in Raphael's 'Dispute About the Sacrament.' A portrait by Ghirlandajo emphasises a point which specially reveals what may be called the neglected Italian quality in the man. It also emphasises points that are very important in the mystic and the philosopher. It is universally attested that Aquinas was what is commonly called an absent-minded man. That type has often been rendered in painting, humorous or serious; but almost always in one of two or three conventional ways. Sometimes the expression of the eyes is merely vacant, as it absent-mindedness did really mean a permanent absence of mind. Sometimes it is rendered more respectfully as a wistful expression, as of one yearning for something afar off, that he cannot see and can only faintly desire. Look at the eyes in Ghirlandajo's portrait of St. Thomas; and you will see a sharp difference. While the eyes are indeed completely torn away from the immediate surroundings, so that the pot of flowers above the philosopher's head might fall on it without attracting his attention, they are not in the least wistful, let alone vacant. There is kindled in them a fire of instant inner excitement; they are vivid and very Italian eyes. The man is thinking about something; and something that has reached a crisis; not about nothing or about anything; or, what is almost worse, about everything. There must have been that smouldering vigilance in his eyes, the moment before he smote the table and startled the banquet hall of the King.

Of the personal habits that go with the personal physique, we have also a few convincing and confirming impressions. When he was not sitting still, reading a book, he walked round and round the cloisters and walked fast and even furiously, a very characteristic action of men who fight their battles in the mind. Whenever he was interrupted, he was very polite and more apologetic than the apologizer. But there was that about him, which suggested that he was rather happier when he was not interrupted. He was ready to stop his truly Peripatetic tramp: but we feel that when he resumed it, he walked all the faster.

All this suggests that his superficial abstraction, that which the world saw, was of a certain kind. It will be well to understand the quality, for there are several kinds of absence of mind, including that of some pretentious poets and intellectuals, in whom the mind has never been noticeably present. There is the abstraction of the contemplative, whether he is the true sort of Christian contemplative, who is contemplating Something, or the wrong sort of Oriental contemplative, who is contemplating Nothing. Obviously St. Thomas was not a Buddhist mystic; but I do not think his fits of abstraction were even those of a Christian mystic. If he had trances of true Christian mysticism, he took jolly good care that *they* should not occur at other people's dinner-tables. I think he had the sort of bemused fit, which really belongs to the practical man rather than the entirely mystical man. He uses the recognised distinction between the active life and the contemplative life, but in the cases concerned here, I think even his contemplative life was an active life. It had nothing to do with his higher life, in the sense of ultimate sanctity. It rather reminds us that Napoleon would fall into a fit of apparent boredom at the Opera, and afterwards confess that he was thinking how he could get three army corps at Frankfurt to combine with two army corps at Cologne. So, in the case of Aquinas, if his daydreams were dreams, they were dreams of the day; and dreams of the day of battle. If he talked to himself, it was because he was arguing with somebody else. We can put it another way, by saying that his daydreams, like the dreams of a dog, were dreams of hunting; of pursuing the error as well as pursuing the truth; of following all the twists and turns of evasive falsehood, and tracking it at last to its lair in hell. He would have been the first to admit that the erroneous thinker would probably be more surprised to learn where his thought came from, than anybody else to discover where it went to. But this notion of *pursuing* he certainly had, and it was the beginning of a thousand mistakes and misunderstandings that pursuing is called in Latin Persecution. Nobody had less than he had of what is commonly called the temper of a persecutor; but he had the quality which in desperate times is often driven to persecute; and that is simply the sense that everything lives somewhere, and nothing dies unless it dies in its own home. That he did sometimes, in this sense, "urge in dreams the shadowy chase" even in broad daylight, is quite true. But he was an active dreamer, if not what is commonly called a man of action; and in that chase he was truly to be counted among the *domini canes*; and surely the mightiest and most magnanimous of the Hounds of Heaven.

There may be many who do not understand the nature even of this sort of abstraction. But then, unfortunately, there are many who do not understand the nature of any sort of argument. Indeed, I think there are fewer people now alive who understand argument than there were twenty or thirty years ago; and St. Thomas might have preferred the society of the atheists of the early nineteenth century to that of the blank sceptics of the early twentieth. Anyhow, one of the real disadvantages of the great and glorious sport, that is called argument, is its inordinate length. If you argue honestly, as St. Thomas always did, you will find that the subject sometimes seems as if it would never end. He was strongly conscious of this fact, as appears in many places; for instance his argument that most men must have a revealed religion, because they have not time to argue. No time, that is, to argue fairly. There is always time to argue unfairly; not least in a time like ours. Being himself resolved to argue, to argue honestly, to answer everybody, to deal with everything, he produced books enough to sink a ship or stock a library; though he died in comparatively early middle age. Probably he could not have done it at all, if he had not been thinking even when he was not writing; but above all thinking *combatively*. This, in his case, certainly did not mean bitterly or spitefully or uncharitably; but it did mean combatively. As a matter of fact, it is generally the man who is not ready to argue, who is ready to sneer. That is why, in recent literature, there has been so little argument and so much sneering.

We have noted that there are barely one or two occasions on which St. Thomas indulged in a denunciation. There is not a single occasion on which he indulged in a sneer. His curiously simple character, his lucid but laborious intellect, could not be better summed up than by saying that he did not know how to sneer. He was in a double sense an intellectual aristocrat: but he was never an intellectual snob. He never troubled at all whether those to whom he talked were more or less of the sort whom the world thinks worth talking to; and it was apparent by the impression of his contemporaries that those who received the ordinary scraps of his wit or wisdom were quite as likely to be nobodies as somebodies, or even quite as likely to be noodles as clever people. He was interested in the souls of all his fellow creatures, but not in classifying the minds of any of them; in a sense it was too personal and in another sense too arrogant for his particular mind and temper. He was very much interested in the subject he was talking about; and may sometimes have talked for a long time, though he was probably silent for a much longer time. But he had all the unconscious contempt which the really intelligent have for an intelligentsia.

Like most men concerned with the common problems of men, he seems to have had a considerable correspondence; considering that correspondence was so much more difficult in his time. We have records of a great many cases in which complete strangers wrote to ask him questions, and sometimes rather ridiculous questions. To all of these he replied with a characteristic mixture of patience and that sort of rationality, which in some rational people tends to be impatience. Somebody, for instance, asked him whether the names of all the blessed were written on a scroll exhibited in heaven. He wrote back, with untiring calm; "So far as I can see, this is not the case; but there is no harm in saying so."

I have remarked on the portrait of St. Thomas by an Italian painter, which shows him alert even in abstraction; and only silent as if about to speak. Pictures in that great tradition are generally full of small touches that show a very large imagination. I mean the sort of imagination on which Ruskin remarked, when he saw that in Tintoretto's sunlit scene of the Crucifixion the face of Christ is dark and undecipherable; but the halo round his head unexpectedly faint and grey like the colour of ashes. It would be hard to put more powerfully the idea of Divinity itself in eclipse. There is a touch, which it may be fanciful to find equally significant, in the portrait of Thomas Aquinas. The artist, having given so much vividness and vigilance to the eyes, may have felt that he stressed too much the merely combative concentration of the saint; but anyhow for some reason he has blazoned upon his breast a rather curious emblem, as if it were some third symbolic and cyclopean eye. At least it is no normal Christian sign; but something more like the disk of the sun such as held the face of a heathen god; but the face itself is dark and occult, and only the rays breaking from it are a ring of fire. I do not know whether any traditional meaning has been attached to this; but its imaginative meaning is strangely apt. That secret sun, dark with excess of light, or not showing its light save in the enlightenment of others, might well be the exact emblem of that inner and ideal life of the saint, which was not only hidden by his external words and actions, but even hidden by his merely outward and automatic silences and fits of reflection. In short, this spiritual detachment is not to be confused with his common habit of brooding or falling into a brown study. He was a man entirely careless of all casual criticism of his casual demeanour; as are many men built on a big masculine model and unconsciously inheriting a certain social splendour and largesse. But about his real life of sanctity he was intensely secretive. Such secrecy has indeed generally gone with sanctity; for the saint has an unfathomable horror of playing the Pharisee. But in Thomas Aquinas it was even more sensitive, and what many in the world would call morbid. He did not mind being caught wool-gathering over the wine-cups of the King's banquet; for that was merely upon a point of controversy. But when there was some question of his having seen St. Paul in a vision, he was in an agony of alarm lest it should be discussed; and the story remains somewhat uncertain in consequence. Needless to say, his followers and admirers were as eager to collect these strictly miraculous stories as he was eager to conceal them; and one or two seem to be preserved with a fairly solid setting of evidence. But there are certainly fewer of them, known to the world, than in the case of many saints equally sincere and even equally modest, but more preoccupied with zeal and less sensitive about publicity.

The truth is that about all such things, in life and death, there is a sort of enormous quiet hanging about St. Thomas. He was one of those large things who take up little room. There was naturally a certain stir about his miracles after his death; and about his burial at the time when the University of Paris wished to bury him. I do not know in detail the long history of the other plans of sepulture, which have ultimately ended with his sacred bones lying in the church of St. Sernin in Toulouse; at the very base of the battle-fields where his Dominicans had warred down the pestilence of pessimism from the East. But somehow, it is not easy to think of his shrine as the scene of the more jolly, rowdy and vulgar devotion either in its medieval or modern form. He was very far from being a Puritan, in the true sense; he made a provision for a holiday and banquet for his young friends, which has quite a convivial sound. The trend of his writing, especially for his time, is reasonable in its recognition of physical life; and he goes out of his way to say that men must vary their lives with jokes and even with pranks. But for all that, we cannot somehow see his personality as a sort of magnet for mobs; or the road to the tomb of St. Thomas at Toulouse having always been a long street of taverns, like that to the tomb of St. Thomas at Canterbury. I think he rather disliked noise; there is a legend that he disliked thunderstorms; but it is contradicted by the fact that in an actual shipwreck he was supremely calm. However that may be, and it probably concerned his health, in some ways sensitive, he certainly was very calm. We have a feeling that we should gradually grow conscious of his presence; as of an immense background.

Here, if this slight sketch could be worthy of its subject, there should stand forth something of that stupendous certitude, in the presence of which all his libraries of philosophy, and even theology, were but a litter of pamphlets. It is certain that this thing was in him from the first, in the form of conviction, long before it could possibly have even begun to take the form of controversy. It was very vivid in his childhood; and his were exactly the circumstances in which the anecdotes of the nursery and the playground are likely enough to have been really preserved. He had from the first that full and final test of truly orthodox Catholicity; the impetuous, impatient intolerant passion for the poor; and even that readiness to be rather a nuisance to the rich, out of a hunger to feed the hungry. This can have had nothing to do with the intellectualism of which he was afterwards accused; still less with any habit of dialectic. It would seem unlikely that at the age of six he had any ambition to answer Averrhoes, or that he knew what Effective Causality is; or even that he had worked out, as he did in later life, the whole theory by which a man's love of himself is Sincere and Constant and Indulgent; and that this should be transferred intact (if possible) to his love of his neighbour. At this early age he did not understand all this. He only did it. But all the atmosphere of his actions carries a sort of conviction with it. It is beautifully typical, for instance, of that sort of aristocratic *ménage*, that his parents seem to have objected mildly, if at all, to his handing out things to beggars and tramps; but it was intensely disliked by the upper servants.

Still, if we take the thing as seriously as all childish things should be taken, we may learn something from that mysterious state of innocence, which is the first and best spring of all our later indignations. We may begin to understand why it was that there grew steadily with his growing mind, a great and very solitary mind, an ambition that was the inversion of all the things about him. We shall guess what had continuously swelled within him, whether in protest or prophecy or prayer for deliverance, before he startled his family by flinging away not only the trappings of nobility, but all forms of ambition, even ecclesiastical ambition. His childhood may contain the hint of that first stride of his manhood, from the house onto the highway; and his proclamation that he also would be a Beggar.

There is another case of a sort of second glimpse or sequel, in which an incident well known in the external sense gives us also a glimpse of the internal. After the affair of the firebrand, and the woman who tempted him in the tower, it is said that he had a dream; in which two angels girded him with a cord of fire, a thing of terrible pain and yet giving a terrible strength; and he awoke with a great cry in the darkness. This also has something very vivid about it, under the circumstances; and probably contains truths that will be some day better understood, when priests and doctors have learned to talk to each other without the stale etiquette of nineteenth-century negations. It would be easy to analyse the dream, as the very nineteenth-century doctor did in *Armadale*,[2] resolving it into the details of the past days; the cord from his struggle against being stripped of his Friar's frock; the thread of fire running through the tapestries of the night, from the firebrand he had snatched from the fireside. But even in *Armadale* the dream was fulfilled mystically as well, and the dream of St. Thomas was fulfilled very mystically indeed. For he did in fact remain remarkably untroubled on that side of his human nature after the incident; though it is likely enough that the incident had caused an upheaval of his normal humanity, which produced a dream stronger than a nightmare.

[2] A novel written by Wilke Collins. In the novel, Allan Armadale has a mysterious dream, the interpretation of which is an important element in the plot. Dr. Hawbury offers a rational analysis of the dream and explains its events as mere reproductions during sleep of images and impressions experienced by Armadale while awake. Armadale's friend Midwinter, however, is convinced that the dream is supernatural in origin and is in fact a premonition of danger for Armadale. It is Midwinter's interpretation which proves accurate in the end.

This is no place to analyse the psychological fact, which puzzles Non-Catholics so much: of the way in which priests do manage to be celibate without ceasing to be virile. Anyhow, it seems probable that in this matter he was less troubled than most. This has nothing to do with true virtue, which is of the will; saints as holy as he have rolled themselves in brambles to distract the pressure of passion; but he never needed much in the way of a counter-irritant; for the simple reason that in this way, as in most ways, he was not very often irritated. Much must remain unexplained, as part of the mysteries of grace; but there is probably some truth in the psychological idea of "sublimation"; that is the lifting of a lower energy to higher ends; so that appetite almost faded in the furnace of his intellectual energy. Between supernatural and natural causes, it is probable that he never knew or suffered greatly on this side of his mind.

There are moments when the most orthodox reader is tempted to hate the hagiographer as much as he loves the holy man. The holy man always conceals his holiness; that is the one invariable rule. And the hagiographer sometimes seems like a persecutor trying to frustrate the holy man; a spy or eavesdropper hardly more respectful than an American interviewer. I admit that these sentiments are fastidious and one-sided, and I will now proceed to prove my penitence by mentioning one or two of the incidents that could only have come to common knowledge in this deplorable way.

It seems certain that he did live a sort of secondary and mysterious life; the divine double of what is called a double life. Somebody seems to have caught a glimpse of the sort of solitary miracle which modern psychic people call Levitation; and he must surely have either been a liar or a literal witness, for there could have been no doubts or degrees about such a prodigy happening to such a person; it must have been like seeing one of the huge pillars of the church suspended like a cloud. Nobody knows, I imagine, what spiritual storm of exaltation or agony produces this convulsion in matter or space; but the thing does almost certainly occur. Even in the case of ordinary Spiritualist mediums, for whatever reason, the evidence is very difficult to refute. But probably the most representative revelation of this side of his life may be found in the celebrated story of the miracle of the crucifix; when in the stillness of the church of St. Dominic in Naples, a voice spoke from the carven Christ, and told the kneeling Friar that he had written rightly, and offered him the choice of a reward among all the things of the world.

Not all, I think, have appreciated the point of this particular story as applied to this particular saint. It is an old story, in so far as it is simply the offer made to a devotee of solitude or simplicity, of the pick of all the prizes of life. The hermit, true or false, the fakir, the fanatic or the cynic, Stylites on his column or Diogenes in his tub, can all be pictured as tempted by the powers of the earth, of the air or of the heavens, with the offer of the best of everything; and replying that they want nothing. In the Greek cynic or stoic it really meant the mere negative; that he wanted nothing. In the Oriental mystic or fanatic, it sometimes meant a sort of positive negative; that he wanted Nothing; that Nothing was really what he wanted. Sometimes it expressed a noble independence, and the twin virtues of antiquity, the love of liberty and the hatred of luxury. Sometimes it only expressed a self-sufficiency that is the very opposite of sanctity. But even the stories of real saints, of this sort, do not quite cover the case of St. Thomas. He was not a person who wanted nothing; and he was a person who was enormously interested in everything. His answer is not so inevitable or simple as some may suppose. As compared with many other saints, and many other philosophers, he was avid in his acceptance of Things; in his hunger and thirst for Things. It was his special spiritual thesis that there really are things; and not only the Thing; that the Many existed as well as the One. I do not mean things to eat or drink or wear, though he never denied to these their place in the noble hierarchy of Being; but rather things to think about, and especially things to prove, to experience and to know. Nobody supposes that Thomas Aquinas, when offered by God his choice among all the gifts of God, would ask for a thousand pounds, or the Crown of Sicily, or a present of rare Greek wine. But he might have asked for things that he really wanted; and he was a man who could want things; as he wanted the lost manuscript of St. Chrysostom. He might have asked for the solution of an old difficulty; or the secret of a new science; or a flash of the inconceivable intuitive mind of the angels; or any one of a thousand things that would really have satisfied his broad and virile appetite for the very vastness and variety of the universe. The point is that for him, when the voice spoke from between the outstretched arms of the Crucified, those arms were truly opened wide, and opening most gloriously the gates of all the worlds; they were arms pointing to the east and to the west, to the ends of the earth and the very extremes of existence. They were truly spread out with a gesture of omnipotent generosity; the Creator himself offering Creation itself; with all its millionfold mystery of separate beings, and the triumphal chorus of the creatures. That is the blazing background of multitudinous Being that gives the particular strength, and even a sort of surprise, to the answer of St. Thomas, when he lifted at last his head and spoke with, and for, that almost blasphemous audacity which is one with the humility of his religion; "I will have Thyself."

Or, to add the crowning and crushing irony to this story, so uniquely Christian for those who can really understand it, there are some who feel that the audacity is softened by insisting that he said, "*Only* Thyself."

Of these miracles, in the strictly miraculous sense, there are not so many as in the lives of less immediately influential saints; but they are probably pretty well authenticated; for he was a well-known public man in a prominent position, and, what is even more convenient for him, he had any number of highly incensed enemies, who could be trusted to sift his claims. There is at least one miracle of healing; that of a woman who touched his gown; and several incidents that may be variants of the story of the crucifix at Naples. One of these stories, however, has a further importance as bringing us to another section of his more private, personal or even emotional religious life; the section that expressed itself in poetry. When he was stationed at Paris, the other Doctors of the Sorbonne put before him a problem about the nature of the mystical change in the elements of the Blessed Sacrament, and he proceeded to write, in his customary manner, a very careful and elaborately lucid statement of his own solution. Needless to say, he felt with hearty simplicity the heavy responsibility and gravity of such a judicial decision; and not unnaturally seems to have worried about it more than he commonly did over his work. He sought for guidance in more than usually prolonged prayer and intercession; and finally, with one of those few but striking bodily gestures that mark the turning points of his life, he threw down his thesis at the foot of the crucifix on the altar, and left it lying there; as if awaiting judgment. Then he turned and came down the altar steps and buried himself once more in prayer; but the other Friars, it is said, were watching; and well they might be. For they declared afterwards that the figure of Christ had come down from the cross before their mortal eyes; and stood upon the scroll, saying "Thomas, thou hast written well concerning the Sacrament of My Body." It was after this vision that the incident is said to have happened, of his being borne up miraculously in mid-air.

An acute observer said of Thomas Aquinas in his own time, "He could alone restore all philosophy, if it had been burnt by fire." That is what is meant by saying that he was an original man, a creative mind; that he could have made his own cosmos out of stones and straws, even without the manuscripts of Aristotle or Augustine. But there is here a not uncommon confusion, between the thing in which a man is most original and that in which he is most interested; or between the thing that he does best and the thing that he loves most. Because St. Thomas was a unique and striking philosopher, it is almost unavoidable that this book should be merely, or mainly, a sketch of his philosophy. It cannot be, and does not pretend to be, a sketch of his theology. But this is because the theology of a saint is simply the theism of a saint; or rather the theism of all saints. It is less individual, but it is much more intense. It is concerned with the common origin; but it is hardly an occasion for originality. Thus we are forced to think first of Thomas as the maker of the Thomist philosophy; as we think first of Christopher Columbus as the discoverer of America, though he may have been quite sincere in his pious hope to convert the Khan of Tartary; or of James Watt as the discoverer of the steam-engine, though he may have been a devout fire-worshipper, or a sincere Scottish Calvinist, or all kinds of curious things. Anyhow, it is but natural that Augustine and Aquinas, Bonaventure and Duns Scotus, all the doctors and the saints, should draw nearer to each other as they approach the divine unity in things; and that there should in that sense be less difference between them in theology than in philosophy. It is true that, in some matters, the critics of Aquinas thought his philosophy had unduly affected his theology. This is especially so, touching the charge that he made the state of Beatitude too intellectual, conceiving it as the satisfaction of the love of truth; rather than specially as the truth of love. It is true that the mystics and the men of the Franciscan school, dwelt more lovingly on the admitted supremacy of love. But it was mostly a matter of emphasis; perhaps tinged faintly by temperament; possibly (to suggest something which is easier to feel than to explain), in the case of St. Thomas, a shadowy influence of a sort of shyness. Whether the supreme ecstasy is more affectional than intellectual is no very deadly matter of quarrel among men who believe it is both, but do not profess even to imagine the actual experience of either. But I have a sort of feeling that, even if St. Thomas had thought it was as emotional as St. Bonaventure did, he would never have been so emotional about it. It would always have embarrassed him to write about love at such length.

The one exception permitted to him was the rare but remarkable output of his poetry. All sanctity is secrecy; and his sacred poetry was really a secretion; like the pearl in a very tightly closed oyster. He may have written more of it than we know; but part of it came into public use through the particular circumstance of his being asked to compose the office for the Feast of Corpus Christi: a festival first established after the controversy to which he had contributed, in the scroll that he laid on the altar. It does certainly reveal an entirely different side of his genius; and it certainly was genius. As a rule, he was an eminently practical prose writer; some would say a very prosaic prose writer. He maintained controversy with an eye on only two qualities; clarity and courtesy. And he maintained these because they were entirely practical qualities; affecting the probabilities of conversion. But the composer of the Corpus Christi service was not merely what even the wild and woolly would call a poet; he was what the most fastidious would call an artist. His double function rather recalls the double activity of some great Renaissance craftsman, like Michelangelo or Leonardo da Vinci, who would work on the outer wall, planning and building the fortifications of the city; and then retire into the inner chamber to carve or model some cup or casket for a reliquary. The Corpus Christi Office is like some old musical instrument, quaintly and carefully inlaid with many coloured stones and metals; the author has gathered remote texts about pasture and fruition like rare herbs; there is a notable lack of the loud and obvious in the harmony; and the whole is strung with two strong Latin lyrics. Father John O'Connor has translated them with an almost miraculous aptitude; but a good translator will be the first to agree that no translation is good; or, at any rate, good enough. How are we to find eight short English words which actually stand for "*Sumit unus, sumunt mille; quantum isti, tantum ille*"?[3] How is anybody really to render the sound of the "*Pange Lingua*", when the very first syllable has a clang like the clash of cymbals?

There was one other channel, besides that of poetry, and it was that of private affections, by which this large and shy man could show that he had really as much *Caritas* as St. Francis; and certainly as much as any Franciscan theologian. Bonaventure was not likely to think that Thomas was lacking in the love of God, and certainly he was never lacking in the love of Bonaventure. He felt for his whole family a steady, we might say a stubborn tenderness; and, considering how his family had treated him, this would seem to call not only for charity, but for his characteristic virtue of patience. Towards the end of his life, he seems to have leaned especially on his love of one of the brethren, a Friar named Reginald, who received from him some strange and rather startling confidences, of the kind that he very seldom gave even to his friends. It was to Reginald that he gave that last and rather extraordinary hint, which was the end of his controversial

[3] This may be translated as "One receives, a thousand receive; however many they, that much is he."

career, and practically of his earthly life; a hint that history has never been able to explain.

He had returned victorious from his last combat with Siger of Brabant; returned and retired. This particular quarrel was the one point, as we may say, in which his outer and his inner life had crossed and coincided; he realised how he had longed from childhood to call up all allies in the battle for Christ; how he had only long afterwards called up Aristotle as an ally; and now in that last nightmare of sophistry, he had for the first time truly realised that some might really wish Christ to go down before Aristotle. He never recovered from the shock. He won his battle, because he was the best brain of his time, but he could not forget such an inversion of the whole idea and purpose of his life. He was the sort of man who hates hating people. He had not been used to hating even their hateful ideas, beyond a certain point. But in the abyss of anarchy opened by Siger's sophistry of the Double Mind of Man, he had seen the possibility of the perishing of all idea of religion, and even of all idea of truth. Brief and fragmentary as are the phrases that record it, we can gather that he came back with a sort of horror of that outer world, in which there blew such wild winds of doctrine, and a longing for the inner world which any Catholic can share, and in which the saint is not cut off from simple men. He resumed the strict routine of religion, and for some time said nothing to anybody. And then something happened (it is said while he was celebrating Mass) the nature of which will never be known among mortal men.

His friend Reginald asked him to return also to his equally regular habits of reading and writing, and following the controversies of the hour. He said with a singular emphasis, "I can write no more." There seems to have been a silence; after which Reginald again ventured to approach the subject; and Thomas answered him with even greater vigour, "I can write no more. I have seen things which make all my writings like straw."

In 1274, when Aquinas was nearly fifty, the Pope, rejoicing in the recent victory over the Arabian sophists, sent word to him, asking him to come to a Council on these controversial matters, to be held at Lyons. He rose in automatic obedience, as a soldier rises; but we may fancy that there was something in his eyes that told those around him that obedience to the outer command would not in fact frustrate obedience to some more mysterious inner command; a signal that only he had seen. He set out with his friend on the journey, proposing to rest for the night with his sister, to whom he was deeply devoted; and when he came into her house he was stricken down with some unnamed malady. We need not discuss the doubtful medical problems. It is true that he had always been one of those men, healthy in the main, who are overthrown by small illnesses; it is equally true that there is no very clear account of this particular illness. He was eventually taken to a monastery at Fossanuova; and his strange end came upon him with great strides. It may be worth remarking, for those who think that he thought too little of the emotional or romantic side of religious truth, that he asked to have The Song of Solomon read through to him from beginning to end. The feelings of the men about him must have been mingled and rather indescribable; and certainly quite different from his own. He confessed his sins and he received his God; and we may be sure that the great philosopher had entirely forgotten philosophy. But it was not entirely so with those who had loved him, or even those who merely lived in his time. The elements of the narrative are so few, yet so essential, that we have a strong sense in reading the story of the two emotional sides of the event. Those men must have known that a great mind was still labouring like a great mill in the midst of them. They must have felt that, for that moment, the inside of the monastery was larger than the outside. It must have resembled the case of some mighty modern engine, shaking the ramshackle building in which it is for the moment enclosed. For truly that machine was made of the wheels of all the worlds; and revolved like that cosmos of concentric spheres which, whatever its fate in the face of changing science, must always be something of a symbol for philosophy; the depth of double and triple transparencies more mysterious than darkness; the sevenfold, the terrible crystal. In the world of that mind there was a wheel of angels, and a wheel of planets, and a wheel of plants or of animals; but there was also a just and intelligible order of all earthly things, a sane authority and a self-respecting liberty, and a hundred answers to a hundred questions in the complexity of ethics or economics. But there must have been a moment, when men knew that the thunderous mill of thought had stopped suddenly; and that after the shock of stillness that wheel would shake the world no more; that there was nothing now within that hollow house but a great hill of clay; and the confessor, who had been with him in the inner chamber, ran forth as if in fear, and whispered that his confession had been that of a child of five.

# VI

# THE APPROACH TO THOMISM

The fact that Thomism is the philosophy of common sense is itself a matter of common sense. Yet it wants a word of explanation, because we have so long taken such matters in a very uncommon sense. For good or evil, Europe since the Reformation, and most especially England since the Reformation, has been in a peculiar sense the home of paradox. I mean in the very peculiar sense that paradox was at home, and that men were at home with it. The most familiar example is the English boasting that they are practical *because* they are not logical. To an ancient Greek or a Chinaman this would seem exactly like saying that London clerks excel in adding up their ledgers, because they are not accurate in their arithmetic. But the point is not that it is a paradox; it is that parodoxy has become orthodoxy; that men repose in a paradox as placidly as in a platitude. It is not that the practical man stands on his head, which may sometimes be a stimulating if startling gymnastic; it is that he *rests* on his head; and even sleeps on his head. This is an important point, because the use of paradox is to awaken the mind. Take a good paradox, like that of Oliver Wendell Holmes: "Give us the luxuries of life and we will dispense with the necessities." It is amusing and therefore arresting; it has a fine air of defiance; it contains a real if romantic truth. It is all part of the fun that it is stated almost in the form of a contradiction in terms. But most people would agree that there would be considerable danger in basing the whole social system on the notion that necessities are not necessary; as some have based the whole British Constitution on the notion that nonsense will always work out as common sense. Yet even here, it might be said that the invidious example has spread, and that the modern industrial system does really say, "Give us luxuries like coal-tar soap, and we will dispense with necessities like corn."

So much is familiar; but what is not even now realised is that not only the practical politics, but the abstract philosophies of the modern world have had this queer twist. Since the modern world began in the sixteenth century, nobody's system of philosophy has really corresponded to everybody's sense of reality; to what, if left to themselves, common men would call common sense. Each started with a paradox; a peculiar point of view demanding the sacrifice of what they would call a sane point of view. That is the one thing common to Hobbes and Hegel, to Kant and Bergson, to Berkeley and William James. A man had to believe something that no normal man would believe, if it were suddenly propounded to his simplicity; as that law is above right, or right is outside reason, or things are only as we think them, or everything is relative to a reality that is not there. The modern philosopher claims, like a sort of confidence man, that if once we will grant him this, the rest will be easy; he will straighten out the world, if once he is allowed to give this one twist to the mind.

It will be understood that in these matters I speak as a fool; or, as our democratic cousins would say, a moron; anyhow as a man in the street; and the only object of this chapter is to show that the Thomist philosophy is nearer than most philosophies to the mind of the man in the street. I am not, like Father D'Arcy, whose admirable book on St. Thomas has illuminated many problems for me, a trained philosopher, acquainted with the technique of the trade. But I hope Father D'Arcy will forgive me if I take one example from his book, which exactly illustrates what I mean. He, being a trained philosopher, is naturally trained to put up with philosophers. Also, being a trained priest, he is naturally accustomed, not only to suffer fools gladly, but (what is sometimes even harder) to suffer clever people gladly. Above all, his wide reading in metaphysics has made him patient with clever people when they indulge in folly. The consequence is that he can write calmly and even blandly sentences like these. "A certain likeness can be detected between the aim and method of St. Thomas and those of Hegel. There are, however, also remarkable differences. For St. Thomas it is impossible that contradictories should exist together, and again reality and intelligibility correspond, but a thing must first be, to be intelligible."

Let the man in the street be forgiven, if he adds that the "remarkable difference" seems to him to be that St. Thomas was sane and Hegel was mad. The moron refuses to admit that Hegel can both exist and not exist; or that it can be possible to understand Hegel, if there is no Hegel to understand. Yet Father D'Arcy mentions this Hegelian paradox as if it were all in the day's work; and of course it is, if the work is reading all the modern philosophers as searchingly and sympathetically as he has done. And this is what I mean by saying that a modern philosophy starts with a stumbling-block. It is surely not too much to say that there *seems* to be a twist, in saying that contraries are not incompatible; or that a thing can "be" intelligible and not as yet "be" at all.

Against all this the philosophy of St. Thomas stands founded on the universal common conviction that eggs are eggs. The Hegelian may say that an egg is really a hen, because it is a part of an endless process of Becoming; the Berkeleian may hold that poached eggs only exist as a dream exists; since it is quite as easy to call the dream the cause of the eggs as the eggs the cause of the dream; the Pragmatist may believe that we get the best out of scrambled eggs by forgetting that they ever were eggs, and only remembering the scramble. But no pupil of St. Thomas needs to addle his brains in order adequately to addle his eggs; to put his head at any peculiar angle in looking at eggs, or squinting at eggs, or winking the other eye in order to see a new simplification of eggs. The Thomist stands in the broad daylight of the brotherhood of men, in their common consciousness that eggs are not hens or dreams or mere practical assumptions; but things attested by the Authority of the Senses, which is from God.

Thus, even those who appreciate the metaphysical depth of Thomism in other matters have expressed surprise that he does not deal at all with what many now think the main metaphysical question; whether we can prove that the primary act of recognition of any reality is real. The answer is that St. Thomas recognised instantly, what so many modern sceptics have begun to suspect rather laboriously; that a man must either answer that question in the affirmative, or else never answer any question, never ask any question, never even exist intellectually, to answer or to ask. I suppose it is true in a sense that a man can be a fundamental sceptic, but he cannot be anything else; certainly not even a defender of fundamental scepticism. If a man feels that all the movements of his own mind are meaningless, then his mind is meaningless, and he is meaningless; and it does not mean anything to attempt to discover his meaning. Most fundamental sceptics appear to survive, because they are not consistently sceptical and not at all fundamental. They will first deny everything and then admit something, if for the sake of argument—or often rather of attack without argument. I saw an almost startling example of this essential frivolity in a professor of final scepticism, in a paper the other day. A man wrote to say that he accepted nothing but Solipsism, and added that he had often wondered it was not a more common philosophy. Now Solipsism simply means that a man believes in his own existence, but not in anybody or anything else. And it never struck this simple sophist, that if his philosophy was true, there obviously were no other philosophers to profess it.

To this question "Is there anything?" St. Thomas begins by answering "Yes"; if he began by answering "No", it would not be the beginning, but the end. That is what some of us call common sense. Either there is no philosophy, no philosophers, no thinkers, no thought, no anything; or else there is a real bridge between the mind and reality. But he is actually less exacting than many thinkers, much less so than most rationalist and materialist thinkers, as to what that first step involves; he is content, as we shall see, to say that it involves the recognition of Ens or Being as something definitely beyond ourselves. Ens is Ens: Eggs are eggs, and it is not tenable that all eggs were found in a mare's nest.

Needless to say, I am not so silly as to suggest that all the writings of St. Thomas are simple and straightforward; in the sense of being easy to understand. There are passages I do not in the least understand myself; there are passages that puzzle much more learned and logical philosophers than I am; there are passages about which the greatest Thomists still differ and dispute. But that is a question of a thing being hard to read or understand: not hard to accept when understood. That is a mere matter of "The Cat sat on the Mat" being written in Chinese characters; or "Mary had a Little Lamb" in Egyptian hieroglyphics. The only point I am stressing here is that Aquinas is almost always on the side of simplicity, and supports the ordinary man's acceptance of ordinary truisms. For instance, one of the most obscure passages, in my very inadequate judgment, is that in which he explains how the mind is certain of an external object and not merely of an impression of that object; and yet apparently reaches it through a concept, though not merely through an impression. But the only point here is that he does explain that the mind is certain of an external object. It is enough for this purpose that his conclusion is what is called the conclusion of common sense; that it is his purpose to justify common sense; even though he justifies it in a passage which happens to be one of rather uncommon subtlety. The problem of later philosophers is that their conclusion is as dark as their demonstration; or that they bring out a result of which the result is chaos.

Unfortunately, between the man in the street and the Angel of the Schools, there stands at this moment a very high brick wall, with spikes on the top, separating two men who in many ways stand for the same thing. The wall is almost a historical accident; at least it was built a very long time ago, for reasons that need not affect the needs of normal men today; least of all the greatest need of normal men; which is for a normal philosophy. The first difficulty is merely a difference of form; not in the medieval but in the modern sense. There is first a simple obstacle of language; there is then a rather more subtle obstacle of logical method. But the language itself counts for a great deal; even when it is translated, it is still a foreign language; and it is, like other foreign languages, very often translated wrong. As with every other literature from another age or country, it carried with it an atmosphere which is beyond the mere translation of words, as they are translated in a traveller's phrase-book. For instance, the whole system of St. Thomas hangs on one huge and yet simple idea; which does actually cover everything there is, and even everything that could possibly be. He represents this cosmic conception by the word *Ens*; and anybody who can read any Latin at all, however rudely, feels it to be the apt and fitting word; exactly as he feels it in a French word in a piece of good French prose. It ought only to be a matter of logic; but it is also a matter of language.

Unfortunately there is no satisfying translation of the word *Ens*. The difficulty is rather verbal than logical, but it is practical. I mean that when the translator says in English 'being', we are aware of a rather different atmosphere. Atmosphere ought not to affect these absolutes of the intellect; but it does. The new psychologists, who are almost eagerly at war with reason, never tire of telling us that the very terms we use are coloured by our subconsciousness, with something we meant to exclude from our consciousness. And one need not be so idealistically irrational as a modern psychologist, in order to admit that the very shape and sound of words do make a difference, even in the baldest prose, as they do in the most beautiful poetry. We cannot quite prevent the imagination from remembering irrelevant associations even in the abstract sciences like mathematics. Jones Minimus, hustled from history to geometry, may for an instant connect the Angles of the isosceles triangle with the Angles of the Anglo-Saxon Chronicle; and even the mature mathematician, if he is as mad as the psychoanalyst hopes, may have in the roots of his subconscious mind something material in his idea of a root. Now it unfortunately happens that the word 'being', as it comes to a modern Englishman, through modern associations, has a sort of hazy atmosphere that is not in the short and sharp Latin word. Perhaps it reminds him of fantastic professors in fiction, who wave their hands and say, "Thus do we mount to the ineffable heights of pure and radiant Being:" or, worse still, of actual professors in real life, who say, "All Being is Becoming; and is but the evolution of Not-Being by the law of its Being." Perhaps it only reminds him of romantic rhapsodies in old love stories; "Beautiful and adorable being, light and breath of my very being". Anyhow it has a wild and woolly sort of sound; as if only very vague people used it; or as if it might mean all sorts of different things.

Now the Latin word *Ens* has a sound like the English word *End*. It is final and even abrupt; it is nothing except itself.

There was once a silly gibe against Scholastics like Aquinas, that they discussed whether angels could stand on the point of a needle. It is at least certain that this first word of Aquinas is as sharp as the point of a pin. For that also is, in an almost ideal sense, an End. But when we say that St. Thomas Aquinas is concerned fundamentally with the idea of Being, we must not admit any of the cloudier generalisations that we may have grown used to, or even grown tired of, in the sort of idealistic writing that is rather rhetoric than philosophy. Rhetoric is a very fine thing in its place, as a medieval scholar would have willingly agreed, as he taught it along with logic in the schools; but St. Thomas Aquinas himself is not at all rhetorical. Perhaps he is hardly even sufficiently rhetorical. There are any number of purple patches in Augustine; but there are no purple patches in Aquinas. He did on certain definite occasions drop into poetry; but he very seldom dropped into oratory. And so little was he in touch with some modern tendencies, that whenever he did write poetry, he actually put it into poems. There is another side to this, to be noted later. He very specially possessed the philosophy that inspires poetry; as he did so largely inspire Dante's poetry. And poetry without philosophy has only inspiration, or, in vulgar language, only wind. He had, so to speak, the imagination without the imagery. And even this is perhaps too sweeping. There is an image of his, that is true poetry as well as true philosophy; about the tree of life bowing down with a huge humility, because of the very load of its living fruitfulness; a thing Dante might have described so as to overwhelm us with the tremendous twilight and almost drug us with the divine fruit. But normally, we may say that his words are brief even when his books are long. I have taken the example of the word *Ens*, precisely because it is one of the cases in which Latin is plainer than plain English. And his style, unlike that of St. Augustine and many Catholic Doctors, is always a penny plain rather than twopence coloured. It is often difficult to understand, simply because the subjects are so difficult that hardly any mind, except one like his own, can fully understand them. But he never darkens it by using words without knowledge, or even more legitimately, by using words belonging only to imagination or intuition. So far as his method is concerned, he is perhaps the one real Rationalist among all the children of men.

This brings us to the other difficulty; that of logical method. I have never understood why there is supposed to be something crabbed or antique about a syllogism; still less can I understand what anybody means by talking as if induction had somehow taken the place of deduction. The whole point of deduction is that true premises produce a true conclusion. What is called induction seems simply to mean collecting a larger number of true premises. or perhaps, in some physical matters, taking rather more trouble to see that they are true. It may be a fact that a modern man can get more out of a great many premises, concerning microbes or asteroids than a medieval man could get out of a very few premises about salamanders and unicorns. But the process of deduction from the data is the same for the modern mind as for the medieval mind; and what is pompously called induction is simply collecting more of the data. And Aristotle or Aquinas, or anybody in his five wits, would of course agree that the conclusion could only be true if the premises were true; and that the more true premises there were the better. It was the misfortune of medieval culture that there were not enough true premises, owing to the rather ruder conditions of travel or experiment. But however perfect were the conditions of travel or experiment, they could only produce premises; it would still be necessary to deduce conclusions. But many modern people talk as if what they call induction were some magic way of reaching a conclusion, without using any of those horrid old syllogisms. But induction does not lead us to a conclusion. Induction only leads us to a deduction. Unless the last three syllogistic steps are all right, the conclusion is all wrong. Thus, the great nineteenth century men of science, whom I was brought up to revere ("accepting the conclusions of science", it was always called), went out and closely inspected the air and the earth, the chemicals and the gases, doubtless more closely than Aristotle or Aquinas, and then came back and embodied their final conclusion in a syllogism. "All matter is made of microscopic little knobs which are indivisible. My body is made of matter. Therefore my body is made of microscopic little knobs which are indivisible." They were not wrong in the form of their reasoning; because it is the only way to reason. In this world there is nothing except a syllogism—and a fallacy. But of course these modern men knew, as the medieval men knew, that their conclusions would not be true unless their premises were true. And that is where the trouble began. For the men of science, or their sons and nephews, went out and took another look at the knobby nature of matter; and were surprised to find that it was not knobby at all. So they came back and completed the process with their syllogism; "All matter is made of whirling protons and electrons. My body is made of matter. Therefore my body is made of whirling protons and electrons." And that again is a good syllogism; though they may have to look at matter once or twice more, before we know whether it is a true premise and a true conclusion. But in the final process of truth there is nothing else except a good syllogism. The only other thing is a bad syllogism; as in the familiar fashionable shape; "All matter is made of protons and electrons. I should very much like to think that mind is much the same as matter. So I will announce, through the microphone or the megaphone, that my mind is made of protons and electrons." But that is not induction; it is only a very bad blunder in deduction. That is not another or new way of thinking; it is only ceasing to think.

What is really meant, and what is much more reasonable, is that the old syllogists sometimes set out the syllogism at length; and certainly that is not always necessary. A man can run down the three steps much more quickly than that; but a man cannot run down the three steps if they are not there. If he does, he will break his neck, as if he walked out of a fourth-story window. The truth about this false antithesis of induction and deduction is simply this; that as premises or data accumulated, the emphasis and detail was shifted to them, from the final deduction to which they lead. But they did lead to a final deduction; or else they led to nothing. The logician had so much to say about electrons or microbes that he dwelt most on these data and shortened or assumed his ultimate syllogism. But if he reasoned rightly, however rapidly, he reasoned syllogistically.

As a matter of fact, Aquinas does not usually argue in syllogisms; though he always argues syllogistically. I mean he does not set out all the steps of the logic in each case; the legend that he does so is part of that loose and largely unverified legend of the Renaissance; that the Schoolmen were all crabbed and mechanical medieval bores. But he does argue with a certain austerity, and disdain of ornament, which may make him seem monotonous to anyone specially seeking the modern forms of wit or fancy. But all this has nothing to do with the question asked at the beginning of this chapter and needing to be answered at the end of it; the question of what he is arguing for. In that respect it can be repeated, most emphatically, that he is arguing for common sense. He is arguing for a common sense which would even now commend itself to most of the common people. He is arguing for the popular proverbs that seeing is believing; that the proof of the pudding is in the eating; that a man cannot jump down his own throat or deny the fact of his own existence. He often maintains the view by the use of abstractions; but the abstractions are no more abstract than Energy or Evolution or Space-Time; and they do not land us, as the others often do, in hopeless contradictions about common life. The Pragmatist sets out to be practical, but his practicality turns out to be entirely theoretical. The Thomist begins by being theoretical, but his theory turns out to be entirely practical. That is why a great part of the world is returning to it today.

Finally, there is some real difficulty in the fact of a foreign language; apart from the ordinary fact of the Latin language. Modern philosophical terminology is not always exactly identical with plain English; and medieval philosophical terminology is not at all identical even with modern philosophical terminology. It is not really very difficult to learn the meaning of the main terms; but their medieval meaning is sometimes the exact opposite of their modern meaning. The obvious example is in the pivotal word "form". We say nowadays, "I wrote a formal apology to the Dean", or "The proceedings when we wound up the Tip-Cat Club were purely formal." But we mean that they were purely fictitious; and St. Thomas, had he been a member of the Tip-Cat Club, would have meant just the opposite. He would have meant that the proceedings dealt with the very heart and soul and secret of the whole being of the Tip-Cat Club; and that the apology to the Dean was so essentially apologetic that it tore the very heart out in tears of true contrition. For "formal" in Thomist language means actual, or possessing the real decisive quality that makes a thing itself. Roughly when he describes a thing as made out of Form and Matter, he very rightly recognises that Matter is the more mysterious and indefinite and featureless element; and that what stamps anything with its own identity is its Form. Matter, so to speak, is not so much the solid as the liquid or gaseous thing in the cosmos; and in this most modern scientists are beginning to agree with him. But the form is the fact; it is that which makes a brick a brick, and a bust a bust, and not the shapeless and trampled clay of which either may be made. The stone that broke a statuette, in some Gothic niche, might have been itself a statuette; and under chemical analysis, the statuette is only a stone. But such a chemical analysis is entirely false as a philosophical analysis. The reality, the thing that makes the two things real, is in the idea of the image and in the idea of the image-breaker. This is only a passing example of the mere idiom of the Thomist terminology; but it is not a bad prefatory specimen of the truth of Thomist thought. Every artist knows that the form is not superficial but fundamental; that the form is the foundation. Every sculptor knows that the form of the statue is not the outside of the statue, but rather the inside of the statue; even in the sense of the inside of the sculptor. Every poet knows that the sonnet-form is not only the form of the poem; but the poem. No modern critic who does not understand what the medieval Schoolman meant by form can meet the Schoolman as an intellectual equal.

## VII

# THE PERMANENT PHILOSOPHY

It is a pity that the word Anthropology has been degraded to the study of Anthropoids. It is now incurably associated with squabbles between prehistoric professors (in more senses than one) about whether a chip of stone is the tooth of a man or an ape; sometimes settled as in that famous case, when it was found to be the tooth of a pig. It is very right that there should be a purely physical science of such things; but the name commonly used might well, by analogy, have been dedicated to things not only wider and deeper, but rather more relevant. Just as, in America, the new Humanists have pointed out to the old Humanitarians that their humanitarianism has been largely concentrated on things that are *not* specially human, such as physical conditions, appetites, economic needs, environment and so on—so in practice those who are called Anthropologists have to narrow their minds to the materialistic things that are *not* notably anthropic. They have to hunt through history and pre-history something which emphatically is not *Homo Sapiens*, but is always in fact regarded as *Simius Insipiens*. *Homo Sapiens* can only be considered in relation to *Sapientia*; and only a book like that of St. Thomas is really devoted to the intrinsic idea of *Sapientia*. In short, there ought to be a real study called Anthropology corresponding to Theology. In this sense St. Thomas Aquinas, perhaps more than he is anything else, is a great anthropologist.

I apologise for the opening words of this chapter to all those excellent and eminent men of science, who are engaged in the real study of humanity in its relation to biology. But I rather fancy that they will be the last to deny that there has been a somewhat disproportionate disposition, in popular science, to turn the study of human beings into the study of savages. And savagery is not history: it is either the beginning of history or the end of it. I suspect that the greatest scientists would agree that only too many professors have thus been lost in the bush or the jungle; professors who wanted to study anthropology and never got any further than anthropophagy. But I have a particular reason for prefacing this suggestion of a higher anthropology by an apology to any genuine biologists who might seem to be included, but are certainly not included, in a protest against cheap popular science. For the first thing to be said about St. Thomas as an anthropologist, is that he is really remarkably like the best sort of modern biological anthropologist; of the sort who would call themselves Agnostics. This fact is so sharp and decisive a turning point in history, that the history really needs to be recalled and recorded.

St. Thomas Aquinas closely resembles the great Professor Huxley, the Agnostic who invented the word Agnosticism. He is like him in his way of starting the argument, and he is unlike everybody else, before and after, until the Huxleyan age. He adopts almost literally the Huxleyan definition of the Agnostic method; "To follow reason as far as it will go"; the only question is—where does it go? He lays down the almost startlingly modern or materialist statement; "Everything that is in the intellect has been in the senses". This is where he began, as much as any modern man of science, nay, as much as any modern materialist who can now hardly be called a man of science; at the very opposite end of enquiry from that of the mere mystic. The Platonists, or at least the Neo-Platonists, all tended to the view that the mind was lit entirely from within; St. Thomas insisted that it was lit by five windows, that we call the windows of the senses. But he wanted the light from without to shine on what was within. He wanted to study the nature of Man, and not merely of such moss and mushrooms as he might see through the window, and which he valued as the first enlightening experience of man. And starting from this point, he proceeds to climb the House of Man, step by step and story by story, until he has come out on the highest tower and beheld the largest vision.

In other words, he is an anthropologist, with a complete theory of Man, right or wrong. Now the modern Anthropologists, who called themselves Agnostics, completely failed to be Anthropologists at all. Under their limitations, they could not get a complete theory of Man, let alone a complete theory of nature. They began by ruling out something which they called the Unknowable. The incomprehensibility was almost comprehensible, if we could really understand the Unknowable in the sense of the Ultimate. But it rapidly became apparent that all sorts of things were Unknowable, which were exactly the things that a man has got to know. It is necessary to know whether he is responsible or irresponsible, perfect or imperfect, perfectible or unperfectible, mortal or immortal, doomed or free, not in order to understand God, but in order to understand Man. Nothing that leaves these things under a cloud of religious doubt can possibly pretend to be a Science of Man; it shrinks from anthropology as completely as from theology. Has a man free will; or is his sense of choice an illusion? Has he a conscience, or has his conscience any authority; or is it only the prejudice of the tribal past? Is there real hope of settling these things by human reason; and has *that* any authority? Is he to regard death as final; and is he to regard miraculous help as possible? Now it is all nonsense to say that these are unknowable in any remote sense, like the distinction between the Cherubim and the Seraphim, or the Procession of the Holy Ghost. The Schoolmen may have shot too far beyond our limits in pursuing the Cherubim and Seraphim. But in asking whether a man can choose or whether a man will die, they were asking ordinary questions in natural history; like whether a cat can scratch or whether a dog can smell. Nothing calling itself a complete Science of Man can shirk them. And the great Agnostics did shirk them. They may have said they had no scientific evidence; in that case they failed to produce even a scientific hypothesis. What they generally did produce was a wildly unscientific contradiction. Most Monist moralists simply said that Man has no choice; but he must think and act heroically as if he had. Huxley made morality, and even Victorian morality, in the exact sense, supernatural. He said it had arbitrary rights above nature; a sort of theology without theism.

I do not know for certain why St. Thomas was called the Angelic Doctor: whether it was that he had an angelic temper, or the intellectuality of an Angel; or whether there was a later legend that he concentrated on Angels—especially on the points of needles. If so, I do not quite understand how this idea arose; history has many examples of an irritating habit of labelling somebody in connection with something, as if he never did anything else. Who was it who began the inane habit of referring to Dr. Johnson as 'our lexicographer'; as if he never did anything but write a dictionary? Why do most people insist on meeting the large and far-reaching mind of Pascal at its very narrowest point; the point at which it was sharpened into a spike by the spite of the Jansenists against the Jesuits? It is just possible, for all I know, that this labelling of Aquinas as a specialist was an obscure depreciation of him as a universalist. For that is a very common trick for the belittling of literary or scientific men. St. Thomas must have made a certain number of enemies, though he hardly ever treated them as enemies. Unfortunately, good temper is sometimes more irritating than bad temper. And he had, after all, done a great deal of damage, as many medieval men would have thought; and, what is more curious, a great deal of damage to both sides. He had been a revolutionist against Augustine and a traditionalist against Averrhoes. He might appear to some to have tried to wreck that ancient beauty of the city of God, which bore some resemblance to the Republic of Plato. He might appear to others to have inflicted a blow on the advancing and levelling forces of Islam, as dramatic as that of Godfrey storming Jerusalem. It is possible that these enemies, by way of damning with faint praise, talked about his very respectable little work on Angels: as a man might say that Darwin was really reliable when writing on coral-insects; or that some of Milton's Latin poems were very creditable indeed. But this is only a conjecture, and many other conjectures are possible. And I am disposed to think that St. Thomas really was rather specially interested in the nature of Angels, for the same reason that made him even more interested in the nature of Men. It was a part of that strong personal interest in things subordinate and semidependent, which runs through his whole system: a hierarchy of higher and lower liberties. He was interested in the problem of the Angel, as he was interested in the problem of the Man, because it was a problem; and especially because it was a problem of an intermediate creature. I do not pretend to deal here with this mysterious quality, as he conceives it to exist in that inscrutable intellectual being, who is less than God but more than Man. But it was this quality of a link in the chain, or a rung in the ladder, which mainly concerned the theologian, in developing his own particular theory of degrees. Above all, it is this which chiefly moves him, when he finds so fascinating the central mystery of Man. And for him the point is always that Man is not a balloon going up into the sky, nor a mole burrowing merely in the earth; but rather a thing like a tree, whose roots are fed from the earth, while its highest branches seem to rise almost to the stars.

I have pointed out that mere modern free-thought has left everything in a fog, including itself. The assertion that thought is free led first to the denial that will is free; but even about that there was no real determination among the Determinists. In practice, they told men that they must treat their will as free though it was not free. In other words, Man must live a double life; which is exactly the old heresy of Siger of Brabant about the Double Mind. In other words, the nineteenth century left everything in chaos; and the importance of Thomism to the twentieth century is that it may give us back a cosmos. We can give here only the rudest sketch of how Aquinas, like the Agnostics, beginning in the cosmic cellars, yet climbed to the cosmic towers.

Without pretending to span within such limits the essential Thomist idea, I may be allowed to throw out a sort of rough version of the fundamental question, which I think I have known myself, consciously or unconsciously since my childhood. When a child looks out of the nursery window and sees anything, say the green lawn of the garden, what does he actually know; or does he know anything? There are all sorts of nursery games of negative philosophy played round this question. A brilliant Victorian scientist delighted in declaring that the child does not see any grass at all; but only a sort of green mist reflected in a tiny mirror of the human eye. This piece of rationalism has always struck me as almost insanely irrational. If he is not sure of the existence of the grass, which he sees through the glass of a window, how on earth can he be sure of the existence of the retina, which he sees through the glass of a microscope? If sight deceives, why can it not go on deceiving? Men of another school answer that grass is a mere green impression on the mind; and that he can be sure of nothing except the mind. They declare that he can only be conscious of his own consciousness; which happens to be the one thing that we know the child is not conscious of at all. In that sense, it would be far truer to say that there is grass and no child, than to say that there is a conscious child but no grass. St. Thomas Aquinas, suddenly intervening in this nursery quarrel, says emphatically that the child is aware of *Ens*. Long before he knows that grass is grass, or self is self, he knows that something is something. Perhaps it would be best to say very emphatically (with a blow on the table), "There *is* an Is". That is as much monkish credulity as St. Thomas asks of us at the start. Very few unbelievers start by asking us to believe so little. And yet, upon this sharp pin-point of reality, he rears by long logical processes that have never really been successfully overthrown, the whole cosmic system of Christendom.

Thus, Aquinas insists very profoundly, but very practically, that there *instantly* enters, with this idea of affirmation, the idea of contradiction. It is instantly apparent, even to the child, that there cannot be both affirmation and contradiction. Whatever you call the thing he sees, a moon or a mirage or a sensation or a state of consciousness, when he sees it, he knows it is not true that he does not see it. Or whatever you call what he is supposed to be doing, seeing or dreaming or being conscious of an impression, he knows that if he is doing it, it is a lie to say he is not doing it. Therefore there has already entered *something* beyond even the first fact of being; there follows it like its shadow the first fundamental creed or commandment; that a thing cannot be and not be. Henceforth, in common or popular language, there is a false and true. I say in popular language, because Aquinas is nowhere more subtle than in pointing out that being is not strictly the same as truth; seeing truth must mean the appreciation of being by some mind capable of appreciating it. But in a general sense there has entered that primeval world of pure actuality, the division and dilemma that brings the ultimate sort of war into the world; the everlasting duel between Yes and No. This is the dilemma that many sceptics have darkened the universe and dissolved the mind, solely in order to escape. They are those who maintain that there is something that is both Yes and No. I do not know whether they pronounce it Yo.

The next step following on this acceptance of actuality or certainty, or whatever we call it in popular language, is much more difficult to explain in that language. But it represents exactly the point at which nearly all other systems go wrong, and in taking the third step abandon the first. Aquinas has affirmed that our first sense of fact is a fact; and he cannot go back on it without falsehood. But when we come to look at the fact or facts, as we know them, we observe that they have a rather queer character; which has made many moderns grow strangely and restlessly sceptical about them. For instance, they are largely in a state of change, from being one thing to being another; or their qualities are relative to other things; or they appear to move incessantly; or they appear to vanish entirely. At this point, as I say, many sages lose hold of the first principle of reality, which they would concede at first; and fall back on saying that there is nothing except change; or nothing except comparison; or nothing except flux; or in effect that there is nothing at all. Aquinas turns the whole argument the other way, keeping in line with his first realisation of reality. There is no doubt about the being of being, even if it does sometimes look like becoming; that is because what we see is not the fullness of being; or (to continue a sort of colloquial slang) we never see being being as much as it can. Ice is melted into cold water and cold water is heated into hot water; it cannot be all three at once. But this does not make water unreal or even relative; it only means that its being is limited to being one thing at a time. But the fullness of being is everything that it can be; and without it the lesser or approximate forms of being cannot be explained as anything; unless they are explained away as nothing.

This crude outline can only at the best be historical rather than philosophical. It is impossible to compress into it the metaphysical proofs of such an idea; especially in the medieval metaphysical language. But this distinction in philosophy is tremendous as a turning point in history. Most thinkers, on realising the apparent mutability of being, have really forgotten their own realisation of the being, and believed only in the mutability. They cannot even say that a thing changes into another thing; for them there is no instant in the process at which it is a thing at all. It is only a change. It would be more logical to call it nothing changing into nothing, than to say (on these principles) that there ever was or will be a moment when the thing is itself. St. Thomas maintains that the ordinary thing at any moment is something; but it is not everything that it could be. There is a fullness of being, in which it could be everything that it can be. Thus, while most sages come at last to nothing but naked change, he comes to the ultimate thing that is unchangeable, because it is all the other things at once. While they describe a change which is really a change in nothing, he describes a changelessness which includes the changes of everything. Things change because they are not complete; but their reality can only be explained as part of something that is complete. It is God.

Historically, at least, it was round this sharp and crooked corner that all the sophists have followed each other while the great Schoolman went up the high road of experience and expansion; to the beholding of cities, to the building of cities. They all failed at this early stage because, in the words of the old game, they took away the number they first thought of. The recognition of something, of a thing or things, is the first act of the intellect. But because the examination of a thing shows it is not a fixed or final thing, they inferred that there is nothing fixed or final. Thus, in various ways, they all began to see a thing as something thinner than a thing; a wave; a weakness; an abstract instability. St. Thomas, to use the same rude figure, saw a thing that was thicker than a thing; that was even more solid than the solid but secondary facts he had started by admitting as facts. Since we know them to be real, any elusive or bewildering element in their reality cannot really be unreality; and must be merely their relation to the real reality. A hundred human philosophies, ranging over the earth from Nominalism to Nirvana and Maya, from formless evolution to mindless quietism, all come from this first break in the Thomist chain; the notion that, because what we see does not satisfy us or explain itself, it is not even what we see. That cosmos is a contradiction in terms and strangles itself; but Thomism cuts itself free. The defect we see, in what is, is simply that it is not all that is. God is more actual even than Man; more actual even than Matter; for God with all His powers at every instant is immortally in action.

A cosmic comedy of a very curious sort occurred recently; involving the views of very brilliant men, such as Mr. Bernard Shaw and the Dean of St. Paul's. Briefly, freethinkers of many sorts had often said they had no need of a Creation, because the cosmos had always existed and always would exist. Mr. Bernard Shaw said he had become an atheist because the universe had gone on making itself from the beginning, or without a beginning; Dean Inge later displayed consternation at the very idea that the universe could have an end. Most modern Christians, living by tradition where medieval Christians could live by logic or reason, vaguely felt that it was a dreadful idea to deprive them of the Day of Judgment. Most modern agnostics (who are delighted to have their ideas called dreadful) cried out all the more, with one accord, that the self-producing, self-existent, truly scientific universe had never needed to have a beginning and could not come to an end. At this very instant, quite suddenly, like the look-out man on a ship who shouts a warning about a rock, the *real* man of science, the expert who was examining the facts, announced in a loud voice that the universe *was* coming to an end. He had not been listening, of course, to the talk of the amateurs; he had been actually examining the texture of matter; and he said it was disintegrating: the world was apparently blowing itself up by a gradual explosion called energy; the whole business would certainly have an end and had presumably had a beginning. This was very shocking indeed; not to the orthodox, but rather specially to the unorthodox; who are rather more easily shocked. Dean Inge, who had been lecturing the orthodox for years on their stern duty of accepting all scientific discoveries, positively wailed aloud over this truly tactless scientific discovery; and practically implored the scientific discoverers to go away and discover something different. It seems almost incredible; but it is a fact that he asked what God would have to amuse Him, if the universe ceased. That is a measure of how much the modern mind needs Thomas Aquinas. But even without Aquinas, I can hardly conceive any educated man, let alone such a learned man, believing in God at all without assuming that God contains in Himself every perfection including eternal joy; and does not require the solar system to entertain him like a circus.

To step out of these presumptions, prejudices and private disappointments, into the world of St. Thomas, is like escaping from a scuffle in a dark room into the broad daylight. St. Thomas says, quite straightforwardly, that he himself believes this world has a beginning and end; because such seems to be the teaching of the Church; the validity of which mystical message to mankind he defends elsewhere with dozens of quite different arguments. Anyhow, the Church said the world would end; and apparently the Church was right; always supposing (as we are always supposed to suppose) that the latest men of science are right. But Aquinas says he sees no particular reason, in reason, why this world should not be a world without end; or even without beginning. And he is quite certain that, if it were entirely without end or beginning, there would still be exactly the same logical need of a Creator. Anybody who does not see that, he gently implies, does not really understand what is meant by a Creator.

For what St. Thomas means is not a medieval picture of an old king; but this second step in the great argument about *Ens* or Being; the second point which is so desperately difficult to put correctly in popular language. That is why I have introduced it here in the particular form of the argument that there must be a Creator even if there is no Day of Creation. Looking at Being as it is now, as the baby looks at the grass, we see a second thing about it; in quite popular language, it *looks* secondary and dependent. Existence exists; but it is not sufficiently self-existent; and would never become so merely by going on existing. The same primary sense which tells us it is Being, tells us that it is not perfect Being; not merely imperfect in the popular controversial sense of containing sin or sorrow; but imperfect as Being; less actual than the actuality it implies. For instance, its Being is often only Becoming; beginning to Be or ceasing to Be; it implies a more constant or complete thing of which it gives in itself no example. That is the meaning of that basic medieval phrase, "Everything that is moving is moved by another"; which, in the clear subtlety of St. Thomas, means inexpressibly more than the mere Deistic "somebody wound up the clock" with which it is probably often confounded. Anyone who thinks deeply will see that motion has about it an essential incompleteness, which approximates to something more complete.

The actual argument is rather technical; and concerns the fact that potentiality does not explain itself; moreover, in any case, unfolding must be of something folded. Suffice it to say that the mere modern evolutionists, who would ignore the argument, do not do so because they have discovered any flaw in the argument; for they have never discovered the argument itself. They do so because they are too shallow to see the flaw in their own argument; for the weakness of their thesis is covered by fashionable phraseology, as the strength of the old thesis is covered by old-fashioned phraseology. But for those who really think, there is always something really unthinkable about the whole evolutionary cosmos, as they conceive it; because it is something coming out of nothing; an ever-increasing flood of water pouring out of an empty jug. Those who can simply accept that, without even seeing the difficulty, are not likely to go so deep as Aquinas and see the solution of his difficulty. In a word, the world does not explain itself, and cannot do so merely by continuing to expand itself. But anyhow, it is absurd for the Evolutionist to complain that it is unthinkable for an admittedly unthinkable God to make everything out of nothing and then pretend that it is *more* thinkable that nothing should turn itself into everything.

We have seen that most philosophers simply fail to philosophise about things because they change; they also fail to philosophise about things because they differ. We have no space to follow St. Thomas through all these negative heresies; but a word must be said about Nominalism, or the doubt founded on the things that differ. Everyone knows that the Nominalist declared that things differ too much to be really classified; so that they are only labelled. Aquinas was a firm but moderate Realist, and therefore held that there really are general qualities; as that human beings are human, and other paradoxes. To be an extreme Realist would have taken him too near to being a Platonist. He recognized that individuality is real, but said that it coexists with a common character making some generalisation possible; in fact, as in most things, he said exactly what all common sense would say, if no intelligent heretics had ever disturbed it. Nevertheless, they still continue to disturb it. I remember when Mr. H. G. Wells had an alarming fit of Nominalist philosophy; and poured forth book after book to argue that everything is unique and untypical; as that a man is so much an individual that he is not even a man. It is a quaint and almost comic fact, that this chaotic negation especially attracts those who are always complaining of social chaos, and who propose to replace it by the most sweeping social regulations. It is the very men who say that nothing can be classified, who say that everything must be codified. Thus Mr. Bernard Shaw said that the only golden rule is that there is no golden rule. He prefers an iron rule; as in Russia.

But this is only a small inconsistency in some moderns as individuals. There is a much deeper inconsistency in them as theorists in relation to the general theory called Creative Evolution. They seem to imagine that they avoid the metaphysical doubt about mere change by assuming (it is not very clear why) that the change will always be for the better. But the mathematical difficulty of finding a corner in a curve is not altered by turning the chart upside down, and saying that a downward curve is now an upward curve. The point is that there is no point in the curve; no place at which we have a logical right to say that the curve has reached its climax, or revealed its origin, or come to its end. It makes no difference that they choose to be cheerful about it, and say, "It is enough that there is always a beyond"; instead of lamenting, like the more realistic poets of the past, over the tragedy of mere Mutability. It is not enough that there is always a beyond; because it might be beyond bearing. Indeed the only defence of this view is that sheer boredom is such an agony, that any movement is a relief. But the truth is that they have never read St. Thomas, or they would find, with no little terror, that they really agree with him. What they really mean is that change is not mere change; but is the unfolding of something; and if it is thus unfolded, though the unfolding takes twelve million years, it must be there already. In other words, they agree with Aquinas that there is everywhere potentiality that has not reached its end in act. But if it is a definite potentiality, and if it can only end in a definite act, why then there is a Great Being, in whom all potentialities already exist as a plan of action. In other words, it is impossible even to say that the change is for the better, unless the best exists somewhere, both before and after the change. Otherwise it is indeed mere change, as the blankest sceptics or the blackest pessimists would see it. Suppose two entirely new paths open before the progress of Creative Evolution. How is the evolutionist to know which Beyond is the better; unless he accepts from the past and present some standard of the best? By their superficial theory everything can change; everything can improve, even the nature of improvement. But in their submerged common sense, they do not really think that an ideal of kindness could change to an ideal of cruelty. It is typical of them that they will sometimes rather timidly use the word Purpose; but blush at the very mention of the word Person.

St. Thomas is the very reverse of anthropomorphic, in spite of his shrewdness as an anthropologist. Some theologians have even claimed that he is too much of an agnostic; and has left the nature of God too much of an intellectual abstraction. But we do not need even St. Thomas, we do not need anything but our own common sense, to tell us that if there has been from the beginning anything that can possibly be called a Purpose, it must reside in something that has the essential elements of a Person. There cannot be an intention hovering in the air all by itself, any more than a memory that nobody remembers or a joke that nobody has made. The only chance for those supporting such suggestions is to take refuge in blank and bottomless irrationality; and even then it is impossible to prove that anybody has any right to be unreasonable, if St. Thomas has no right to be reasonable.

In a sketch that aims only at the baldest simplification, this does seem to me the simplest truth about St. Thomas the philosopher. He is one, so to speak, who is faithful to his first love; and it is love at first sight. I mean that he immediately recognised a real quality in things; and afterwards resisted all the disintegrating doubts arising from the nature of those things. That is why I emphasise, even in the first few pages, the fact that there is a sort of purely Christian humility and fidelity underlying his philosophic realism. St. Thomas could as truly say, of having seen merely a stick or a stone, what St. Paul said of having seen the rending of the secret heavens, "I was not disobedient to the heavenly vision". For though the stick or the stone is an earthly vision, it is through them that St. Thomas finds his way to heaven; and the point is that he is obedient to the vision; he does not go back on it. Nearly all the other sages who have led or misled mankind do, on one excuse or another, go back on it. They dissolve the stick or the stone in chemical solutions of scepticism; either in the medium of mere time and change; or in the difficulties of classification of unique units; or in the difficulty of recognising variety while admitting unity. The first of these three is called debate about flux or formless transition; the second is the debate about Nominalism and Realism, or the existence of general ideas; the third is called the ancient metaphysical riddle of the One and the Many. But they can all be reduced under a rough image to this same statement about St. Thomas. He is still true to the first truth and refusing the first treason. He will not deny what he has seen, though it be a secondary and diverse reality. He will not take away the numbers he first thought of, though there may be quite a number of them.

He has seen grass; and will not say he has not seen grass, because it today is and tomorrow is cast into the oven. That is the substance of all scepticism about change, transition, transformism and the rest. He will not say that there is no grass but only growth. If grass grows and withers, it can only mean that it is part of a greater thing, which is even more real; not that the grass is less real than it looks. St. Thomas has a really logical right to say, in the words of the modern mystic, A. E.: "I begin by the grass to be bound again to the Lord".

He has seen grass and grain; and he will not say that they do not differ, because there is something common to grass and grain. Nor will he say that there is nothing common to grass and grain, because they do really differ. He will not say, with the extreme Nominalists, that because grain can be differentiated into all sorts of fruitage, or grass trodden into mire with any kind of weed, therefore there can be no *classification* to distinguish weeds from slime or to draw a fine distinction between cattle-food and cattle. He will not say with the extreme Platonists, on the other hand, that he saw the perfect fruit in his own head by shutting his eyes, *before* he saw any difference between grain and grass. He saw one thing and then another thing, and then a common quality; but he does not really pretend that he saw the quality before the thing.

He has seen grass and gravel; that is to say, he has seen things really different; things not classified together like grass and grain. The first flash of fact shows us a world of really strange things; not merely strange to us, but strange to each other. The separate things need have nothing in common except Being. Everything is Being; but it is not true that everything is Unity. It is here, as I have said, that St. Thomas does definitely, one might say defiantly, part company with the Pantheist and Monist. All things are; but among the things that are is the thing called difference, quite as much as the thing called similarity. And here again we begin to be bound again to the Lord, not only by the universality of grass, but by the incompatibility of grass and gravel. For this world of different and varied beings is especially the world of the Christian Creator; the world of created things, like things made by an artist; as compared with the world that is only one thing, with a sort of shimmering and shifting veil of misleading change; which is the conception of so many of the ancient religions of Asia and the modern sophistries of Germany. In the face of these, St. Thomas still stands stubborn in the same obstinate objective fidelity. He has seen grass and gravel; and he is not disobedient to the heavenly vision.

To sum up; the reality of things, the mutability of things, the diversity of things, and all other such things that can be attributed to things, is followed carefully by the medieval philosopher, without losing touch with the original point of the reality. There is no space in this book to specify the thousand steps of thought by which he shows that he is right. But the point is that, even apart from being right he is real. He is a realist in a rather curious sense of his own, which is a third thing, distinct from the almost contrary medieval and modern meanings of the word. Even the doubts and difficulties about reality have driven him to believe in more reality rather than less. The *deceitfulness* of things which has had so sad an effect on so many sages, has almost a contrary effect on this sage. If things deceive us, it is by being more real than they seem. As ends in themselves they always deceive us; but as things tending to a greater end, they are even more real than we think them. If they seem to have a relative unreality (so to speak) it is because they are potential and not actual; they are unfulfilled, like packets of seeds or boxes of fireworks. They have it in them to be more real than they are. And there is an upper world of what the Schoolman called Fruition, or Fulfillment, in which all this relative relativity becomes actuality; in which the trees burst into flower or the rockets into flame.

Here I leave the reader, on the very lowest rung of those ladders of logic, by which St. Thomas besieged and mounted the House of Man. It is enough to say that by arguments as honest and laborious, he climbed up to the turrets and talked with angels on the roofs of gold. This is, in a very rude outline, his philosophy; it is impossible in such an outline to describe his theology. Anyone writing so small a book about so big a man, must leave out something. Those who know him best will best understand why, after some considerable consideration, I have left out the only important thing.

# VIII

## THE SEQUEL TO ST. THOMAS

It is often said that St. Thomas, unlike St. Francis, did not permit in his work the indescribable element of poetry: As, for instance, that there is little reference to any pleasure in the actual flowers and fruit of natural things, though any amount of concern with the buried roots of nature. And yet I confess that, in reading his philosophy, I have a very peculiar and powerful impression analogous to poetry. Curiously enough, it is in some ways more analogous to painting, and reminds me very much of the effect produced by the *best* of the modern painters, when they throw a strange and almost crude light upon stark and rectangular objects, or seem to be groping for rather than grasping the very pillars of the subconscious mind. It is probably because there is in his work a quality which is Primitive, in the best sense of a badly misused word; but anyhow, the pleasure is definitely not only of the reason, but also of the imagination.

Perhaps the impression is connected with the fact that painters deal with things without words. An artist draws quite gravely the grand curves of a pig; because he is not thinking of the *word* pig. There is no thinker who is so unmistakably thinking about things, and not being misled by the indirect influence of words, as St. Thomas Aquinas. It is true in that sense that he has not the advantage of words, any more than the disadvantage of words. Here he differs sharply, for instance, from St. Augustine who was, among other things, a wit. He was also a sort of prose poet, with a power over words in their atmospheric and emotional aspect; so that his books abound with beautiful passages that rise in the memory like strains of music; the *illi in vos saeviant*;[1] or the unforgettable cry, "Late I have loved thee, O Ancient Beauty!" It is true that there is little or nothing of this kind in St. Thomas; but if he was without the higher uses of the mere magic of words, he was also free from that abuse of it, by mere sentimentalists or self-centred artists, which can become merely morbid and a very black magic indeed. And truly it is by some such comparison with the purely introspective intellectual, that we may find a hint about the real nature of the thing I describe, or rather fail to describe; I mean the elemental and primitive poetry that shines through all his thoughts; and especially through the thought with which all his thinking begins. It is the intense rightness of his sense of the relation between the mind and the real thing outside the mind.

That *strangeness* of things, which is the light in all poetry, and indeed in all art, is really connected with their otherness; or what is called their objectivity. What is subjective must be stale; it is exactly what is objective that is in this imaginative manner strange. In this the great contemplative is the complete contrary of that false contemplative, the mystic who looks only into his own soul, the selfish artist who shrinks from the world and lives only in his own mind. According to St. Thomas, the mind acts freely of itself, but its freedom exactly consists in finding a way out to liberty and the light of day; to reality and the land of the living. In the subjectivist, the pressure of the world forces the imagination inwards. In the Thomist, the energy of the mind forces the imagination outwards, but because the images it seeks are real things. All their romance and glamour, so to speak, lie in the fact that they are real things; things *not* to be found by

[1] This may be translated as "let them rage against you."

staring inwards at the mind. The flower is a vision because it is not only a vision. Or, if you will, it is a vision because it is not a dream. This is for the poet the strangeness of stones and trees and solid things; they are strange because they are solid. I am putting it first in the poetical manner, and indeed it needs much more technical subtlety to put it in the philosophical manner. According to Aquinas, the object becomes a part of the mind; nay, according to Aquinas, the mind actually becomes the object. But, as one commentator acutely puts it, it only becomes the object and does not create the object. In other words, the object *is* an object; it can and does exist outside the mind, or in the absence of the mind. And *therefore* it enlarges the mind of which it becomes a part. The mind conquers a new province like an emperor; but only because the mind has answered the bell like a servant. The mind has opened the doors and windows, because it is the natural activity of what is inside the house to find out what is outside the house. If the mind is sufficient to itself, it is insufficient for itself. For this feeding upon fact *is* itself; as an organ it has an object which is objective; this eating of the strange strong meat of reality.

Note how this view avoids both pitfalls; the alternative abysses of impotence. The mind is not merely receptive, in the sense that it absorbs sensations like so much blotting-paper; on that sort of softness has been based all that cowardly materialism, which conceives man as wholly servile to his environment. On the other hand, the mind is not purely creative, in the sense that it paints pictures on the windows and then mistakes them for a landscape outside. But the mind is active, and its activity consists in following, so far as the will chooses to follow, the light outside that does really shine upon real landscapes. That is what gives the indefinably virile and even adventurous quality to this view of life; as compared with that which holds that material inferences pour in upon an utterly helpless mind, or that which holds that psychological influences pour out and create an entirely baseless phantasmagoria. In other words, the essence of the Thomist common sense is that two agencies are at work; reality and the recognition of reality; and their meeting is a sort of marriage. Indeed it is very truly a marriage, because it is fruitful; the only philosophy now in the world that really is fruitful. It produces practical results, precisely because it is the combination of an adventurous mind and a strange fact.

M. Maritain has used an admirable metaphor, in his book *Theonas*, when he says that the external fact *fertilises* the internal intelligence, as the bee fertilises the flower. Anyhow, upon that marriage, or whatever it may be called, the whole system of St. Thomas is founded; God made Man so that he was capable of coming in contact with reality; and those whom God hath joined, let no man put asunder.

Now, it is worthy of remark that it is the only working philosophy. Of nearly all other philosophies it is strictly true that their followers work in spite of them, or do not work at all. No sceptics work sceptically; no fatalists work fatalistically; all without exception work on the principle that it is possible to assume what it is not possible to believe. No materialist who thinks his mind was made up for him, by mud and blood and heredity, has any hesitation in making up his mind. No sceptic who believes that truth is subjective has any hesitation about treating it as objective.

Thus St. Thomas's work has a constructive quality absent from almost all cosmic systems after him. For he is already building a house, while the newer speculators are still at the stage of testing the rungs of a ladder, demonstrating the hopeless softness of the unbaked bricks, chemically analysing the spirit in the spirit-level, and generally quarrelling about whether they can even make the tools that will make the house. Aquinas is whole intellectual aeons ahead of them, over and above the common chronological sense of saying a man is in advance of his age; he is ages in advance of our age. For he has thrown out a bridge across the abyss of the first doubt, and found reality beyond and begun to build on it. Most modern philosophies are not philosophy but philosophic doubt; that is, doubt about whether there can be any philosophy. If we accept St. Thomas's fundamental act or argument in the acceptance of reality, the further deductions from it will be equally real; they will be things and not words. Unlike Kant and most of the Hegelians, he has a faith that is not merely a doubt about doubt. It is not merely what is commonly called a faith about faith; it is a faith about fact. From this point he can go forward, and deduce and develop and decide, like a man planning a city and sitting in a judgment-seat. But never since that time has any thinking man of that eminence thought that there is any real evidence for anything, not even the evidence of his senses, that was strong enough to bear the weight of a definite deduction.

From all this we may easily infer that this philosopher does not merely touch on social things, or even take them in his stride to spiritual things; though that is always his direction. He takes hold of them, he has not only a grasp of them, but a grip. As all his controversies prove, he was perhaps a perfect example of the iron hand in the velvet glove. He was a man who always turned his full attention to anything; and he seems to fix even passing things as they pass. To him even what was momentary was momentous. The reader feels that any small point of economic habit or human accident is for the moment almost scorched under the converging rays of a magnifying lens. It is impossible to put in these pages a thousandth part of the decisions on details of life that may be found in his work; it would be like reprinting the law-reports of an incredible century of just judges and sensible magistrates. We can only touch on one or two obvious topics of this kind.

I have noted the need to use modern atmospheric words for certain ancient atmospheric things; as in saying that St. Thomas was what most modern men vaguely mean by an Optimist. In the same way, he was very much what they vaguely mean by a Liberal. I do not mean that any of his thousand political suggestions would suit any such definite political creed; if there are nowadays any definite political creeds. I mean, in the same sense, that he has a sort of atmosphere of believing in breadth and balance and debate. He may not be a Liberal by the extreme demands of the moderns for we seem always to mean by the moderns the men of the last century, rather than this. He was very much of a Liberal compared with the most modern of all moderns; for they are nearly all of them turning into Fascists and Hitlerites. But the point is that he obviously preferred the sort of decisions that are reached by deliberation rather than despotic action; and while, like all his contemporaries and co-religionists, he has no doubt that true authority may be authoritative, he is rather averse to the whole savour of its being arbitrary. He is much less of an Imperialist than Dante, and even his Papalism is not very Imperial. He is very fond of phrases like "a mob of free men" as the essential material of a city; and he is emphatic upon the fact that law, when it ceases to be justice, ceases even to be law.

If this work were controversial, whole chapters could be given to the economics as well as the ethics of the Thomist system. It would be easy to show that, in this matter, he was a prophet as well as a philosopher. He foresaw from the first the peril of that mere reliance on trade and exchange, which was beginning about his time; and which has culminated in a universal commercial collapse in our time. He did not merely assert that Usury is unnatural, though in saying that he only followed Aristotle and obvious common sense, which was never contradicted by anybody until the time of the commercialists, who have involved us in the collapse. The modern world began by Bentham writing the Defence of Usury, and it has ended after a hundred years in even the vulgar newspaper opinion finding Finance indefensible. But St. Thomas struck much deeper than that. He even mentioned the truth, ignored during the long idolatry of trade, that things which men produce only to sell are likely to be worse in quality than the things they produce in order to consume. Something of our difficulty about the fine shades of Latin will be felt when we come to his statement that there is always a certain *inhonestas* about trade. For *inhonestas* does not exactly mean dishonesty. It means approximately "something unworthy," or, more nearly perhaps, "something not quite handsome." And he was right; for trade, in the modern sense, does mean selling something for a little more than it is worth, nor would the nineteenth century economists have denied it. They would only have said that he was not practical; and this seemed sound while their view led to practical prosperity. Things are a little different now that it has led to universal bankruptcy.

Here, however, we collide with a colossal paradox of history. The Thomist philosophy and theology, quite fairly compared with other philosophies like the Buddhist or the Monist, with other theologies like the Calvinist or the Christian Scientist, is quite obviously a working and even a fighting system; full of common sense and constructive confidence; and therefore normally full of hope and promise. Nor is this hope vain or this promise unfulfilled. In this not very hopeful modern moment, there are no men so hopeful as those who are today looking to St. Thomas as a leader in a hundred crying questions of craftsmanship and ownership and economic ethics. There is undoubtedly a hopeful and creative Thomism in our time. But we are none the less puzzled by the fact that this did not immediately follow on St. Thomas's time. It is true that there was a great march of progress in the thirteenth century; and in some things, such as the status of the peasant, matters had greatly improved by the end of the Middle Ages. But nobody can honestly say that Scholasticism had greatly improved by the end of the Middle Ages. Nobody can tell how far the popular spirit of the Friars had helped the later popular medieval movements; or how far this great Friar, with his luminous rules of justice and his lifelong sympathy with the poor, may have indirectly contributed to the improvement that certainly occurred. But those who followed his method, as distinct from his moral spirit, degenerated with a strange rapidity; and it was certainly not in the Scholastics that the improvement occurred. Of some of the Scholastics we can only say that they took everything that was worst in Scholasticism and made it worse. They continued to count the steps of logic; but every step of logic took them further from common sense. They forgot how St. Thomas had started almost as an agnostic; and seemed resolved to leave nothing in heaven or hell about which anybody could be agnostic. They were a sort of rabid rationalists, who would have left no mysteries in the Faith at all. In the earliest Scholasticism there is something that strikes a modern as fanciful and pedantic; but, properly understood, it has a fine spirit in its fancy. It is the spirit of freedom; and especially the spirit of free will. Nothing seems more quaint, for instance, than the speculations about what would have happened to every vegetable or animal or angel, if Eve had chosen *not* to eat the fruit of the tree. But this was originally full of the thrill of choice; and the feeling that she might have chosen otherwise. It was this detailed detective method that was followed, without the thrill of the original detective story. The world was cumbered with countless tomes, proving by logic a thousand things that can be known only to God. They developed all that was really sterile in

Scholasticism, and left for us all that is really fruitful in Thomism.

There are many historical explanations. There is the Black Death, which broke the back of the Middle Ages; the consequent decline in clerical culture, which did so much to provoke the Reformation. But I suspect that there was another cause also; which can only be stated by saying that the contemporary fanatics, who controverted with Aquinas, left their own school behind them; and in a sense that school triumphed after all. The really narrow Augustinians, the men who saw the Christian life only as the narrow way, the men who could not even comprehend the great Dominican's exultation in the blaze of Being, or the glory of God in all his creatures, the men who continued to insist feverishly on every text, or even on every truth, that appeared pessimistic or paralysing, these gloomy Christians could not be extirpated from Christendom; and they remained and waited for their chance. The narrow Augustinians, the men who would have no science or reason or rational use of secular things, might have been defeated in controversy, but they had an accumulated passion of conviction. There was an Augustinian monastery in the North where it was near to explosion.

Thomas Aquinas had struck his blow; but he had not entirely settled the Manichees. The Manichees are not so easily settled; in the sense of settled forever. He had insured that the main outline of the Christianity that has come down to us should be supernatural but not anti-natural; and should never be darkened with a false spirituality to the oblivion of the Creator and the Christ who was made Man. But as his tradition trailed away into less liberal or less creative habits of thought, and as his medieval society fell away and decayed through other causes, the thing against which he had made war crept back into Christendom. A certain spirit or element in the Christian religion, necessary and sometimes noble but always needing to be balanced by more gentle and generous elements in the Faith, began once more to strengthen, as the framework of Scholasticism stiffened or split. The Fear of the Lord, that is the beginning of wisdom, and therefore belongs to the beginnings, and is felt in the first cold hours before the dawn of civilisation; the power that comes out of the wilderness and rides on the whirlwind and breaks the gods of stone; the power before which the eastern nations are prostrate like a pavement; the power before which the primitive prophets run naked and shouting, at once proclaiming and escaping from their god; the fear that is rightly rooted in the beginnings of every religion, true or false: the fear of the Lord, that is the beginning of wisdom; but not the end.

It is often remarked, as showing the ironical indifference of rulers to revolutions, and especially the frivolity of those who are called the Pagan Popes of the Renaissance, in their attitude to the Reformation, that when the Pope first heard of the first movements of Protestantism, which had started in Germany, he only said in an offhand manner that it was "some quarrel of monks". Every Pope of course was accustomed to quarrels among the monastic orders; but it has always been noted as a strange and almost uncanny negligence that he could see no more than this in the beginnings of the great sixteenth century schism. And yet, in a somewhat more recondite sense, there is something to be said for what he has been blamed for saying. In one sense, the schismatics had a sort of spiritual ancestry even in medieval times.

It will be found earlier in this book; and it *was* a quarrel of monks. We have seen how the great name of Augustine, a name never mentioned by Aquinas without respect but often mentioned without agreement, covered an Augustinian school of thought naturally lingering longest in the Augustinian Order. The difference, like every difference between

Catholics, was only a difference of emphasis. The Augustinians stressed the idea of the impotence of man before God, the omniscience of God about the destiny of man, the need for holy fear and the humiliation of intellectual pride, more than the opposite and corresponding truths of free will or human dignity or good works. In this they did in a sense continue the distinctive note of St. Augustine, who is even now regarded as relatively the determinist doctor of the Church. But there is emphasis and emphasis; and a time was coming when emphasising the one side was to mean flatly contradicting the other. Perhaps, after all, it did begin with a quarrel of monks; but the Pope was yet to learn how quarrelsome a monk could be. For there was one particular monk, in that Augustinian monastery in the German forests, who may be said to have had a single and special talent for emphasis; for emphasis and nothing except emphasis; for emphasis with the quality of earthquake. He was the son of a slatecutter; a man with a great voice and a certain volume of personality; brooding, sincere, decidedly morbid; and his name was Martin Luther. Neither Augustine nor the Augustinians would have desired to see the day of that vindication of the Augustinian tradition; but in one sense, perhaps, the Augustinian tradition was avenged after all.

It came out of its cell again, in the day of storm and ruin, and cried out with a new and mighty voice for an elemental and emotional religion, and for the destruction of all philosophies. It had a peculiar horror and loathing of the great Greek philosophies, and of the Scholasticism that had been founded on those philosophies. It had one theory that was the destruction of all theories; in fact it had its own theology which was itself the death of theology. Man could say nothing to God, nothing from God, nothing about God, except an almost inarticulate cry for mercy and for the supernatural help of Christ, in a world where all natural things were useless. Reason was useless. Will was useless. Man could not move himself an inch any more than a stone. Man could not trust what was in his head any more than a turnip. Nothing remained in earth or heaven, but the name of Christ lifted in that lonely imprecation; awful as the cry of a beast in pain.

We must be just to those huge human figures, who are in fact the hinges of history. However strong, and rightly strong, be our own controversial conviction, it must never mislead us into thinking that something trivial has transformed the world. So it is with that great Augustinian monk, who avenged all the ascetic Augustinians of the Middle Ages; and whose broad and burly figure has been big enough to block out for four centuries the distant human mountain of Aquinas. It is not, as the moderns delight to say, a question of theology. The Protestant theology of Martin Luther was a thing that no modern Protestant would be seen dead in a field with; or if the phrase be too flippant, would be specially anxious to touch with a barge-pole. That Protestantism was pessimism; it was nothing but bare insistence on the hopelessness of all human virtue, as an attempt to escape hell. That Lutheranism is now quite unreal; more modern phases of Lutheranism are rather more unreal; but Luther was not unreal. He was one of those great elemental barbarians, to whom it is indeed given to change the world. To compare those two figures bulking so big in history, in any philosophical sense, would of course be futile and even unfair. On a great map like the mind of Aquinas, the mind of Luther would be almost invisible. But it is not altogether untrue to say, as so many journalists have said without caring whether it was true or untrue, that Luther opened an epoch; and began the modern world.

He was the first man who ever consciously used his consciousness; or what was later called his Personality. He had as a fact a rather strong personality. Aquinas had an even stronger personality; he had a massive and magnetic presence; he had an intellect that could act like a huge system of artillery spread over the whole world; he had that instantaneous presence of mind in debate, which alone really deserves the name of wit. But it never occurred to him to use anything except his wits, in defence of a truth distinct from himself. It never occurred to Aquinas to use Aquinas as a weapon. There is not a trace of his ever using his personal advantages, of birth or body or brain or breeding, in debate with anybody. In short, he belonged to an age of intellectual unconsciousness, to an age of intellectual innocence, which was very intellectual. Now Luther did begin the modern mood of depending on things not merely intellectual. It is not a question of praise or blame; it matters little whether we say that he was a strong personality, or that he was a bit of a big bully. When he quoted a Scripture text, inserting a word that is not in Scripture, he was content to shout back at all hecklers: "Tell them that Dr. Martin Luther will have it so!" That is what we now call Personality. A little later it was called Psychology. After that it was called Advertisement or Salesmanship. But we are not arguing about advantages or disadvantages. It is due to this great Augustinian pessimist to say, not only that he did triumph at last over the Angel of the Schools, but that he did in a very real sense make the modern world. He destroyed Reason; and substituted Suggestion.

It is said that the great Reformer publicly burned the *Summa Theologica* and the works of Aquinas; and with the bonfire of such books this book may well come to an end. They say it is very difficult to burn a book; and it must have been exceedingly difficult to burn such a mountain of books as the Dominican had contributed to the controversies of Christendom. Anyhow, there is something lurid and apocalyptic about the idea of such destruction, when we consider the compact complexity of all that encyclopaedic survey of social and moral and theoretical things. All the close-packed definitions that excluded so many errors and extremes; all the broad and balanced judgments upon the clash of loyalties or the choice of evils; all the liberal speculations upon the limits of government or the proper conditions of justice; all the distinctions between the use and abuse of private property; all the rules and exceptions about the great evil of war; all the allowances for human weakness and all the provisions for human health; all this mass of medieval humanism shrivelled and curled up in smoke before the eyes of its enemy; and that great passionate peasant rejoiced darkly, because the day of the Intellect was over. Sentence by sentence it burned, and syllogism by syllogism; and the golden maxims turned to golden flames in that last and dying glory of all that had once been the great wisdom of the Greeks. The great central Synthesis of history, that was to have linked the ancient with the modern world, went up in smoke and, for half the world, was forgotten like a vapour.

For a time it seemed that the destruction was final. It is still expressed in the amazing fact that (in the North) modern men can still write histories of philosophy, in which philosophy stops with the last little sophists of Greece and Rome; and is never heard of again until the appearance of such a third-rate philosopher as Francis Bacon. And yet this small book, which will probably do nothing else, or have very little other value, will be at least a testimony to the fact that the tide has turned once more. It is four hundred years after; and this book, I hope (and I am happy to say I believe) will probably be lost and forgotten in the flood of better books about St. Thomas Aquinas, which are at this moment pouring from every printing-press in Europe, and even in England and America. Compared with such books it is obviously a very slight and amateurish production; but it is not likely to be burned, and if it were, it would not leave even a noticeable gap in the pouring mass of new and magnificent work, which is now daily dedicated to the *philosophia perennis*; to the Everlasting Philosophy.

# ST. FRANCIS OF ASSISI

# ST. FRANCIS OF ASSISI

## AN INTRODUCTION

by Joseph Pearce

Chesterton enjoyed a lifelong friendship with St Francis of Assisi. As a small boy, long before he had an inkling of the nature of Catholicism, he was read a story by his parents about a man who gave up all his possessions, even the clothes he was wearing on his back, to follow Christ in holy poverty. From the moment the wide-eyed Gilbert first heard the story of St. Francis he knew he had found a friend. As such, long before he had submitted to the reason of Rome, Chesterton had succumbed to the romance of Assisi.

Perhaps inevitably, child-like wonder was followed by adolescent doubt. As Chesterton groped towards manhood during the early 1890s, he succumbed temporarily to the beguiling power of the Decadents. Under the charismatic and iconoclastic seduction of Oscar Wilde, the world of Chesterton's youth seemed under the mad and maddening influence of those who preferred the shadows of sin and cynicism to the light of virtue and verity. Romance itself had donned the mask of darkness. It was in this gloom-laden atmosphere that the young Chesterton wrote a poem on St. Francis of Assisi, published in November 1892. The questions it asks were a quest for answers in a world of doubt.

> Is there not a question rises from his word of "brother, sister",
> Cometh from that lonely dreamer that today we shrink to find?

Shall the lives that moved our brethren leave us at the gates
of darkness,
What were heaven if ought we cherished shall be wholly
left behind?
Is it God's bright house we dwell in, or a vault of dark
confusion . . . ?

This poem, dedicated to the 'lonely dreamer' of Assisi, illuminates the darkness of Chesterton's adolescence. The young poet, seeking to make sense of the conflicting visions of reality vying for his allegiance, was beginning to perceive that the Decadents had cast out Brother Sun so that they could worship Sister Moon. Within three years of the publication of this poem Wildean Decadence had decayed in the squalor of the police courts. Wilde himself would repent and would be received into the Catholic Church on his deathbed. In his conversion, he was merely following many of the other Decadents, both in England and France, who, having dipped their toes in the antechambers of Hell, had decided, prudently, that it wasn't somewhere they wished to spend eternity. Baudelaire, Verlaine, Huysmans, Beardsley, Johnson, and Dowson had all followed the 'Decadent path to Christ', repenting of their sin and embracing the loving forgiveness to be found in Mother Church. Paradoxically, the path to Christ was always to be found in the implicit Christian morality of much of the art of the Decadents, particularly, and most memorably, in Wilde's masterpiece, *The Picture of Dorian Gray*. Incidentally, and continuing the 'Decadent' aside, John Gray, a young friend of Wilde's who was the original inspiration for 'Dorian', also became a Catholic convert. He went on to study for the priesthood in Rome and became a parish priest in Edinburgh until his death in the 1930s. Truth, it seems, is not only stranger than fiction; it has a happier ending!

Chesterton's own response, and riposte, to the Decadence of the 1890s can be found in his novel, *The Man Who Was*

*Thursday*. Whereas the Decadents—taking their own perverse inspiration from the Dark Romanticism of Byron, Shelley, and Keats—had stripped the masks off 'reality' and discovered darkness, Chesterton stripped the masks off 'reality' (from the 'anarchists' in his novel) and discovered light. By the dawn of the new century, Chesterton had emerged from the subreal dream of decadence into the real awakening of a Christian perception of the cosmos. In this journey from darkness to light he had, as his constant ally and companion, the 'lonely dreamer' of Assisi. On 1 December 1900, the day after Wilde had died a Catholic in Paris, Chesterton, not yet a Catholic, was singing the praises of St. Francis in an article published in *The Speaker*.

> To most people . . . there is a fascinating inconsistency in the position of St Francis. He expressed in loftier and bolder language than any earthly thinker the conception that laughter is as divine as tears. He called his monks the mountebanks of God. He never forgot to take pleasure in a bird as it flashed past him, or a drop of water as it fell from his finger: he was, perhaps, the happiest of the sons of men. Yet this man undoubtedly founded his whole polity on the negation of what we think the most imperious necessities; in his three vows of poverty, chastity, and obedience, he denied to himself and those he loved most, property, love, and liberty. Why was it that the most large-hearted and poetic spirits in that age found their most congenial atmosphere in these awful renunciations? Why did he who loved where all men were blind, seek to blind himself where all men loved? Why was he a monk and not a troubadour? These questions are far too large to be answered fully here, but in any life of Francis they ought at least to have been asked; we have a suspicion that if they were answered we should suddenly find that much of the enigma of this sullen time of ours was answered also.

These words, which could have served as the introduction to Chesterton's biography of St. Francis published twenty-three years later, indicated that the saint had served as an antidote to the poison of the previous decade.

In 1902, in *Twelve Types*, Chesterton again lauded St Francis with the lucidity and faith that had been almost wholly absent in the questioning ambivalence of his poem of ten years earlier.

In July 1922 Chesterton was finally received into the Catholic Church. Eight weeks later he received the Sacrament of Confirmation, choosing Francis as his confirmation name. It would, perhaps, be easy to suggest that the obvious motive for the choice was a desire to show love and respect for Frances, his wife. It was, however, hardly surprising that he should have chosen the saint who had been the friend of his childhood, the ally in his confused adolescence, and the companion in his approach to the Faith. In any case, the two motives are not mutually exclusive. In pleasing his wife, he was also pleasing himself.

At the time of his reception into the Church, Chesterton was already planning a full-length biography of St. Francis, which would be published in the following year. Confirming the saint's importance, he wrote that the figure of St. Francis 'stands on a sort of bridge connecting my boyhood with my conversion to many other things'. With these words in mind, it is not difficult to imagine that Chesterton took on the writing of *St. Francis of Assisi*, so soon after his conversion, as an act of thanksgiving to the saint who, above all others, had accompanied him on his journey to the Faith.

The admiration that Chesterton felt towards St. Francis was inextricably bound up with his belief in the superiority of childlike innocence over all forms of cynicism. St. Francis and his followers were called the Jongleurs de Dieu because of the innocence of their jollity and the jollity of their innocence. 'The jongleur was properly a joculator or jester; sometimes he was what we should call a juggler.' It was this mystical synthesis of laughter and humility, a belief that playing and praying go hand in hand, which was the secret of the saint's success. Ultimately, however, the laughter and the humility were rooted in gratitude because, as Chesterton discerned with characteristic and Franciscan sagacity: 'There is no way in which a man can earn a star or deserve a sunset.'

Chesterton's life of St. Francis was destined to be one of the most commercially and critically successful of all his books. Typical of the enthusiastic response of the critics was that of Patrick Braybrooke who described the book as 'astoundingly brilliant': 'The Catholic Church has found in Mr Chesterton the greatest interpreter of her greatest saint.' Ultimately, however, the book's brilliance shone from the blurring of the distinction between the Chestertonian and the Franciscan. It is, at times, difficult to distinguish between Chesterton's exposition of the Franciscan spirit and his elucidation of Chestertonian philosophy. Throughout the pages of the book Chesterton chases the saint, complaining that all explanations of the saint's enigmatic character were 'too slight for satisfaction'. The book unravels like a heaven-sent game of hide-and-seek, similar to the plot of *The Man Who was Thursday*, with the Man who was Francis remaining as difficult to pin down as the Man who was Sunday. Yet, as with the plot to the novel, there is something thrilling in the chase.

Whatever the book's shortcomings as an entirely satisfying explanation of the saint, it remains an emphatically successful romp and romance in the true Franciscan and Chestertonian spirit. From start to finish Chesterton plays cat and mouse with the Jongleur de Dieu. And, in keeping with the poetry of the saint, it doesn't really matter that sister cat fails to catch brother mouse. The charm is in the chase. For those reading Chesterton's *St. Francis of Assisi* for the first time, you are in for a rare treat. Prepare to be charmed. Enjoy the chase!

# I

# THE PROBLEM OF ST. FRANCIS

A sketch of St. Francis of Assisi in modern English may be written in one of three ways. Between these the writer must make his selection; and the third way, which is adopted here, is in some respects the most difficult of all. At least, it would be the most difficult if the other two were not impossible.

First, he may deal with this great and most amazing man as a figure in secular history and a model of social virtues. He may describe this divine demagogue as being, as he probably was, the world's one quite sincere democrat. He may say (what means very little) that St. Francis was in advance of his age. He may say (what is quite true) that St. Francis anticipated all that is most liberal and sympathetic in the modern mood; the love of nature; the love of animals; the sense of social compassion; the sense of the spiritual dangers of prosperity and even of property. All those things that nobody understood before Wordsworth were familiar to St. Francis. All those things that were first discovered by Tolstoy had been taken for granted by St. Francis. He could be presented, not only as a human but a humanitarian hero; indeed as the first hero of humanism. He has been described as a sort of morning star of the Renaissance. And in comparison with all these things, his ascetical theology can be ignored or dismissed as a contemporary accident, which was fortunately not a fatal accident. His religion can be regarded as a superstition, but an inevitable superstition, from which not even genius could wholly free itself; in the consideration of which it would be unjust to condemn St. Francis for his self-denial or unduly chide him for his chastity. It is quite true that even from so detached a standpoint his stature would still appear heroic. There would still be a great deal to be said about the man who tried to end the Crusades by talking to the Saracens or who interceded with the Emperor for the birds. The writer might describe in a purely historical spirit the whole of that great Franciscan inspiration that was felt in the painting of Giotto, in the poetry of Dante, in the miracle plays that made possible the modern drama, and in so many other things that are already appreciated by the modern culture. He may try to do it, as others have done, almost without raising any religious question at all. In short, he may try to tell the story of a saint without God; which is like being told to write the life of Nansen[1] and forbidden to mention the North Pole.

Second, he may go to the opposite extreme, and decide, as it were, to be defiantly devotional. He may make the theological enthusiasm as thoroughly the theme as it was the theme of the first Franciscans. He may treat religion as the real thing that it was to the real Francis of Assisi. He can find an austere joy, so to speak, in parading the paradoxes of asceticism and all the holy topsy-turvydom of humility. He can stamp the whole history with the Stigmata, record fasts like fights against a dragon; till in the vague modern mind St. Francis is as dark a figure as St. Dominic. In short he can produce what many in our world will regard as a sort of photographic negative, the reversal of all lights and shades; what the foolish will find as impenetrable as darkness and even many of the wise will find almost as invisible as if it were written in silver upon white. Such a study of St. Francis would be unintelligible to anyone who does not share his religion, perhaps only partly

[1] Fridtjof Nansen was a Norwegian explorer. His great achievement was the partial accomplishment of his scheme for reaching the North Pole by letting his ship get frozen into the ice north of Siberia and drift with a current toward Greenland.

intelligible to anyone who does not share his vocation. According to degrees of judgment, it will be regarded as something too bad or too good for the world. The only difficulty about doing the thing in this way is that it cannot be done. It would really require a saint to write the life of a saint. In the present case the objections to such a course are insuperable.

Third, he may try to do what I have tried to do here; and, as I have already suggested, the course has peculiar problems of its own. The writer may put himself in the position of the ordinary modern outsider and enquirer; as indeed the present writer is still largely and was once entirely in that position. He may start from the standpoint of a man who already admires St. Francis, but only for those things which such a man finds admirable. In other words he may assume that the reader is at least as enlightened as Renan[2] or Matthew Arnold;[3] but in the light of that enlightenment he may try to illuminate what Renan and Matthew Arnold left dark. He may try to use what is understood to explain what is not understood. He may say to the modern English reader: "Here is an historical character which is admittedly attractive to many of us already, by its gaiety, its romantic imagination, its spiritual courtesy and camaraderie, but which also contains elements (evidently equally sincere and emphatic) which seem to you quite remote and repulsive. But after all, this man was a man and not half a dozen men. What seems inconsistency to you did not seem inconsistency to him. Let us see whether we can understand, with the help of the existing understanding, these other things that seem now to be doubly dark, by their intrinsic gloom and their ironic contrast." I do not mean, of course, that I can really reach such a psychological completeness in this crude and curt outline. But I mean that this

[2] Ernest Renan (1823–1892), French critic, writer and sceptic.

[3] Matthew Arnold (1822–1888), English critic and poet.

is the only controversial condition that I shall here assume; that I am dealing with the sympathetic outsider. I shall not assume any more or any less agreement than this. A materialist may not care whether the inconsistencies are reconciled or not. A Catholic may not see any inconsistencies to reconcile. But I am here addressing the ordinary modern man, sympathetic but sceptical, and I can only rather hazily hope that, by approaching the great saint's story through what is evidently picturesque and popular about it, I may at least leave the reader understanding a little more than he did before of the consistency of a complete character; that by approaching it in this way, we may at least get a glimmering of why the poet who praised his lord the sun, often hid himself in a dark cavern, of why the saint who was so gentle with his Brother the Wolf was so harsh to his Brother the Ass (as he nicknamed his own body), of why the troubadour who said that love set his heart on fire separated himself from women, of why the singer who rejoiced in the strength and gaiety of the fire deliberately rolled himself in the snow, of why the very song which cries with all the passion of a pagan, "Praised be God for our Sister, Mother Earth, which brings forth varied fruits and grass and glowing flowers," ends almost with the words "Praised be God for our Sister, the death of the body."

Renan and Matthew Arnold failed utterly at this test. They were content to follow Francis with their praises until they were stopped by their prejudices; the stubborn prejudices of the sceptic. The moment Francis began to do something they did not understand or did not like, they did not try to understand it, still less to like it; they simply turned their backs on the whole business and "walked no more with him." No man will get any further along a path of historical enquiry in that fashion. These sceptics are really driven to drop the whole subject in despair, to leave the most simple and sincere of all historical characters as a mass of contradictions, to be praised on the principle of the curate's egg.[4] Arnold refers to the asceticism of Alverno almost hurriedly, as if it were an unlucky but undeniable blot on the beauty of the story; or rather as if it were a pitiable break-down and bathos at the end of the story. Now this is simply to be stone-blind to the whole point of any story. To represent Mount Alverno as the mere collapse of Francis is exactly like representing Mount Calvary as the mere collapse of Christ. Those mountains are mountains, whatever else they are, and it is nonsense to say (like the Red Queen) that they are comparative hollows or negative holes in the ground. They were quite manifestly meant to be culminations and landmarks. To treat the Stigmata as a sort of scandal, to be touched on tenderly but with pain, is exactly like treating the original five wounds of Jesus Christ as five blots on His character. You may dislike the idea of asceticism; you may dislike equally the idea of martyrdom; for that matter you may have an honest and natural dislike of the whole conception of sacrifice symbolised by the cross. But if it is an intelligent dislike, you will still retain the capacity for seeing the point of a story; of the story of a martyr or even the story of a monk. You will not be able rationally to read the Gospel and regard the Crucifixion as an afterthought or an anti-climax or an accident in the life of Christ; it is obviously the point of the story like the point of a sword, the sword that pierced the heart of the Mother of God.

And you will not be able rationally to read the story of a man presented as a Mirror of Christ without understanding

[4] "Among the catch-phrases that *Punch* has introduced into the language, 'Good in parts, like the curate's egg' is proverbial. The illustration shows a nervous young curate at his bishop's breakfast table. Asked by his lordship whether the egg is to his liking, he is terrified to say that it is bad and stammers out 'Parts of it are excellent!'" (*Brewer's Dictionary of Phrase and Fable*).

his final phase as a Man of Sorrows, and at least artistically appreciating the appropriateness of his receiving, in a cloud of mystery and isolation, inflicted by no human hand, the unhealed everlasting wounds that heal the world.

The practical reconciliation of the gaiety and austerity I must leave the story itself to suggest. But since I have mentioned Matthew Arnold and Renan and the rationalistic admirers of St. Francis, I will here give the hint of what it seems to me most advisable for such readers to keep in mind. These distinguished writers found things like the Stigmata a stumbling-block because to them a religion was a philosophy. It was an impersonal thing; and it is only the most personal passion that provides here an approximate earthly parallel. A man will not roll in the snow for a stream of tendency by which all things fulfil the law of their being. He will not go without food in the name of something, not ourselves, that makes for righteousness. He will do things like this, or pretty nearly like this, under quite a different impulse. He will do these things when he is in love. The first fact to realise about St. Francis is involved in the first fact with which his story starts; that when he said from the first that he was a Troubadour, and said later that he was a Troubadour of a newer and nobler romance, he was not using a mere metaphor, but understood himself much better than the scholars understand him. He was, to the last agonies of asceticism, a Troubadour. He was a Lover. He was a lover of God and he was really and truly a lover of men; possibly a much rarer mystical vocation. A lover of men is very nearly the opposite of a philanthropist; indeed the pedantry of the Greek word carries something like a satire on itself. A philanthropist may be said to love anthropoids. But as St. Francis did not love humanity but men, so he did not love Christianity but Christ. Say, if you think so, that he was a lunatic loving an imaginary person; but an imaginary person, not an imaginary idea. And for the modern reader the clue to the asceticism and all the rest can best be found in the stories of lovers when they seemed to be rather like lunatics. Tell it as the tale of one of the Troubadours, and the wild things he would do for his lady, and the whole of the modern puzzle disappears. In such a romance there would be no contradiction between the poet gathering flowers in the sun and enduring a freezing vigil in the snow, between his praising all earthly and bodily beauty and then refusing to eat, between his glorifying gold and purple and perversely going in rags, between his showing pathetically a hunger for a happy life and a thirst for a heroic death. All these riddles would easily be resolved in the simplicity of any noble love; only this was so noble a love that nine men out of ten have hardly even heard of it. We shall see later that this parallel of the earthly lover has a very practical relation to the problems of his life, as to his relations with his father and with his friends and their families. The modern reader will almost always find that if he could only feel this kind of love as a reality, he could feel this kind of extravagance as a romance. But I only note it here as a preliminary point because, though it is very far from being the final truth in the matter, it is the best approach to it. The reader cannot even begin to see the sense of a story that may well seem to him a very wild one, until he understands that to this great mystic his religion was not a thing like a theory but a thing like a love-affair. And the only purpose of this prefatory chapter is to explain the limits of this present book; which is only addressed to that part of the modern world which finds in St. Francis a certain modern difficulty; which can admire him yet hardly accept him, or which can appreciate the saint almost without the sanctity. And my only claim even to attempt such a task is that I myself have for so long been in various stages of such a condition. Many thousand things that I now partly comprehend I should have thought utterly incomprehensible, many things I now hold sacred I should have scouted as utterly superstitious, many things that seem to me lucid and enlightened now they are seen from the inside I should honestly have called dark and barbarous seen from the outside, when long ago in those days of boyhood my fancy first caught fire with the glory of Francis of Assisi. I too have lived in Arcady; but even in Arcady I met one walking in a brown habit who loved the woods better than Pan. The figure in the brown habit stands above the hearth in the room where I write, and alone among many such images, at no stage of my pilgrimage has he ever seemed to me a stranger. There is something of harmony between the hearth and the firelight and my own first pleasure in his words about his brother fire; for he stands far enough back in my memory to mingle with all those more domestic dreams of the first days. Even the fantastic shadows thrown by fire make a sort of shadow pantomime that belongs to the nursery; yet the shadows were even then the shadows of his favourite beasts and birds, as be saw them, grotesque but haloed with the love of God. His Brother Wolf and Brother Sheep seemed then almost like the Brer Fox and Brer Rabbit of a more Christian Uncle Remus. I have come slowly to see many and more marvellous aspects of such a man, but I have never lost that one. His figure stands on a sort of bridge connecting my boyhood with my conversion to many other things; for the romance of his religion had penetrated even the rationalism of that vague Victorian time. In so far as I have had this experience, I may be able to lead others a little further along that road; but only a very little further. Nobody knows better than I do now that it is a road upon which angels might fear to tread; but though I am certain of failure I am not altogether overcome by fear; for he suffered fools gladly.

# II

# THE WORLD ST. FRANCIS FOUND

The modern innovation which has substituted journalism for history, or for that tradition that is the gossip of history, has had at least one definite effect. It has insured that everybody should only hear the end of every story. Journalists are in the habit of printing above the very last chapters of their serial stories (when the hero and heroine are just about to embrace in the last chapter, as only an unfathomable perversity prevented them from doing in the first) the rather misleading words, "You can begin this story here." But even this is not a complete parallel; for the journals do give some sort of a summary of the story, while they never give anything remotely resembling a summary of the history. Newspapers not only deal with news, but they deal with everything as if it were entirely new. Tutankamen, for instance, was entirely new. It is exactly in the same fashion that we read that Admiral Bangs has been shot, which is the first intimation we have that he has ever been born. There is something singularly significant in the use which journalism makes of its stores of biography. It never thinks of publishing the life until it is publishing the death. As it deals with individuals it deals with institutions and ideas. After the Great War our public began to be told of all sorts of nations being emancipated. It had never been told a word about their being enslaved. We were called upon to judge of the justice of the settlements, when we had never been allowed to hear of the very existence of the quarrels. People would think it pedantic to talk about the Serbian epics and they prefer to speak in plain every-day modern language about the Yugo-Slavonic international new diplomacy; and they are quite excited about something they call Czecho-Slovakia without apparently having ever heard of Bohemia. Things that are as old as Europe are regarded as more recent than the very latest claims pegged out on the prairies of America. It is very exciting; like the last act of a play to people who have only come into the theatre just before the curtain falls. But it does not conduce exactly to knowing what it is all about. To those content with the mere fact of a pistol-shot or a passionate embrace, such a leisurely manner of patronising the drama may be recommended. To those tormented by a merely intellectual curiosity about who is kissing or killing whom, and why, it is unsatisfactory.

Most modern history, especially in England, suffers from the same imperfection as journalism. At best it only tells half of the history of Christendom; and that the second half without the first half. Men for whom reason begins with the Revival of Learning, men for whom religion begins with the Reformation, can never give a complete account of anything, for they have to start with institutions whose origin they cannot explain, or generally even imagine. Just as we hear of the admiral being shot but have never heard of his being born, so we all heard a great deal about the dissolution of the monasteries, but we heard next to nothing about the creation of the monasteries. Now this sort of history would be hopelessly insufficient, even for an intelligent man who hated the monasteries. It is hopelessly insufficient in connection with institutions that many intelligent men do in a quite healthy spirit hate. For instance, it is possible that some of us have occasionally seen some mention, by our learned leader-writers, of an obscure institution called the Spanish Inquisition. Well, it really is an obscure institution, according to them and the histories they read. It is obscure because its origin is obscure. Protestant history simply begins with the horrible thing in possession, as the pantomime begins with the demon king in the goblin kitchen. It is likely enough that it was, especially towards the end, a horrible thing that might be haunted by demons; but if we say this was so, we have no notion why it was so. To understand the Spanish Inquisition it would be necessary to discover two things that we have never dreamed of bothering about; what Spain was and what an Inquisition was. The former would bring in the whole great question about the Crusade against the Moors; and by what heroic chivalry a European nation freed itself of an alien domination from Africa. The latter would bring in the whole business of the other Crusade against the Albigensians, and why men loved and hated that nihilistic vision from Asia. Unless we understand that there was in these things originally the rush and romance of a Crusade, we cannot understand how they came to deceive men or drag them on towards evil. The Crusaders doubtless abused their victory, but there was a victory to abuse. And where there is victory there is valour in the field and popularity in the forum. There is some sort of enthusiasm that encourages excesses or covers faults. For instance, I for one have maintained from very early days the responsibility of the English for their atrocious treatment of the Irish. But it would be quite unfair to the English to describe even the devilry of '98[1] and leave out altogether all mention of the war with Napoleon. It would be unjust to suggest that the English mind was bent on nothing but the death of Emmett, when it was more probably full of the glory of the death of Nelson. Unfortunately '98 was very far from

[1] The United Irishmen (a society which sought to bring Catholics and Protestants together in the cause of radical political reform and to put an end to religious discrimination) planned an uprising in 1798. After some bitter fighting, accompanied by harsh reprisals by the yeomancy and other military units, the rising was suppressed. Though Robert Emmet was to lead a short-lived outbreak in Dublin in 1803, the militant republican movement was, in effect, brought to an end by the defeats of 1798.

being the last date of such dirty work; and only a few years ago our politicians started trying to rule by random robbing and killing, while gently remonstrating with the Irish for their memory of old unhappy far-off things and battles long ago. But however badly we may think of the Black-and-Tan[2] business, it would be unjust to forget that most of us were not thinking of Black-and-Tan but of khaki; and that khaki had just then a noble and national connotation covering many things. To write of the war in Ireland and leave out the war against Prussia, and the English sincerity about it, would be unjust to the English. So to talk about the torture-engine as if it had been a hideous toy is unjust to the Spanish. It does not tell sensibly from the start the story of what the Spaniard did, and why. We may concede to our contemporaries that in any case it is not a story that ends well. We do not insist that in their version it should begin well. What we complain of is that in their version it does not begin at all. They are only in at the death; or even, like Lord Tom Noddy, too late for the hanging. It is quite true that it was sometimes more horrible than any hanging; but they only gather, so to speak, the very ashes of the ashes; the fag-end of the faggot.

The case of the Inquisition is here taken at random, for it is one among any number illustrating the same thing; and not because it is especially connected with St. Francis, in whatever sense it may have been connected with St. Dominic. It may well be suggested later indeed that St. Francis is unintelligible, just as St. Dominic is unintelligible, unless we do understand something of what the thirteenth century

[2] The Black and Tans were members of the irregular force enlisted in England for service in Ireland as auxiliaries to the Royal Irish Constabulary during the disturbances of 1919–1922. They received this name because their original uniform was khaki with black leather accouterments.

meant by heresy and a crusade. But for the moment I use it as a lesser example for a much larger purpose. It is to point out that to begin the story of St. Francis with the birth of St. Francis would be to miss the whole point of the story, or rather not to tell the story at all. And it is to suggest that the modern tail-foremost type of journalistic history perpetually fails us. We learn about reformers without knowing what they had to reform, about rebels without a notion of what they rebelled against, of memorials that are not connected with any memory and restorations of things that had apparently never existed before. Even at the expense of this chapter appearing disproportionate, it is necessary to say something about the great movements that led up to the entrance of the founder of the Franciscans. It may seem to mean describing a world, or even a universe, in order to describe a man. It will inevitably mean that the world or the universe will be described with a few desperate generalisations in a few abrupt sentences. But so far from its meaning that we see a very small figure under so large a sky, it will mean that we must measure the sky before we can begin to measure the towering stature of the man.

And this phrase alone brings me to the preliminary suggestions that seem necessary before even a slight sketch of the life of St. Francis. It is necessary to realise, in however rude and elementary a fashion, into what sort of a world St. Francis entered and what has been the history of that world, at least in so far as it affected him. It is necessary to have, if only in a few sentences, a sort of preface in the form of an Outline of History, if we may borrow the phrase of Mr. Wells. In the case of Mr. Wells himself, it is evident that the distinguished novelist suffered the same disadvantage as if he had been obliged to write a novel of which he hated the hero. To write history and hate Rome, both pagan and papal, is practically to hate nearly everything that has happened.

It comes very near to hating humanity on purely humanitarian grounds. To dislike both the priest and the soldier, both the laurels of the warrior and the lilies of the saint, is to suffer a division from the mass of mankind for which not all the dexterities of the finest and most flexible of modern intelligences can compensate. A much wider sympathy is needed for the historical setting of St. Francis, himself both a soldier and a saint. I will therefore conclude this chapter with a few generalisations about the world that St. Francis found.

Men will not believe because they will not broaden their minds. As a matter of individual belief, I should of course express it by saying that they are not sufficiently catholic to be Catholic. But I am not going to discuss here the doctrinal truths of Christianity, but simply the broad historical fact of Christianity, as it might appear to a really enlightened and imaginative person even if he were not a Christian. What I mean at the moment is that the majority of doubts are made out of details. In the course of random reading a man comes across a pagan custom that strikes him as picturesque or a Christian action that strikes him as cruel; but he does not enlarge his mind sufficiently to see the main truth about pagan custom or the Christian reaction against it. Until we understand, not necessarily in detail, but in their big bulk and proportion that pagan progress and that Christian reaction, we cannot really understand the point of history at which St. Francis appears or what his great popular mission was all about.

Now everybody knows, I imagine, that the twelfth and thirteenth centuries were an awakening of the world. They were a fresh flowering of culture and the creative arts after a long spell of much sterner and even more sterile experience which we call the Dark Ages. They may be called an emancipation; they were certainly an end; an end of what may at least seem a harsher and more inhuman time. But what was it that was ended? From what was it that men were emancipated? That is where there is a real collision and point at issue between the different philosophies of history. On the merely external and secular side, it has been truly said that men awoke from a sleep; but there had been dreams in that sleep of a mystical and sometimes of a monstrous kind. In that rationalistic routine into which most modern historians have fallen, it is considered enough to say that they were emancipated from mere savage superstition and advanced towards mere civilised enlightenment. Now this is the big blunder that stands as a stumbling-block at the very beginning of our story. Anybody who supposes that the Dark Ages were plain darkness and nothing else, and that the dawn of the thirteenth century was plain daylight and nothing else, will not be able to make head or tail of the human story of St. Francis of Assisi. The truth is that the joy of St. Francis and his Jongleurs de Dieu was not merely an awakening. It was something which cannot be understood without understanding their own mystical creed. The end of the Dark Ages was not merely the end of a sleep. It was certainly not merely the end of a superstitious enslavement. It was the end of something belonging to a quite definite but quite different order of ideas.

It was the end of a penance; or, if it be preferred, a purgation. It marked the moment when a certain spiritual expiation had been finally worked out and certain spiritual diseases had been finally expelled from the system. They had been expelled by an era of asceticism, which was the only thing that could have expelled them. Christianity had entered the world to cure the world; and she had cured it in the only way in which it could be cured.

Viewed merely in an external and experimental fashion, the whole of the high civilisation of antiquity had ended in the learning of a certain lesson; that is, in its conversion to Christianity. But that lesson was a psychological fact as well as a theological faith. That pagan civilisation had indeed been a very high civilisation. It would not weaken our thesis, it might even strengthen it, to say that it was the highest that humanity ever reached. It had discovered its still unrivalled arts of poetry and plastic representation; it had discovered its own permanent political ideals; it had discovered its own clear system of logic and of language. But above all, it had discovered its own mistake.

That mistake was too deep to be ideally defined; the shorthand of it is to call it the mistake of nature-worship. It might almost as truly be called the mistake of being natural; and it was a very natural mistake. The Greeks, the great guides and pioneers of pagan antiquity, started out with the idea of something splendidly obvious and direct; the idea that if man walked straight ahead on the high road of reason and nature, he could come to no harm; especially if he was, as the Greek was, eminently enlightened and intelligent. We might be so flippant as to say that man was simply to follow his nose, so long as it was a Greek nose. And the case of the Greeks themselves is alone enough to illustrate the strange but certain fatality that attends upon this fallacy. No sooner did the Greeks themselves begin to follow their own noses and their own notion of being natural, than the queerest thing in history seems to have happened to them. It was much too queer to be an easy matter to discuss. It may be remarked that our more repulsive realists never give us the benefit of their realism. Their studies of unsavoury subjects never take note of the testimony which they bear to the truths of a traditional morality. But if we had the taste for such things, we could cite thousands of such things as part of the case for Christian morals. And an instance of this is found in the fact that nobody has written, in this sense, a real moral history of the

Greeks. Nobody has seen the scale or the strangeness of the story. The wisest men in the world set out to be natural; and the most unnatural thing in the world was the very first thing they did. The immediate effect of saluting the sun and the sunny sanity of nature was a perversion spreading like a pestilence. The greatest and even the purest philosophers could not apparently avoid this low sort of lunacy. Why? It would seem simple enough for the people whose poets had conceived Helen of Troy, whose sculptors had carved the Venus of Milo, to remain healthy on the point. The truth is that people who worship health cannot remain healthy. When Man goes straight he goes crooked. When he follows his nose he manages somehow to put his nose out of joint, or even to cut off his nose to spite his face; and that in accordance with something much deeper in human nature than nature-worshippers could ever understand. It was the discovery of that deeper thing, humanly speaking, that constituted the conversion to Christianity. There is a bias in man like the bias in the bowl; and Christianity was the discovery of how to correct the bias and therefore hit the mark. There are many who will smile at the saying; but it is profoundly true to say that the glad good news brought by the Gospel was the news of original sin.

Rome rose at the expense of her Greek teachers largely because she did not entirely consent to be taught these tricks. She had a much more decent domestic tradition; but she ultimately suffered from the same fallacy in her religious tradition; which was necessarily in no small degree the heathen tradition of nature-worship. What was the matter with the whole heathen civilization was that there was nothing for the mass of men in the way of mysticism, except that concerned with the mystery of the nameless forces of nature, such as sex and growth and death. In the Roman Empire also, long before the end, we find nature-worship inevitably producing things that are against nature. Cases like that of Nero have passed into a proverb, when Sadism sat on a throne brazen in the broad daylight. But the truth I mean is something much more subtle and universal than a conventional catalogue of atrocities. What had happened to the human imagination, as a whole, was that the whole world was coloured by dangerous and rapidly deteriorating passions; by natural passions becoming unnatural passions. Thus the effect of treating sex as only one innocent natural thing was that every other innocent natural thing became soaked and sodden with sex. For sex cannot be admitted to a mere equality among elementary emotions or experiences like eating and sleeping. The moment sex ceases to be a servant it becomes a tyrant. There is something dangerous and disproportionate in its place in human nature, for whatever reason; and it does really need a special purification and dedication. The modern talk about sex being free like any other sense, about the body being beautiful like any tree or flower, is either a description of the Garden of Eden or a piece of thoroughly bad psychology, of which the world grew weary two thousand years ago.

This is not to be confused with mere self-righteous sensationalism about the wickedness of the pagan world. It was not so much that the pagan world was wicked as that it was good enough to realise that its paganism was becoming wicked, or rather was on the logical high road to wickedness. I mean that there was no future for "natural magic"; to deepen it was only to darken it into black magic. There was no future for it; because in the past it had only been innocent because it was young. We might say it had only been innocent because it was shallow. Pagans were wiser than paganism; that is why the pagans became Christians. Thousands of them had philosophy and family virtues and military honour to hold them up; but by this time the purely popular thing called religion was certainly dragging them down. When this reaction against the evil is allowed for, it is true to repeat that it was an evil that was everywhere. In another and more literal sense its name was Pan.

It was no metaphor to say that these people needed a new heaven and a new earth; for they had really defiled their own earth and even their own heaven. How could their case be met by looking at the sky, when erotic legends were scrawled in stars across it; how could they learn anything from the love of birds and flowers after the sort of love stories that were told of them? It is impossible here to multiply evidences, and one small example may stand for the rest. We know what sort of sentimental associations are called up to us by the phrase "a garden"; and how we think mostly of the memory of melancholy and innocent romances, or quite as often of some gracious maiden lady or kindly old parson pottering under a yew hedge, perhaps in sight of a village spire. Then, let anyone who knows a little Latin poetry recall suddenly what would once have stood in place of the sun-dial or the fountain, obscene and monstrous in the sun; and of what sort was the god of their gardens.

Nothing could purge this obsession but a religion that was literally unearthly. It was no good telling such people to have a natural religion full of stars and flowers; there was not a flower or even a star that had not been stained. They had to go into the desert where they could find no flowers or even into the cavern where they could see no stars. Into that desert and that cavern the highest human intellect entered for some four centuries; and it was the very wisest thing it could do. Nothing but the stark supernatural stood up for its salvation; if God could not save it, certainly the gods could not. The Early Church called the gods of paganism devils; and the Early Church was perfectly right. Whatever natural religion may have had to do with their beginnings, nothing but fiends now inhabited those hollow shrines. Pan was nothing but panic. Venus was nothing but venereal vice. I do not mean for a moment, of course, that all the individual pagans were of this character even to the end; but it was as individuals that they differed from it. Nothing distinguishes paganism from Christianity so dearly as the fact that the individual thing called philosophy had little or nothing to do with the social thing called religion. Anyhow it was no good to preach natural religion to people to whom nature had grown as unnatural as any religion. They knew much better than we do what was the matter with them and what sort of demons at once tempted and tormented them; and they wrote across that great space of history the text: "This sort goeth not out but by prayer and fasting."

Now the historic importance of St. Francis and the transition from the twelfth to the thirteenth century, lies in the fact that they marked the end of this expiation. Men at the close of the Dark Ages may have been rude and unlettered and unlearned in everything but wars with heathen tribes, more barbarous than themselves, but they were clean. They were like children; the first beginnings of their rude arts have all the clean pleasure of children. We have to conceive them in Europe as a whole living under little local governments, feudal in so far as they were a survival of fierce wars with the barbarians, often monastic and carrying a more friendly and fatherly character, still faintly imperial in so far as Rome still ruled as a great legend. But in Italy something had survived more typical of the finer spirit of antiquity; the republic. Italy was dotted with little states, largely democratic in their ideals, and often filled with real citizens. But the city no longer lay open as under the Roman peace, but was pent in high walls for defence against feudal war and all the citizens had to be soldiers. One of these stood in a steep and striking position on the wooded hills of Umbria; and its name was

Assisi. Out of its deep gate under its high turrets was to come the message that was the gospel of the hour, "Your warfare is accomplished, your iniquity is pardoned." But it was out of all these fragmentary things of feudalism and freedom and remains of Roman Law that there was to rise, at the beginning of the thirteenth century, vast and almost universal, the mighty civilisation of the Middle Ages.

It is an exaggeration to attribute it entirely to the inspiration of any one man, even the most original genius of the thirteenth century. Its elementary ethics of fraternity and fair play had never been entirely extinct and Christendom had never been anything less than Christian. The great truisms about justice and pity can be found in the rudest monastic records of the barbaric transition or the stiffest maxims of the Byzantine decline. And early in the eleventh and twelfth centuries a larger moral movement had clearly begun. But what may fairly be said of it is this, that over all those first movements there was still something of that ancient austerity that came from the long penitential period. It was the twilight of morning; but it was still a grey twilight. This may be illustrated by the mere mention of two or three of these reforms before the Franciscan reform. The monastic institution itself, of course, was far older than all these things; indeed it was undoubtedly almost as old as Christianity. Its counsels of perfection had always taken the form of vows of chastity and poverty and obedience. With these unworldly aims it had long ago civilised a great part of the world. The monks had taught people to plough and sow as well as to read and write; indeed they had taught the people nearly everything that the people knew. But it may truly be said that the monks were severely practical, in the sense that they were not only practical but also severe; though they were generally severe with themselves and practical for other people. All this early monastic movement had long ago settled down and doubtless often deteriorated; but when we come to the first medieval movements this sterner character is still apparent. Three examples may be taken to illustrate the point.

First, the ancient social mould of slavery was already beginning to melt. Not only was the slave turning into the serf, who was practically free as regards his own farm and family life, but many lords were freeing slaves and serfs altogether. This was done under the pressure of the priests; but especially it was done in the spirit of a penance. In one sense, of course, any Catholic society must have an atmosphere of penance; but I am speaking of that rather sterner spirit of penance which had expiated the excesses of paganism. There was about such restitutions the atmosphere of the death-bed; as many of them doubtless were examples of death-bed repentance. A very honest atheist with whom I once debated made use of the expression, "Men have only been kept in slavery by the fear of hell." As I pointed out to him, if he had said that men had only been freed from slavery by the fear of hell, he would at least have been referring to an unquestionable historical fact.

Another example was the sweeping reform of Church discipline by Pope Gregory[3] the Seventh. It really was a reform, undertaken from the highest motives and having the healthiest results; it conducted a searching inquisition against simony or the financial corruptions of the clergy; it insisted on a more serious and self-sacrificing ideal for the life of a parish priest. But the very fact that this largely took the form

[3] St. Gregory VII (1020–1085), was pope from 1073 to 1085, and he ended lay investiture of the clergy. Gregory excommunicated Henry IV of Germany for suppressing the Church and Henry did penance in the snow before Gregory's palace at Canossa in 1077. Henry was absolved, but in 1078 the pope renewed the excommunication. Henry declared war and captured Rome in 1084. St. Gregory died in exile at Salerno in 1085.

of making universal the obligation of celibacy will strike the note of something which, however noble, would seem to many to be vaguely negative. The third example is in one sense the strongest of all. For the third example was a war; a heroic war and for many of us a holy war; but still something having all the stark and terrible responsibilities of war. There is no space here to say all that should be said about the true nature of the Crusades. Everybody knows that in the very darkest hour of the Dark Ages a sort of heresy had sprung up in Arabia and become a new religion of a military but nomadic sort, invoking the name of Mahomet. Intrinsically it had a character found in many heresies from the Moslem to the Monist. It seemed to the heretic a sane simplification of religion; while it seems to the Catholic an insane simplification of religion, because it simplifies all to a single idea and so loses the breadth and balance of Catholicism. Anyhow its objective character was that of a military danger to Christendom and Christendom had struck at the very heart of it, in seeking to reconquer the Holy Places. The great Duke Godfrey and the first Christians who stormed Jerusalem were heroes if there were ever any in the world; but they were the heroes of a tragedy.

Now I have taken these two or three examples of the earlier medieval movements in order to note about them one general character, which refers back to the penance that followed paganism. There is something in all these movements that is bracing even while it is still bleak, like a wind blowing between the clefts of the mountains. That wind, austere and pure, of which the poet speaks, is really the spirit of the time, for it is the wind of a world that has at last been purified. To anyone who can appreciate atmospheres there is something clear and clean about the atmosphere of this crude and often harsh society. Its very lusts are clean; for they have no longer any smell of perversion. Its very cruelties are clean; they are not the luxurious cruelties of the amphitheatre. They come either of a very simple horror at blasphemy or a very simple fury at insult. Gradually against this grey background beauty begins to appear, as something really fresh and delicate and above all surprising. Love returning is no longer what was once called platonic but what is still called chivalric love. The flowers and stars have recovered their first innocence. Fire and water are felt to be worthy to be the brother and sister of a saint. The purge of paganism is complete at last.

For water itself has been washed. Fire itself has been purified as by fire. Water is no longer that water into which slaves were flung to feed the fishes. Fire is no longer that fire through which children were passed to Moloch. Flowers smell no more of the forgotten garlands gathered in the garden of Priapus; stars stand no more as signs of the far frigidity of gods as cold as those cold fires. They are all like things newly made and awaiting new names, from one who shall come to name them. Neither the universe nor the earth have now any longer the old sinister significance of the world. They await a new reconciliation with man, but they are already capable of being reconciled. Man has stripped from his soul the last rag of nature-worship, and can return to nature.

While it was yet twilight a figure appeared silently and suddenly on a little hill above the city, dark against the fading darkness. For it was the end of a long and stern night, a night of vigil, not unvisited by stars. He stood with his hands lifted, as in so many statues and pictures, and about him was a burst of birds singing; and behind him was the break of day.

# III

# FRANCIS THE FIGHTER

According to one tale, which if not true would be none the less typical, the very name of St. Francis was not so much a name as a nickname. There would be something akin to his familiar and popular instinct in the notion that he was nicknamed very much as an ordinary schoolboy might be called "Frenchy" at school. According to this version, his name was not Francis at all but John; and his companions called him "Francesco" or "The little Frenchman" because of his passion for the French poetry of the Troubadours. The more probable story is that his mother had named him John when he was born in the absence of his father, who shortly returned from a visit to France, where his commercial success had filled him with so much enthusiasm for French taste and social usage that he gave his son the new name signifying the Frank or Frenchman. In either case the name has a certain significance, as connecting Francis from the first with what he himself regarded as the romantic fairyland of the Troubadours.

The name of the father was Pietro Bernardone and he was a substantial citizen of the guild of the cloth merchants in the town of Assisi. It is hard to describe the position of such a man without some appreciation of the position of such a guild and even of such a town. It did not exactly correspond to anything that is meant in modern times either by a merchant or a man of business or a tradesman, or anything that exists under the conditions of capitalism. Bernardone may have employed people but he was not an employer; that is, he did not belong to an employing class as distinct from an employed class. The person we definitely hear of his employing is his son Francis; who, one is tempted to guess, was about the last person that any man of business would employ if it were convenient to employ anybody else. He was rich, as a peasant may be rich by the work of his own family; but he evidently expected his own family to work in a way almost as plain as a peasant's. He was a prominent citizen, but he belonged to a social order which existed to prevent him being too prominent to be a citizen. It kept all such people on their own simple level, and no prosperity connoted that escape from drudgery by which in modern times the lad might have seemed to be a lord or a fine gentleman or something other than the cloth merchant's son. This is a rule that is proved even in the exception. Francis was one of those people who are popular with everybody in any case; and his guileless swagger as a Troubadour and leader of French fashions made him a sort of romantic ringleader among the young men of the town. He threw money about both in extravagance and benevolence, in a way native to a man who never, all his life, exactly understood what money was. This moved his mother to mingled exultation and exasperation and she said, as any tradesman's wife might say anywhere: "He is more like a prince than our son." But one of the earliest glimpses we have of him shows him as simply selling bales of cloth from a booth in the market; which his mother may or may not have believed to be one of the habits of princes. This first glimpse of the young man in the market is symbolic in more ways than one. An incident occurred which is perhaps the shortest and sharpest summary that could be given of certain curious things which were a part of his character, long before it was transfigured by transcendental faith. While he was selling velvet and fine embroideries to some solid merchant of the town, a beggar came imploring alms; evidently in a somewhat tactless manner. It was a rude and simple society and there were no laws to punish a starving man for expressing his need for food, such as have been established in a more humanitarian age; and the lack of any organised police permitted such persons to pester the wealthy without any great danger. But there was, I believe, in many places a local custom of the guild forbidding outsiders to interrupt a fair bargain; and it is possible that some such thing put the mendicant more than normally in the wrong. Francis had all his life a great liking for people who had been put hopelessly in the wrong. On this occasion he seems to have dealt with the double interview with rather a divided mind; certainly with distraction, possibly with irritation. Perhaps he was all the more uneasy because of the almost fastidious standard of manners that came to him quite naturally. All are agreed that politeness flowed from him from the first, like one of the public fountains in such a sunny Italian market place. He might have written among his own poems as his own motto that verse of Mr. Belloc's poem—

> 'Of Courtesy, it is much less
> Than courage of heart or holiness,
> Yet in my walks it seems to me
> That the grace of God is in Courtesy.'

Nobody ever doubted that Francis Bernardone had courage of heart, even of the most ordinary manly and military sort; and a time was to come when there was quite as little doubt about the holiness and the grace of God. But I think that if there was one thing about which he was punctilious, it was punctiliousness. If there was one thing of which so humble a man could be said to be proud, he was proud of good manners. Only behind his perfectly natural urbanity were wider and even wilder possibilities, of which we get the first flash in this trivial incident. Anyhow Francis was evidently torn two ways with the botheration of two talkers, but finished his business with the merchant somehow; and when he had finished it, found the beggar was gone. Francis leapt from his booth, left all the bales of velvet and embroidery behind him apparently unprotected, and went racing across the market-place like an arrow from the bow. Still running, he threaded the labyrinth of the narrow and crooked streets of the little town, looking for his beggar, whom he eventually discovered; and loaded that astonished mendicant with money. Then he straightened himself, so to speak, and swore before God that he would never all his life refuse help to a poor man. The sweeping simplicity of this undertaking is extremely characteristic. Never was any man so little afraid of his own promises. His life was one riot of rash vows; of rash vows that turned out right.

The first biographers of Francis, naturally alive with the great religious revolution that he wrought, equally naturally looked back to his first years chiefly for omens and signs of such a spiritual earthquake. But writing at a greater distance, we shall not decrease that dramatic effect, but rather increase it, if we realise that there was not at this time any external sign of anything particularly mystical about the young man. He had not anything of that early sense of his vocation that has belonged to some of the saints. Over and above his main ambition to win fame as a French poet, he would seem to have most often thought of winning fame as a soldier. He was born kind; he was brave in the normal boyish fashion; but he drew the line both in kindness and bravery pretty well where most boys would have drawn it; for instance, he had the human horror of leprosy of which few normal people felt any need to be ashamed. He had the love of gay and bright apparel which was inherent in the heraldic taste of medieval times and seems altogether to have been rather a festive figure. If he did not paint the town red, he would probably have preferred to paint it all the colours of the rainbow, as in a medieval picture. But in this story of the young man in gay garments scampering after the vanishing beggar in rags there are certain notes of his natural individuality that must be assumed from first to last.

For instance, there is the spirit of swiftness. In a sense he continued running for the rest of his life, as he ran after the beggar. Because nearly all the errands he ran on were errands of mercy, there appeared in his portraiture a mere element of mildness which was true in the truest sense, but is easily misunderstood. A certain precipitancy was the very poise of his soul. This saint should be represented among the other saints as angels were sometimes represented in pictures of angels; with flying feet or even with feathers; in the spirit of the text that makes angels winds and messengers a flaming fire. It is a curiosity of language that courage actually means running; and some of our sceptics will no doubt demonstrate that courage really means running away. But his courage was running, in the sense of rushing. With all his gentleness, there was originally something of impatience in his impetuosity. The psychological truth about it illustrates very well the modern muddle about the word "practical." If we mean by what is practical what is most immediately practicable, we mean merely what is easiest. In that sense St. Francis was very impractical, and his ultimate aims were very unworldly. But if we mean by practicality a preference for prompt effort and energy over doubt or delay, he was very practical indeed. Some might call him a madman, but he was the very reverse of a dreamer. Nobody would be likely to call him a man of business; but he was very emphatically a man of action. In some of his early experiments he was rather too much of a man of action; he acted too soon and was too practical to be prudent. But at every turn of his extraordinary career we shall find him flinging himself round corners in the most unexpected fashion, as when he flew through the crooked streets after the beggar.

Another element implied in the story, which was already partially a natural instinct, before it became a supernatural ideal, was something that had never perhaps been wholly lost in those little republics of medieval Italy. It was something very puzzling to some people; something clearer as a rule to Southerners than to Northerners, and I think to Catholics than to Protestants; the quite natural assumption of the equality of men. It has nothing necessarily to do with the Franciscan love for men; on the contrary one of its merely practical tests is the equality of the duel. Perhaps a gentleman will never be fully as egalitarian until he can really quarrel with his servant. But it was an antecedent condition of the Franciscan brotherhood; and we feel it in this early and secular incident. Francis, I fancy, felt a real doubt about which he must attend to, the beggar or the merchant; and having attended to the merchant, he turned to attend to the beggar; he thought of them as two men. This is a thing much more difficult to describe, in a society from which it is absent, but it was the original basis of the whole business; it was why the popular movement arose in that sort of place and that sort of man. His imaginative magnanimity afterwards rose like a tower to starry heights that might well seem dizzy and even crazy; but it was founded on this high table-land of human equality.

I have taken this the first among a hundred tales of the youth of St. Francis, and dwelt on its significance a little, because until we have learned to look for the significance there will often seem to be little but a sort of light sentiment in telling the story. St. Francis is not a proper person to be patronised with merely "pretty" stories. There are any number of them; but they are too often used so as to be a sort of sentimental sediment of the medieval world, instead of being, as the saint emphatically is, a challenge to the modern world. We must take his real human development somewhat more seriously; and the next story in which we get a real glimpse of it is in a very different setting. But in exactly the same way it opens, as if by accident, certain abysses of the mind and perhaps of the unconscious mind. Francis still looks more or less like an ordinary young man; and it is only when we look at him as an ordinary young man, that we realise what an extraordinary young man he must be.

War had broken out between Assisi and Perugia. It is now fashionable to say in a satirical spirit that such wars did not so much break out as go on indefinitely between the city-states of medieval Italy. It will be enough to say here that if one of these medieval wars had really gone on without stopping for a century, it might possibly have come within a remote distance of killing as many people as we kill in a year, in one of our great modern scientific wars between our great modern industrial empires. But the citizens of the medieval republic were certainly under the limitation of only being asked to die for the things with which they had always lived, the houses they inhabited, the shrines they venerated and the rulers and representatives they knew; and had not the larger vision calling them to die for the latest rumours about remote colonies as reported in anonymous newspapers. And if we infer from our own experience that war paralysed civilisation, we must at least admit that these warring towns turned out a number of paralytics who go by the names of Dante and Michael Angelo, Ariosto and Titian, Leonardo and Columbus, not to mention Catherine of Siena and the subject of this story. While we lament all this local patriotism as a hubbub of the Dark Ages, it must seem a rather curious fact that about three quarters of the greatest men who ever lived came out of these little towns and were often engaged in these little wars. It remains to be seen what will ultimately come out of our large towns; but there has been no sign of anything of this sort since they became large; and I have sometimes been haunted by a fancy of my youth, that these things will not come till there is a city wall round Clapham and the tocsin is rung at night to arm the citizens of Wimbledon.

Anyhow, the tocsin was rung in Assisi and the citizens armed, and among them Francis the son of the cloth merchant. He went out to fight with some company of lancers and in some fight or foray or other he and his little band were taken prisoners. To me it seems most probable that there had been some tale of treason or cowardice about the disaster; for we are told that there was one of the captives with whom his fellow-prisoners flatly refused to associate even in prison; and when this happens in such circumstances, it is generally because the military blame for the surrender is thrown on some individual. Anyhow, somebody noted a small but curious thing, though it might seem rather negative than positive. Francis, we are told, moved among his captive companions with all his characteristic courtesy and even conviviality, "liberal and hilarious" as somebody said of him, resolved to keep up their spirits and his own. And when he came across the mysterious outcast, traitor or coward or whatever he was called, he simply treated him exactly like all the rest, neither with coldness nor compassion, but with the same unaffected gaiety and good fellowship. But if there had been present in that prison someone with a sort of second sight about the truth and trend of spiritual things, he might have known he was in the presence of something new and seemingly almost anarchic; a deep tide driving out to uncharted seas of charity. For in this sense there was really something wanting in Francis of Assisi, something to which he was blind that he might see better and more beautiful things. All those limits in good fellowship and good form, all those landmarks of social life that divide the tolerable and the intolerable, all those social scruples and conventional conditions that are normal and even noble in ordinary men, all those things that hold many decent societies together, could never hold this man at all. He liked as he liked; he seems to have liked everybody, but especially those whom everybody disliked him for liking. Something very vast and universal was already present in that narrow dungeon; and such a seer might have seen in its darkness that red halo of *caritas caritatum* which marks one saint among saints as well as among men. He might have heard the first whisper of that wild blessing that afterwards took the form of a blasphemy; "He listens to those to whom God himself will not listen."

But though such a seer might have seen such a truth, it is exceedingly doubtful if Francis himself saw it. He had acted out of an unconscious largeness, or in the fine medieval phrase largesse, within himself, something that might almost have been lawless if it had not been reaching out to a more divine law; but it is doubtful whether he yet knew that the law was divine. It is evident that he had not at this time any notion of abandoning the military, still less of adopting the monastic life. It is true that there is not, as pacifists and prigs imagine, the least inconsistency between loving men and fighting them, if we fight them fairly and for a good cause. But it seems to me that there was more than this involved; that the mind of the young man was really running towards a military morality in any case. About this time the first calamity crossed his path in the form of a malady which was to revisit him many times and hamper his headlong career. Sickness made him more serious; but one fancies it would only have made him a more serious soldier, or even more serious about soldiering. And while he was recovering, something rather larger than the little feuds and raids of the Italian towns opened an avenue of adventure and ambition. The crown of Sicily, a considerable centre of controversy at the time, was apparently claimed by a certain Gauthier de Brienne, and the Papal cause to aid which Gauthier was called in aroused enthusiasm among a number of young Assisians, including Francis, who proposed to march into Apulia on the count's behalf; perhaps his French name had something to do with it. For it must never be forgotten that though that world was in one sense a world of little things, it was a world of little things concerned about great things. There was more internationalism in the lands dotted with tiny republics than in the huge homogeneous impenetrable national divisions of to-day. The legal authority of the Assisian magistrates might hardly reach further than a bow-shot from their high embattled city walls. But their sympathies might be with the ride of the Normans through Sicily or the palace of the Troubadours at Toulouse; with the Emperor throned in the German forests or the great Pope[1] dying in the exile of Salerno. Above all, it must be remembered that when the interests of an age are mainly religious they must be universal. Nothing can be more universal than the universe. And there are several things about the religious position at that particular moment which modern people not unnaturally fail to realise. For one thing, modern people naturally think of people so remote as ancient people, and even early people. We feel vaguely that these things happened in the first ages of the Church. The Church was already a good deal more than a thousand years old. That is, the Church was then rather older than France is now, a great deal older than England is now. And she looked old then; almost as old as she does now; possibly older than she does now. The Church looked like great Charlemagne with the long white beard, who had already fought a hundred wars with the heathen, and in the legend was bidden by an angel to go forth and fight once more though he was two hundred years old. The Church had topped her thousand

[1] See Chapter II, footnote 3, page 212.

years and turned the corner of the second thousand; she had come through the Dark Ages in which nothing could be done except desperate fighting against the barbarians and the stubborn repetition of the creed. The creed was still being repeated after the victory or escape; but it is not unnatural to suppose that there was something a little monotonous about the repetition. The Church looked old then as now; and there were some who thought her dying then as now. In truth orthodoxy was not dead but it may have been dull; it is certain that some people began to think it dull. The Troubadours of the Provençal movement had already begun to take that turn or twist towards Oriental fancies and the paradox of pessimism, which always come to Europeans as something fresh when their own sanity seems to be something stale. It is likely enough that after all those centuries of hopeless war without and ruthless asceticism within, the official orthodoxy seemed to be something stale. The freshness and freedom of the first Christians seemed then as much as now a lost and almost prehistoric age of gold. Rome was still more rational than anything else; the Church was really wiser but it may well have seemed wearier than the world. There was something more adventurous and alluring, perhaps, about the mad metaphysics that had been blown across out of Asia. Dreams were gathering like dark clouds over the Midi to break in a thunder of anathema and civil war. Only the light lay on the great plain round Rome; but the light was blank and the plain was flat; and there was no stir in the still air and the immemorial silence about the sacred town.

High in the dark house of Assisi Francesco Bernardone slept and dreamed of arms. There came to him in the darkness a vision splendid with swords, patterned after the cross in the Crusading fashion, of spears and shields and helmets hung in a high armoury, all bearing the sacred sign. When he awoke he accepted the dream as a trumpet bidding him to the battlefield, and rushed out to take horse and arms. He delighted in all the exercises of chivalry; and was evidently an accomplished cavalier and fighting man by the tests of the tournament and the camp. He would doubtless at any time have preferred Christian sort of chivalry; but it seems clear that he was also in a mood which thirsted for glory, though in him that glory would always have been identical with honour. He was not without some vision of that wreath of laurel which Cæsar has left for all the Latins. As he rode out to war the great gate in the deep wall of Assisi resounded with his last boast, "I shall come back a great prince."

A little way along his road his sickness rose again and threw him. It seems highly probable, in the light of his impetuous temper, that he had ridden away long before he was fit to move. And in the darkness of this second and far more desolating interruption, he seems to have had another dream in which a voice said to him, "You have mistaken the meaning of the vision. Return to your own town." And Francis trailed back in his sickness to Assisi, a very dismal and disappointed and perhaps even derided figure, with nothing to do but to wait for what should happen next. It was his first descent into a dark ravine that is called the valley of humiliation, which seemed to him very rocky and desolate, but in which he was afterwards to find many flowers.

But he was not only disappointed and humiliated; he was also very much puzzled and bewildered. He still firmly believed that his two dreams must have meant something; and he could not imagine what they could possibly mean. It was while he was drifting, one may even say mooning, about the streets of Assisi and the fields outside the city wall, that an incident occurred to him which has not always been immediately connected with the business of the dreams, but which seems to me the obvious culmination of them. He was riding listlessly in some wayside place, apparently in the open country, when he saw a figure coming along the road towards him and halted; for he saw it was a leper. And he knew instantly that his courage was challenged, not as the world challenges, but as one would challenge who knew the secrets of the heart of a man. What he saw advancing was not the banner and spears of Perugia, from which it never occurred to him to shrink; not the armies that fought for the crown of Sicily, of which he had always thought as a courageous man thinks of mere vulgar danger. Francis Bernardone saw his fear coming up the road towards him; the fear that comes from within and not without; though it stood white and horrible in the sunlight. For once in the long rush of his life his soul must have stood still. Then he sprang from his horse, knowing nothing between stillness and swiftness, and rushed on the leper and threw his arms round him. It was the beginning of a long vocation of ministry among many lepers, for whom he did many services; to this man he gave what money he could and mounted and rode on. We do not know how far he rode, or with what sense of the things around him; but it is said that when he looked back, he could see no figure on the road.

# IV

# FRANCIS THE BUILDER

We have now reached the great break in the life of Francis of Assisi; the point at which something happened to him that must remain greatly dark to most of us, who are ordinary and selfish men whom God has not broken to make anew.

In dealing with this difficult passage, especially for my own purpose of making things moderately easy for the more secular sympathiser, I have hesitated as to the proper course; and have eventually decided to state first of all what happened, with little more than a hint of what I imagine to have been the meaning of what happened. The fuller meaning may be debated more easily afterwards, when it was unfolded in the full Franciscan life. Anyhow what happened was this. The story very largely revolves round the ruins of the Church of St. Damian, an old shrine in Assisi which was apparently neglected and falling to pieces. Here Francis was in the habit of praying before the crucifix during these dark and aimless days of transition that followed the tragical collapse of all his military ambitions, probably made bitter by some loss of social prestige terrible to his sensitive spirit. As he did so he heard a voice saying to him, "Francis, seest thou not that my house is in ruins? Go and restore it for me."

Francis sprang up and went. To go and do something was one of the driving demands of his nature; probably he had gone and done it before he had at all thoroughly thought out what he had done. In any case what he had done was something very decisive and immediately very disastrous for his singular social career. In the coarse conventional language of the uncomprehending world, he stole. From his own enthusiastic point of view, he extended to his venerable father Peter Bernardone the exquisite excitement and inestimable privilege of assisting, more or less unconsciously, in the rebuilding of St. Damian's Church. In point of fact what he did was first to sell his own horse and then to go off and sell several bales of his father's cloth, making the sign of the cross over them to indicate their pious and charitable destination. Peter Bernardone did not see things in this light. Peter Bernardone indeed had not very much light to see by, so far as understanding the genius and temperament of his extraordinary son was concerned. Instead of understanding in what sort of a wind and flame of abstract appetites the lad was living, instead of simply telling him (as the priest practically did later) that he had done an indefensible thing with the best intentions, old Bernardone took up the matter in the hardest style; in a legal and literal fashion. He used absolute political powers like a heathen father, and himself put his son under lock and key as a vulgar thief. It would appear that the cry was caught up among many with whom the unlucky Francis had once been popular; and altogether, in his efforts to build up the house of God he had only succeeded in bringing his own house about his ears and lying buried under the ruins. The quarrel dragged drearily through several stages; at one time the wretched young man seems to have disappeared underground, so to speak, into some cavern or cellar where he remained huddled hopelessly in the darkness. Anyhow, it was his blackest moment; the whole world had turned over; the whole world was on top of him.

When he came out, it was only perhaps gradually that anybody grasped that something had happened. He and his father were summoned in the court of the bishop; for Francis had refused the authority of all legal tribunals. The bishop addressed some remarks to him, full of that excellent common sense which the Catholic Church keeps permanently as the background for all the fiery attitudes of her saints. He told Francis that he must unquestionably restore the money to his father; that no blessing could follow a good work done by unjust methods; and in short (to put it crudely) if the young fanatic would give back his money to the old fool, the incident would then terminate. There was a new air about Francis. He was no longer crushed, still less crawling, so far as his father was concerned; yet his words do not, I think, indicate either just indignation or wanton insult or anything in the nature of a mere continuation of the quarrel. They are rather remotely akin to mysterious utterances of his great model, "What have I to do with thee?" or even the terrible "Touch me not."

He stood up before them all and said, "Up to this time I have called Pietro Bernardone father, but now I am the servant of God. Not only the money but everything that can be called his I will restore to my father, even the very clothes he has given me." And he rent off all his garments except one; and they saw that that was a hair-shirt.

He piled the garments in a heap on the floor and tossed the money on top of them. Then he turned to the bishop, and received his blessing, like one who turns his back on society; and, according to the account, went out as he was into the cold world. Apparently it was literally a cold world at the moment, and snow was on the ground. A curious detail, very deep in its significance, I fancy, is given in the same account of this great crisis in his life. He went out half-naked in his hair-shirt into the winter woods, walking the frozen ground between the frosty trees; a man without a father. He was penniless, he was parentless, he was to all appearance without a trade or a plan or a hope in the world; and as he went under the frosty trees, he burst suddenly into song.

It was apparently noted as remarkable that the language in which he sang was French, or that Provençal which was called for convenience French. It was not his native language; and it was in his native language that he ultimately won fame as a poet; indeed St. Francis is one of the very first of the national poets in the purely national dialects of Europe. But it was the language with which all his most boyish ardours and ambitions had been identified; it was for him pre-eminently the language of romance. That it broke from him in this extraordinary extremity seems to me something at first sight very strange and in the last analysis very significant. What that significance was, or may well have been, I will try to suggest in the subsequent chapter; it is enough to indicate here that the whole philosophy of St. Francis revolved round the idea of a new supernatural light on natural things, which meant the ultimate recovery not the ultimate refusal of natural things. And for the purpose of this purely narrative part of the business, it is enough to record that while he wandered in the winter forest in his hair-shirt, like the very wildest of the hermits, he sang in the tongue of the Troubadours.

Meanwhile the narrative naturally reverts to the problem of the ruined or at least neglected church, which had been the starting point of the saint's innocent crime and beatific punishment. That problem still predominated in his mind and was soon engaging his insatiable activities; but they were activities of a new sort; and he made no more attempts to interfere with the commercial ethics of the town of Assisi. There had dawned on him one of those great paradoxes that are also platitudes. He realised that the way to build a church is not to become entangled in bargains and, to him, rather bewildering questions of legal claim. The way to build a church is not to pay for it, certainly not with somebody else's money. The way to build a church is not even to pay for it with your own money. The way to build a church is to build it.

He went about by himself collecting stones. He begged all the people he met to give him stones. In fact he became a new sort of beggar, reversing the parable; a beggar who asks not for bread but a stone. Probably, as happened to him again and again throughout his extraordinary existence, the very queerness of the request gave it a sort of popularity; and all sorts of idle and luxurious people fell in with the benevolent project, as they would have done with a bet. He worked with his own hands at the rebuilding of the church, dragging the material like a beast of burden and learning the very last and lowest lessons of toil. A vast number of stories are told about Francis at this as at every other period of his life; but for the purpose here, which is one of simplification, it is best to dwell on this definite reentrance of the saint into the world by the low gate of manual labour. There does indeed run through the whole of his life a sort of double meaning, like his shadow thrown upon the wall. All his action had something of the character of an allegory; and it is likely enough that some leaden-witted scientific historian may some day try to prove that he himself was never anything but an allegory. It is true enough in this sense that he was labouring at a double task, and rebuilding something else as well as the church of St. Damian. He was not only discovering the general lesson that his glory was not to be in overthrowing men in battle but in building up the positive and creative monuments of peace. He was truly building up something else, or beginning to build it up; something that has often enough fallen into ruin but has never been past rebuilding; a church that could always be built anew though it had rotted away to its first foundation-stone, against which the gates of hell shall not prevail.

The next stage in his progress is probably marked by his transferring the same energies of architectural reconstruction to the little church of St. Mary of the Angels at the Portiuncula. He had already done something of the same kind at a church dedicated to St. Peter; and that quality in his life noted above, which made it seem like a symbolical drama, led many of his most devout biographers to note the numerical symbolism of the three churches. There was at any rate a more historical and practical symbolism about two of them. For the original church of St. Damian afterwards became the seat of his striking experiment of a female order, and of the pure and spiritual romance of St. Clare. And the church of the Portiuncula will remain for ever as one of the great historic buildings of the world; for it was there that he gathered the little knot of friends and enthusiasts; it was the home of many homeless men. At this time, however, it is not clear that he had the definite idea of any such monastic developments. How early the plan appeared in his own mind it is of course impossible to say; but on the face of events it first takes the form of a few friends who attached themselves to him one by one because they shared his own passion for simplicity. The account given of the form of their dedication is, however, very significant; for it was that of an invocation of the simplification of life as suggested in the New Testament. The adoration of Christ had been a part of the man's passionate nature for a long time past. But the imitation of Christ, as a sort of plan or ordered scheme of life, may in that sense be said to begin here.

The two men who have the credit, apparently, of having first perceived something of what was happening in the world of the soul were a solid and wealthy citizen named Bernard of Quintavalle and a canon from a neighbouring church named Peter. It is the more to their credit because Francis, if one may put it so, was by this time wallowing in poverty and association with lepers and ragged mendicants; and these two were men with much to give up; the one of comforts in the world and the other of ambition in the Church. Bernard the rich burgher did quite literally and finally sell all he had and give to the poor. Peter did even more; for he descended from a chair of spiritual authority, probably when he was already a man of mature years and therefore of fixed mental habits, to follow an extravagant young eccentric whom most people probably regarded as a maniac. What it was of which they had caught a glimpse, of which Francis had seen the glory, may be suggested later so far as it can be suggested at all. At this stage we need profess to see no more than all Assisi saw, and that something not altogether unworthy of comment. The citizens of Assisi only saw the camel go in triumph through the eye of the needle and God doing impossible things because to him all things were possible; only a priest who rent his robes like the Publican and not like the Pharisee and a rich man who went away joyful, for he had no possessions.

These three strange figures are said to have built themselves a sort of hut or den adjoining the leper hospital. There they talked to each other, in the intervals of drudgery and danger (for it needed ten times more courage to look after a leper than to fight for the crown of Sicily), in the terms of their new life, almost like children talking a secret language. Of these individual elements on their first friendship we can say little with certainty; but it is certain that they remained friends to the end. Bernard of Quintavalle occupies in the story something of the position of Sir Bedivere, "first made and latest left of Arthur's knights," for he reappears again at the right hand of the saint on his deathbed and receives some sort of special blessing. But all those things belong to another historical world and were quite remote from the ragged and fantastic trio in their tumble-down hut. They were not monks except perhaps in the most literal and archaic sense which was identical with hermits. They were, so to speak, three solitaries living together socially, but not as a society. The whole thing seems to have been intensely individual, as seen from the outside doubtless individual to the point of insanity. The stir of something that had in it the promise of a movement or a mission can first be felt as I have said in the affair of the appeal to the New Testament.

It was a sort of *sors virgiliana* applied to the Bible; a practice not unknown among Protestants though open to their criticism, one would think, as being rather a superstition of pagans. Anyhow it seems almost the opposite of searching the Scriptures to open them at random; but St. Francis certainly opened them at random. According to one story, he merely made the sign of the cross over the volume of the Gospel and opened it at three places reading three texts. The first was the tale of the rich young man whose refusal to sell all his goods was the occasion of the great paradox about the camel and the needle. The second was the commandment to the disciples to take nothing with them on their journey, neither scrip nor staff nor any money. The third was that saying, literally to be called crucial, that the follower of Christ must also carry his cross. There is a somewhat similar story of Francis finding one of these texts, almost as accidentally, merely in listening to what happened to be the Gospel of the day. But from the former version at least it would seem that the incident occurred very early indeed in his new life, perhaps soon after his breach with his father; for it was after this oracle, apparently, that Bernard the first disciple rushed forth and scattered all his goods among the poor. If this be so, it would seem that nothing followed it for the moment except the individual ascetical life with the hut for a hermitage. It must of course have been a rather public sort of hermitage, but it was none the less in a very real sense withdrawn from the world. St. Simeon Stylites on the top of his pillar was in one sense an exceedingly public character; but there was something a little singular in his situation for all that. It may be presumed that most people thought the situation of Francis singular, that some even thought it too singular. There was inevitably indeed in any Catholic society something ultimate and even subconscious that was at least capable of comprehending it better than a pagan or puritan society could comprehend it. But we must not at this stage, I think, exaggerate this potential public sympathy. As has already been suggested, the Church and all its institutions had already the air of being old and settled and sensible things, the monastic institutions among the rest. Common sense was commoner in the Middle Ages, I think, than in our own rather jumpy journalistic age; but men like Francis are not common in any age, nor are they to be fully understood merely by the exercise of common sense. The thirteenth century was certainly a progressive period; perhaps the only really progressive period in human history. But it can truly be called progressive precisely because its progress was very orderly. It is really and truly an example of an epoch of reforms without revolutions. But the reforms were not only progressive but very practical; and they were very much to the advantage of highly practical institutions; the towns and the trading guilds and the manual crafts. Now the solid men of town and guild in the time of Francis of Assisi were probably very solid indeed. They were much more economically equal, they were much more justly governed in their own economic environment, than the moderns who struggle madly between starvation and the monopolist prizes of capitalism; but it is likely enough that the majority of such citizens were as hardheaded as peasants. Certainly the behaviour of the venerable Peter Bernardone does not indicate a delicate sympathy with the fine and almost fanciful subtleties of the Franciscan spirit. And we cannot measure the beauty and originality of this strange spiritual adventure, unless we have the humour and human sympathy to put into plain words how it would have looked to such an unsympathetic person at the time when it happened. In the next chapter I shall make an attempt, inevitably inadequate, to indicate the inside of this story of the building of the three churches and the little hut. In this chapter I have but outlined it from the outside. And in concluding that chapter I ask the reader to remember and realise what that story really looked like, when thus seen from the outside. Given a critic of rather coarse common sense, with no feeling about the incident except annoyance, and how would the story seem to stand?

A young fool or rascal is caught robbing his father and selling goods which he ought to guard; and the only explanation he will offer is that a loud voice from nowhere spoke in his ear and told him to mend the cracks and holes in a particular wall. He then declares himself naturally independent of all powers corresponding to the police or the magistrates, and takes refuge with an amiable bishop who is forced to remonstrate with him and tell him he is wrong. He then proceeds to take off his clothes in public and practically throw them at his father; announcing at the same time that his father is not his father at all. He then runs about the town asking everybody he meets to give him fragments of buildings or building materials, apparently with reference to his old monomania about mending the wall. It may be an excellent thing that cracks should be filled up, but preferably not by somebody who is himself cracked; and architectural restoration like other things is not best performed by builders who, as we should say, have a tile loose. Finally the wretched youth relapses into rags and squalor and practically crawls away into the gutter. That is the spectacle that Francis must have presented to a very large number of his neighbours and friends.

How he lived at all must have seemed to them dubious; but presumably he already begged for bread as he had begged for building materials. But he was always very careful to beg for the blackest or worst bread he could get, for the stalest crusts or something rather less luxurious than the crumbs which the dogs eat, and which fall from the rich man's table. Thus he probably fared worse than an ordinary beggar; for the beggar would eat the best he could get and the saint ate the worst he could get. In plain fact he was ready to live on refuse; and it was probably something much uglier as an experience than the refined simplicity which vegetarians and waterdrinkers would call the simple life. As he dealt with the question of food, so he apparently dealt with the question of clothing. He dealt with it, that is, upon the same principle of taking what he could get, and not even the best of what he could get. According to one story he changed clothes with a beggar; and he would doubtless have been content to change them with a scarecrow. In another version he got hold of the rough brown tunic of a peasant, but presumably only because the peasant gave him his very oldest brown tunic, which was probably very old indeed. Most peasants have few changes of clothing to give away; and some peasants are not specially inclined to give them away until it is absolutely necessary. It is said that in place of the girdle which he had flung off (perhaps with the more symbolic scorn because it probably carried the purse or wallet by the fashion of the period) he picked up a rope more or less at random, because it was lying near, and tied it round his waist. He undoubtedly meant it as a shabby expedient; rather as the very destitute tramp will sometimes tie his clothes together with a piece of string. He meant to strike the note of collecting his clothes anyhow, like rags from a succession of dust-bins. Ten years later that make-shift costume was the uniform of five thousand men; and a hundred years later, in that, for a pontifical panoply, they laid great Dante in the grave.

## V

# LE JONGLEUR DE DIEU

Many signs and symbols might be used to give a hint of what really happened in the mind of the young poet of Assisi. Indeed they are at once too numerous for selection and yet too slight for satisfaction. But one of them may be adumbrated in this small and apparently accidental fact: that when he and his secular companions carried their pageant of poetry through the town, they called themselves Troubadours. But when he and his spiritual companions came out to do their spiritual work in the world, they were called by their leader the Jongleurs de Dieu.

Nothing has been said here at any length of the great culture of the Troubadours as it appeared in Provence or Languedoc, great as was their influence in history and their influence on St. Francis. Something more may be said of them when we come to summarise his relation to history; it is enough to note here in a few sentences the facts about them that were relevant to him, and especially the particular point now in question, which was the most relevant of all. Everybody knows who the Troubadours were; everybody knows that very early in the Middle Ages, in the twelfth and early thirteenth centuries, there arose a civilisation in Southern France which threatened to rival or eclipse the rising tradition of Paris. Its chief product was a school of poetry, or rather more especially a school of poets. They were primarily love-poets, though they were often also satirists and critics of things in general. Their picturesque posture in history is largely due to the fact that they sang their own poems and often played their own accompaniments, on the light musical instruments of the period; they were minstrels as well as men of letters. Allied to their love-poetry were other institutions of a decorative and fanciful kind concerned with the same theme. There was what was called the "Gay Science," the attempt to reduce to a sort of system the fine shades of flirtation and philandering. There were the things called Courts of Love, in which the same delicate subjects were dealt with with legal pomp and pedantry. There is one point in this part of the business that must be remembered in relation to St. Francis. There were manifest moral dangers in all this superb sentimentalism; but it is a mistake to suppose that its only danger of exaggeration was in the direction of sensualism. There was a strain in the southern romance that was actually an excess of spirituality; just as the pessimist heresy it produced was in one sense an excess of spirituality. The love was not always animal; sometimes it was so airy as to be almost allegorical. The reader realises that the lady is the most beautiful being that can possibly exist, only he has occasional doubts as to whether she does exist. Dante owed something to the Troubadours; and the critical debates about his ideal woman are an excellent example of these doubts. We know that Beatrice was not his wife, but we should in any case be equally sure that she was not his mistress; and some critics have even suggested that she was nothing at all, so to speak, except his muse. This idea of Beatrice as an allegorical figure is, I believe, unsound; it would seem unsound to any man who has read the *Vita Nuova* and has been in love. But the very fact that it is possible to suggest it illustrates something abstract and scholastic in these medieval passions. But though they were abstract passions they were very passionate passions. These men could feel almost like lovers, even about allegories and abstractions. It is necessary to remember this in order to realise that St. Francis was talking the true language of a troubadour when he said that he also had a most glorious and gracious lady and that her name was Poverty.

But the particular point to be noted here is not concerned so much with the word Troubadour as with the word Jongleur. It is especially concerned with the transition from one to the other; and for this it is necessary to grasp another detail about the poets of the Gay Science. A jongleur was not the same thing as a troubadour, even if the same man were both a troubadour and a jongleur. More often, I believe, they were separate men as well as separate trades. In many cases apparently the two men would walk the world together like companions in arms, or rather companions in arts. The jongleur was properly a joculator or jester; sometimes he was what we should call a juggler. This is the point, I imagine, of the tale about Taillefer the Jongleur at the battle of Hastings, who sang of the death of Roland while he tossed up his sword and caught it, as a juggler catches balls. Sometimes he may have been even a tumbler; like that acrobat in the beautiful legend who was called "The Tumbler of Our Lady," because he turned head over heels and stood on his head before the image of the Blessed Virgin, for which he was nobly thanked and comforted by her and the whole company of heaven. In the ordinary way, we may imagine, the troubadour would exalt the company with earnest and solemn strains of love and then the jongleur would do his turn as a sort of comic relief. A glorious medieval romance remains to be written about two such companions wandering through the world. At any rate, if there is one place in which the true Franciscan spirit can be found outside the true Franciscan story, it is in that tale of the Tumbler of Our Lady. And when St. Francis called his followers the Jongleurs de Dieu, he meant something very like the Tumblers of Our Lord.

Somewhere in that transition from the ambition of the Troubadour to the antics of the Tumbler is hidden, as under a parable, the truth of St. Francis. Of the two minstrels or entertainers, the jester was presumably the servant or at least the secondary figure. St. Francis really meant what he said when he said he had found the secret of life in being the servant and the secondary figure. There was to be found ultimately in such service a freedom almost amounting to frivolity. It was comparable to the condition of the jongleur because it almost amounted to frivolity. The jester could be free when the knight was rigid; and it was possible to be a jester in the service which is perfect freedom. This parallel of the two poets or minstrels is perhaps the best preliminary and external statement of the Franciscan change of heart, being conceived under an image with which the imagination of the modern world has a certain sympathy. There was, of course, a great deal more than this involved; and we must endeavour however insufficiently to penetrate past the image to the idea. It is so far like the tumblers that it is really to many people a topsy-turvy idea.

Francis, at the time or somewhere about the time when he disappeared into the prison or the dark cavern, underwent a reversal of a certain psychological kind; which was really like the reversal of a complete somersault, in that by coming full circle it came back, or apparently came back, to the same normal posture. It is necessary to use the grotesque simile of an acrobatic antic, because there is hardly any other figure that will make the fact clear. But in the inward sense it was a profound spiritual revolution. The man who went into the cave was not the man who came out again; in that sense he was almost as different as if he were dead, as if he were a ghost or a blessed spirit. And the effects of this on his attitude towards the actual world were really as extravagant as any parallel can make them. He looked at the world as differently from other men as if he had come out of that dark hole walking on his hands.

If we apply this parable of Our Lady's Tumbler to the case, we shall come very near to the point of it. Now it really is a fact that any scene such as a landscape can sometimes be more clearly and freshly seen if it is seen upside down. There have been landscape-painters who adopted the most startling and pantomimic postures in order to look at it for a moment in that fashion. Thus that inverted vision, so much more bright and quaint and arresting, does bear a certain resemblance to the world which a mystic like St. Francis sees every day. But herein is the essential part of the parable. Our Lady's Tumbler did not stand on his head *in order* to see flowers and trees as a clearer or quainter vision. He did not do so; and it would never have occurred to him to do so. Our Lady's Tumbler stood on his head to please Our Lady. If St. Francis had done the same thing, as he was quite capable of doing, it would originally have been from the same motive; a motive of a purely supernatural thought. It would be *after* this that his enthusiasm would extend itself and give a sort of halo to the edges of all earthly things. This is why it is not true to represent St. Francis as a mere romantic forerunner of the Renaissance and a revival of natural pleasures for their own sake. The whole point of him was that the secret of recovering the natural pleasures lay in regarding them in the light of a supernatural pleasure. In other words, he repeated in his own person that historic process noted in the introductory chapter; the vigil of asceticism which ends in the vision of a natural world made new. But in the personal case there was even more than this; there were elements that make the parallel of the Jongleur or Tumbler even more appropriate than this.

It may be suspected that in that black cell or cave Francis passed the blackest hours of his life. By nature he was the sort of man who has that vanity which is the opposite of pride; that vanity which is very near to humility. He never despised his fellow creatures and therefore he never despised the opinion of his fellow creatures; including the admiration of his fellow creatures. All that part of his human nature had suffered the heaviest and most crushing blows. It is possible that after his humiliating return from his frustrated military campaign he was called a coward. It is certain that after his quarrel with his father about the bales of cloth he was called a thief. And even those who had sympathised most with him, the priest whose church he had restored, the bishop whose blessing he had received, had evidently treated him with an almost humorous amiability which left only too clear the ultimate conclusion of the matter. He had made a fool of himself. Any man who has been young, who has ridden horses or thought himself ready for a fight, who has fancied himself as a troubadour and accepted the conventions of comradeship, will appreciate the ponderous and crushing weight of that simple phrase. The conversion of St. Francis, like the conversion of St. Paul, involved his being in some sense flung suddenly from a horse; but in a sense it was an even worse fall; for it was a warhorse. Anyhow, there was not a rag of him left that was not ridiculous. Everybody knew that at the best he had made a fool of himself. It was a solid objective fact, like the stones in the road, that he had made a fool of himself. He saw himself as an object, very small and distinct like a fly walking on a clear window pane; and it was unmistakably a fool. And as he stared at the word "fool" written in luminous letters before him, the word itself began to shine and change.

We used to be told in the nursery that if a man were to bore a hole through the centre of the earth and climb continually down and down, there would come a moment at the centre when he would seem to be climbing up and up. I do not know whether this is true. The reason I do not know whether it is true is that I never happened to bore a hole through the centre of the earth, still less to crawl through it. If I do not know what this reversal or inversion feels like, it is because I have never been there. And this also is an allegory. It is certain that the writer, it is even possible that the reader, is an ordinary person who has never been there. We cannot follow St. Francis to that final spiritual overturn in which complete humiliation becomes complete holiness or happiness, because we have never been there. I for one do not profess to follow it any further than that first breaking down of the romantic barricades of boyish vanity, which I have suggested in the last paragraph. And even that paragraph, of course, is merely conjectural, an individual guess at what he may have felt; but he may have felt something quite different. But whatever else it was, it was so far analogous to the story of the man making a tunnel through the earth that it did mean a man going down and down until at some mysterious moment he begins to go up and up. We have never gone up like that because we have never gone down like that; we are obviously incapable of saying that it does not happen; and the more candidly and calmly we read human history, and especially the history of the wisest men, the more we shall come to the conclusion that it does happen. Of the intrinsic internal essence of the experience I make no pretence of writing at all. But the external effect of it, for the purpose of this narrative, may be expressed by saying that when Francis came forth from his cave of vision, he was wearing the same word "fool" as a feather in his cap; as a crest or even a crown. He would go on being a fool: he would become more and more of a fool; he would be the court fool of the King of Paradise.

This state can only be represented in symbol; but the symbol of inversion is true in another way. If a man saw the world upside down, with all the trees and towers hanging head downwards as in a pool, one effect would be to emphasise the idea of *dependence*. There is a Latin and literal connection; for the very word dependence only means hanging.

It would make vivid the Scriptural text which says that God has hanged the world upon nothing. If St. Francis had seen, in one of his strange dreams, the town of Assisi upside down, it need not have differed in a single detail from itself except in being entirely the other way round. But the point is this: that whereas to the normal eye the large masonry of its walls or the massive foundations of its watchtowers and its high citadel would make it seem safer and more permanent, the moment it was turned over the very same weight would make it seem more helpless and more in peril. It is but a symbol; but it happens to fit the psychological fact. St. Francis might love his little town as much as before, or more than before; but the nature of the love would be altered even in being increased. He might see and love every tile on the steep roofs or every bird on the battlements; but he would see them all in a new and divine light of eternal danger and dependence. Instead of being merely proud of his strong city because it could not be moved, he would be thankful to God Almighty that it had not been dropped; he would be thankful to God for not dropping the whole cosmos like a vast crystal to be shattered into falling stars. Perhaps St. Peter saw the world so, when he was crucified head-downwards.

It is commonly in a somewhat cynical sense that men have said, "Blessed is he that expecteth nothing, for he shall not be disappointed." It was in a wholly happy and enthusiastic sense that St. Francis said, "Blessed is he who expecteth nothing, for he shall enjoy everything." It was by this deliberate idea of starting from zero, from the dark nothingness of his own deserts, that he did come to enjoy even earthly things as few people have enjoyed them; and they are in themselves the best working example of the idea. For there is no way in which a man can earn a star or deserve a sunset. But there is more than this involved, and more indeed than is easily to be expressed in words. It is not only true that the less a man thinks of himself, the more he thinks of his good luck and of all the gifts of God. It is also true that he sees more of the things themselves when he sees more of their origin; for their origin is a part of them and indeed the most important part of them. Thus they become more extraordinary by being explained. He has more wonder at them but less fear of them; for a thing is really wonderful when it is significant and not when it is insignificant; and a monster, shapeless or dumb or merely destructive, may be larger than the mountains, but is still in a literal sense insignificant. For a mystic like St. Francis the monsters had a meaning; that is, they had delivered their message. They spoke no longer in an unknown tongue. That is the meaning of all those stories, whether legendary or historical, in which he appears as a magician speaking the language of beasts and birds. The mystic will have nothing to do with mere mystery; mere mystery is generally a mystery of iniquity.

The transition from the good man to the saint is a sort of revolution; by which one for whom all things illustrate and illuminate God becomes one for whom God illustrates and illuminates all things. It is rather like the reversal whereby a lover might say at first sight that a lady looked like a flower, and say afterwards that all flowers reminded him of his lady. A saint and a poet standing by the same flower might seem to say the same thing; but indeed though they would both be telling the truth, they would be telling different truths. For one the joy of life is a cause of faith, for the other rather a result of faith. But one effect of the difference is that the sense of a divine dependence, which for the artist is like the brilliant levin-blaze, for the saint is like the broad daylight. Being in some mystical sense on the other side of things, he sees things go forth from the divine as children going forth from a familiar and accepted home, instead of meeting them as they come out, as most of us do, upon the roads of the world. And it is the paradox that by this privilege he is more familiar, more free and fraternal, more carelessly hospitable than we. For us the elements are like heralds who tell us with trumpet and tabard that we are drawing near the city of a great king; but he hails them with an old familiarity that is almost an old frivolity. He calls them his Brother Fire and his Sister Water.

So arises out of this almost nihilistic abyss the noble thing that is called Praise; which no one will ever understand while he identifies it with nature-worship or pantheistic optimism. When we say that a poet praises the whole creation, we commonly mean only that he praises the whole cosmos. But this sort of poet does really praise creation, in the sense of the act of creation. He praises the passage or transition from nonentity to entity; there falls here also the shadow of that archetypal image of the bridge, which has given to the priest his archaic and mysterious name. The mystic who passes through the moment when there is nothing but God does in some sense behold the beginningless beginnings in which there was really nothing else. He not only appreciates everything but the nothing of which everything was made. In a fashion he endures and answers even the earthquake irony of the Book of Job; in some sense he is there when the foundations of the world are laid, with the morning stars singing together and the sons of God shouting for joy. That is but a distant adumbration of the reason why the Franciscan, ragged, penniless, homeless and apparently hopeless, did indeed come forth singing such songs as might come from the stars of morning; and shouting, a son of God.

This sense of the great gratitude and the sublime dependence was not a phrase or even a sentiment; it is the whole point that this was the very rock of reality. It was not a fancy but a fact; rather it is true that beside it all facts are fancies. That we all depend in every detail, at every instant, as a Christian would say upon God, as even an agnostic would say upon existence and the nature of things, is not an illusion of imagination; on the contrary, it is the fundamental fact which we cover up, as with curtains, with the illusion of ordinary life. That ordinary life is an admirable thing in itself, just as imagination is an admirable thing in itself. But it is much more the ordinary life that is made of imagination than the contemplative life. He who has seen the whole world hanging on a hair of the mercy of God has seen the truth; we might almost say the cold truth. He who has seen the vision of his city upside-down has seen it the right way up.

Rossetti makes the remark somewhere, bitterly but with great truth, that the worst moment for the atheist is when he is really thankful and has nobody to thank. The converse of this proposition is also true; and it is certain that this gratitude produced, in such men as we are here considering, the most purely joyful moments that have been known to man. The great painter boasted that he mixed all his colours with brains, and the great saint may be said to mix all his thoughts with thanks. All goods look better when they look like gifts. In this sense it is certain that the mystical method establishes a very healthy external relation to everything else. But it must always be remembered that everything else has for ever fallen into a second place, in comparison with this simple fact of dependence on the divine reality. In so far as ordinary social relations have in them something that seems solid and self-supporting, some sense of being at once buttressed and cushioned; in so far as they establish sanity in the sense of security and security in the sense of self-sufficiency, the man who has seen the world hanging on a hair does have some difficulty in taking them so seriously as that. In so far as even the secular authorities and hierarchies, even the most natural superiorities and the most necessary subordinations, tend at once to put a man in his place, and to make him sure of his position, the man who has seen the human hierarchy upside down will always have something of a smile for its superiorities. In this sense the direct vision of divine reality does disturb solemnities that are sane enough in themselves. The mystic may have added a cubit to his stature; but he generally loses something of his status. He can no longer take himself for granted, merely because he can verify his own existence in a parish register or a family Bible. Such a man may have something of the appearance of the lunatic who has lost his name while preserving his nature; who straightway forgets what manner of man he was. "Hitherto I have called Pietro Bernardone father; but now I am the servant of God."

All these profound matters must be suggested in short and imperfect phrases; and the shortest statement of one aspect of this illumination is to say that it is the discovery of an infinite debt. It may seem a paradox to say that a man may be transported with joy to discover that he is in debt. But this is only because in commercial cases the creditor does not generally share the transports of joy; especially when the debt is by hypothesis infinite and therefore unrecoverable. But here again the parallel of a natural love-story of the nobler sort disposes of the difficulty in a flash. There the infinite creditor does share the joy of the infinite debtor; for indeed they are both debtors and both creditors. In other words debt and dependence do become pleasures in the presence of unspoilt love; the word is used too loosely and luxuriously in popular simplifications like the present; but here the word is really the key. It is the key of all the problems of Franciscan morality which puzzle the merely modern mind; but above all it is the key of asceticism. It is the highest and holiest of the paradoxes that the man who really knows he cannot pay his debt will be for ever paying it. He will be for ever giving back what he cannot give back, and cannot be expected to give back. He will be always throwing things away into a bottomless pit of unfathomable thanks. Men who think they are too modern to understand this are in fact too mean to understand it; we are most of us too mean to practise it. We are not generous enough to be ascetics; one might almost say not genial enough to be ascetics. A man must have magnanimity of surrender, of which he commonly only catches a glimpse in first love, like a glimpse of our lost Eden. But whether he sees it or not, the truth is in that riddle; that the whole world has, or is, only one good thing; and it is a bad debt.

If ever that rarer sort of romantic love, which was the truth that sustained the Troubadours, falls out of fashion and is treated as fiction, we may see some such misunderstanding as that of the modern world about asceticism. For it seems conceivable that some barbarians might try to destroy chivalry in love, as the barbarians ruling in Berlin destroyed chivalry in war. If that were ever so, we should have the same sort of unintelligent sneers and unimaginative questions. Men will ask what selfish sort of woman it must have been who ruthlessly exacted tribute in the form of flowers, or what an avaricious creature she can have been to demand solid gold in the form of a ring; just as they ask what cruel kind of God can have demanded sacrifice and self-denial. They will have lost the clue to all that lovers have meant by love; and will not understand that it was because the thing was not demanded that it was done. But whether or no any such lesser things will throw a light on the greater, it is utterly useless to study a great thing like the Franciscan movement while remaining in the modern mood that murmurs against gloomy asceticism. The whole point about St. Francis of Assisi is that he certainly was ascetical and he certainly was not gloomy. As soon as ever he had been unhorsed by the glorious humiliation of his vision of dependence on the divine love, he flung himself into fasting and vigil exactly as he had flung himself furiously into battle. He had wheeled his charger clean round, but there was no halt or check in the thundering impetuosity of his charge. There was nothing negative about it; it was not a regimen or a stoical simplicity of life. It was not self-denial merely in the sense of self-control. It was as positive as a passion; it had all the air of being as positive as a pleasure. He devoured fasting as a man devours food. He plunged after poverty as men have dug madly for gold. And it is precisely the positive and passionate quality of this part of his personality that is a challenge to the modern mind in the whole problem of the pursuit of pleasure. There undeniably is the historical fact; and there attached to it is another moral fact almost as undeniable. It is certain that he held on this heroic or unnatural course from the moment when he went forth in his hair-shirt into the winter woods to the moment when he desired even in his death agony to lie bare upon the bare ground, to prove that he had and that he was nothing. And we can say, with almost as deep a certainty, that the stars which passed above that gaunt and wasted corpse stark upon the rocky floor had for once, in all their shining cycles round the world of labouring humanity, looked down upon a happy man.

## VI

## THE LITTLE POOR MAN

From that cavern, that was a furnace of glowing gratitude and humility, there came forth one of the strongest and strangest and most original personalities that human history has known. He was, among other things, emphatically what we call a character; almost as we speak of a character in a good novel or play. He was not only a humanist but a humorist; a humorist especially in the old English sense of a man always in his humour, going his own way and doing what nobody else would have done. The anecdotes about him have a certain biographical quality of which the most familiar example is Dr. Johnson; which belongs in another way to William Blake or to Charles Lamb. The atmosphere can only be defined by a sort of antithesis; the act is always unexpected and never inappropriate. Before the thing is said or done it cannot even be conjectured; but after it is said or done it is felt to be merely characteristic. It is surprisingly and yet inevitably individual. This quality of abrupt fitness and bewildering consistency belongs to St. Francis in a way that marks him out from most men of his time. Men are learning more and more of the solid social virtues of medieval civilisation; but those impressions are still social rather than individual. The medieval world was far ahead of the modern world in its sense of the things in which all men are at one: death and the daylight of reason and the common conscience that holds communities together. Its generalisations were saner and sounder than the mad materialistic theories of today; nobody would have tolerated a Schopenhauer scorning life or a Nietzsche living only for scorn. But the modern world is more subtle in its sense of the things in which men are not at one; in the temperamental varieties and differentiations that make up the personal problems of life. All men who can think themselves now realize that the great schoolmen had a type of thought that was wonderfully clear; but it was as it were deliberately colourless. All are now agreed that the greatest art of the age was the art of public buildings; the popular and communal art of architecture. But it was not an age for the art of portrait-painting. Yet the friends of St. Francis have really contrived to leave behind a portrait; something almost resembling a devout and affectionate caricature. There are lines and colours in it that are personal almost to the extent of being perverse, if one can use the word perversity of an inversion that was also a conversion. Even among the saints he has the air of a sort of eccentric, if one may use the word of one whose eccentricity consisted in always turning towards the centre.

Before resuming the narrative of his first adventures, and the building of the great brotherhood which was the beginning of so merciful a revolution, I think it well to complete this imperfect personal portrait here; and having attempted in the last chapter a tentative description of the process, to add in this chapter a few touches to describe the result. I mean by the result the real man as he was after his first formative experiences; the man whom men met walking about on the Italian roads in his brown tunic tied with a rope. For that man, saving the grace of God, is the explanation of all that followed; men acted quite differently according to whether they had met him or not. If we see afterwards a vast tumult, an appeal to the Pope, mobs of men in brown habits besieging the seats of authority, Papal pronouncements, heretical sessions, trial and triumphant survival, the world full of a new movement, the friar a household word in every corner of Europe, and if we ask *why* all this happened, we can only approximate to any answer to our own question if we can, in some faint and indirect imaginative fashion, hear one human voice or see one human face under a hood. There is no answer except that Francis Bernardone had happened; and we must try in some sense to see what we should have seen if he had happened to us. In other words, after some groping suggestions about his life from the inside, we must again consider it from the outside; as if he were a stranger coming up the road towards us, along the hills of Umbria, between the olives or the vines.

Francis of Assisi was slight in figure with that sort of slightness which, combined with so much vivacity, gives the impression of smallness. He was probably taller than he looked; middle-sized, his biographers say; he was certainly very active and, considering what he went through, must have been tolerably tough. He was of the brownish Southern colouring, with a dark beard thin and pointed such as appears in pictures under the hoods of elves; and his eyes glowed with the fire that fretted him night and day. There is, something about the description of all he said and did which suggests that, even more than most Italians, he turned naturally to a passionate pantomime of gestures. If this was so it is equally certain that with him, even more than with most Italians, the gestures were all gestures of politeness or hospitality. And both these facts, the vivacity and the courtesy, are the outward signs of something that mark him out very distinctively from many who might appear to be more of his kind than they really are. It is truly said that Francis of Assisi was one of the founders of the medieval drama, and therefore of the modern drama. He was the very reverse of a theatrical person in the selfish sense; but for all that he was pre-eminently a dramatic person. This side of him can best be suggested by taking what is commonly regarded as a reposeful quality; what is commonly described as a love of nature. We are compelled to use the term; and it is entirely the wrong term.

St. Francis was not a lover of nature. Properly understood, a lover of nature was precisely what he was not. The phrase implies accepting the material universe as a vague environment, a sort of sentimental pantheism. In the romantic period of literature, in the age of Byron and Scott, it was easy enough to imagine that a hermit in the ruins of a chapel (preferably by moonlight) might find peace and a mild pleasure in the harmony of solemn forests and silent stars, while he pondered over some scroll or illuminated volume, about the liturgical nature of which the author was a little vague. In short, the hermit might love nature as a background. Now for St. Francis nothing was ever in the background. We might say that his mind had no background, except perhaps that divine darkness out of which the divine love had called up every coloured creature one by one. He saw everything as dramatic, distinct from its setting, not all of a piece like a picture but in action like a play. A bird went by him like an arrow; something with a story and a purpose, though it was a purpose of life and not a purpose of death. A bush could stop him like a brigand; and indeed he was as ready to welcome the brigand as the bush.

In a word, we talk about a man who cannot see the wood for the trees. St. Francis was a man who did not want to see the wood for the trees. He wanted to see each tree as a separate and almost a sacred thing, being a child of God and therefore a brother or sister of man. But he did not want to stand against a piece of stage scenery used merely as a background, and inscribed in a general fashion: "Scene; a wood." In this sense we might say that he was too dramatic for the drama. The scenery would have come to life in his comedies; the walls would really have spoken like Snout the Tinker and the trees would really have come walking to Dunsinane. Everything would have been in the foreground; and in that sense in the footlights. Everything would be in every sense a character. This is the quality in which, as a poet, he is the very opposite of a pantheist. He did not call nature his mother; he called a particular donkey his brother or a particular sparrow his sister. If he had called a pelican his aunt or an elephant his uncle, as he might possibly have done, he would still have meant that they were particular creatures assigned by their Creator to particular places; not mere expressions of the evolutionary energy of things. That is where his mysticism is so close to the common sense of the child. A child has no difficulty about understanding that God made the dog and the cat; though he is well aware that the making of dogs and cats out of nothing is a mysterious process beyond his own imagination. But no child would understand what you meant if you mixed up the dog and the cat and everything else into one monster with a myriad legs and called it nature. The child would resolutely refuse to make head or tail of any such animal. St. Francis was a mystic, but he believed in mysticism and not in mystification. As a mystic he was the mortal enemy of all those mystics who melt away the edges of things and dissolve an entity into its environment. He was a mystic of the daylight and the darkness; but not a mystic of the twilight. He was the very contrary of that sort of oriental visionary who is only a mystic because he is too much of a sceptic to be a materialist. St. Francis was emphatically a realist, using the word realist in its much more real medieval sense. In this matter he really was akin to the best spirit of his age, which had just won its victory over the nominalism of the twelfth century. In this indeed there was something symbolic in the contemporary art and decoration of his period; as in the art of heraldry. The Franciscan birds and beasts were really rather like heraldic birds and beasts; not in the sense of being fabulous animals but in the sense of being treated as if they were facts, clear and positive and unaffected by the illusions of atmosphere and perspective. In that sense he did see a bird sable on a field azure or a sheep argent on a field vert. But the heraldry of humility was richer than the heraldry of pride; for it saw all these things that God had given as something more precious and unique than the blazonry that princes and peers had only given to themselves. Indeed out of the depths of that surrender it rose higher than the highest titles of the feudal age; than the laurel of Cæsar or the Iron Crown of Lombardy. It is an example of extremes that meet, that the Little Poor Man, who had stripped himself of everything and named himself as nothing, took the same title that has been the wild vaunt of the vanity of the gorgeous Asiatic autocrat, and called himself the Brother of the Sun and Moon.

This quality, of something outstanding and even startling in things as St. Francis saw them, is here important as illustrating a character in his own life. As he saw all things dramatically, so he himself was always dramatic. We have to assume throughout, needless to say, that he was a poet and can only be understood as a poet. But he had one poetic privilege denied to most poets. In that respect indeed he might be called the one happy poet among all the unhappy poets of the world. He was a poet whose whole life was a poem. He was not so much a minstrel merely singing his own songs as a dramatist capable of acting the whole of his own play. The things he said were more imaginative than the things he wrote. The things he did were more imaginative than the things he said. His whole course through life was a series of scenes in which he had a sort of perpetual luck in bringing things to a beautiful crisis. To talk about the art of living has come to sound rather artificial than artistic. But St. Francis did in a definite sense make the very act of living an art, though it was an unpremeditated art. Many of his acts will seem grotesque and puzzling to a rationalistic taste. But they were always acts and not explanations; and they always meant what he meant them to mean. The amazing vividness with which he stamped himself on the memory and imagination of mankind is very largely due to the fact that he was seen again and again under such dramatic conditions. From the moment when he rent his robes and flung them at his father's feet to the moment when he stretched himself in death on the bare earth in the pattern of the cross, his life was made up of these unconscious attitudes and unhesitating gestures. It would be easy to fill page after page with examples; but I will here pursue the method found convenient everywhere in this short sketch, and take one typical example, dwelling on it with a little more detail than would be possible in a catalogue, in the hope of making the meaning more clear. The example taken here occurred in the last days of his life, but it refers back in a rather curious fashion to the first; and rounds off the remarkable unity of that romance of religion.

The phrase about his brotherhood with the sun and moon, and with the water and the fire, occurs of course in his famous poem called the Canticle of the Creatures or the Canticle of the Sun. He sang it wandering in the meadows in the sunnier season of his own career, when he was pouring upwards into the sky all the passions of a poet. It is a supremely characteristic work, and much of St. Francis could be reconstructed from that work alone. Though in some ways the thing is as simple and straightforward as a ballad, there is a delicate instinct of differentiation in it. Notice, for instance, the sense of sex in inanimate things, which goes far beyond the arbitrary genders of a grammar. It was not for nothing that he called fire his brother, fierce and gay and strong, and water his sister, pure and clear and inviolate. Remember that St. Francis was neither encumbered nor assisted by all that Greek and Roman polytheism turned into allegory, which has been to European poetry often an inspiration, too often a convention. Whether he gained or lost by his contempt of learning, it never occurred to him to connect Neptune and the nymphs with the water or Vulcan and the Cyclops with the flame. This point exactly illustrates what has already been suggested; that, so far from being a revival of paganism, the Franciscan renascence was a sort of fresh start and first awakening after a forgetfulness of paganism. Certainly it is responsible for a certain freshness in the thing itself. Anyhow St. Francis was, as it were, the founder of a new folk-lore; but he could distinguish his mermaids from his mermen and his witches from his wizards. In short, he had to make his own mythology; but he knew at a glance the goddesses from the gods. This fanciful instinct for the sexes is not the only example of an imaginative instinct of the kind. There is just the same quaint felicity in the fact that he singles out the sun with a slightly more courtly title besides that of brother; a phrase that one king might use of another, corresponding to "Monsieur notre frère." It is like a faint half ironic shadow of the shining primacy that it had held in the pagan heavens. A bishop is said to have complained of a Nonconformist saying Paul instead of Saint Paul; and to have added "He might at least have called him Mr. Paul." So St. Francis is free of all obligation to cry out in praise or terror on the Lord God Apollo, but in his new nursery heavens, he salutes him as Mr. Sun. Those are the things in which he has a sort of inspired infancy, only to be paralleled in nursery tales. Something of the same hazy but healthy awe makes the story of Brer Fox and Brer Rabbit refer respectfully to Mr. Man.

This poem, full of the mirth of youth and the memories of childhood, runs through his whole life like a refrain, and scraps of it turn up continually in the ordinary habit of his talk. Perhaps the last appearance of its special language was in an incident that has always seemed to me intensely impressive, and is at any rate very illustrative of the great manner and gesture of which I speak. Impressions of that kind are a matter of imagination and in that sense of taste. It is idle to argue about them; for it is the whole point of them that they have passed beyond words; and even when they use words, seem to be completed by some ritual movement like a blessing or a blow. So, in a supreme example, there is something far past all exposition, something like the sweeping movement and mighty shadow of a hand, darkening even the darkness of Gethsemane; "Sleep on now, and take your rest. . . ." Yet there are people who have started to paraphrase and expand the story of the Passion.

St. Francis was a dying man. We might say he was an old man, at the time this typical incident occurred; but in fact he was only prematurely old; for he was not fifty when he died, worn out with his fighting and fasting life. But when he came down from the awful asceticism and more awful revelation of Alverno, he was a broken man. As will be apparent when these events are touched on in their turn, it was not only sickness and bodily decay that may well have darkened his life; he had been recently disappointed in his main mission to end the Crusades by the conversion of Islam; he had been still more disappointed by the signs of compromise and a more political or practical spirit in his own order; he had spent his last energies in protest. At this point he was told that he was going blind. If the faintest hint has been given here of what St. Francis felt about the glory and pageantry of earth and sky, about the heraldic shape and colour and symbolism of birds and beasts and flowers, some notion may be formed of what it meant, to him to go blind. Yet the remedy might well have seemed worse than the disease. The remedy, admittedly an uncertain remedy, was to cauterise the eye, and that without any anæsthetic. In other words it was to burn his living eyeballs with a red-hot iron. Many of the tortures of martyrdom, which he envied in martyrology and sought vainly in Syria, can have been no worse. When they took the brand from the furnace, he rose as with an urbane gesture and spoke as to an invisible presence: "Brother Fire, God made you beautiful and strong and useful; I pray you be courteous with me."

If there be any such thing as the art of life, it seems to me that such a moment was one of its masterpieces. Not to many poets has it been given to remember their own poetry at such a moment, still less to live one of their own poems. Even William Blake would have been disconcerted if, while he was re-reading the noble lines "Tiger, tiger, burning bright," a real large live Bengal tiger had put his head in at the window of the cottage in Felpham, evidently with every intention of biting his head off. He might have wavered before politely saluting it, above all by calmly completing the recitation of the poem to the quadruped to whom it was dedicated. Shelley, when he wished to be a cloud or a leaf carried before the wind, might have been mildly surprised to find himself turning slowly head over heels in mid air a thousand feet above the sea. Even Keats, knowing that his hold on life was a frail one, might have been disturbed to discover that the true, the blushful Hippocrene of which he had just partaken freely had indeed contained a drug, which really ensured that he should cease upon the midnight with no pain. For Francis there was no drug; and for Francis there was plenty of pain. But his first thought was one of his first fancies from the songs of his youth. He remembered the time when a flame was a flower, only the most glorious and gaily coloured of the flowers in the garden of God; and when that shining thing returned to him in the shape of an instrument of torture, he hailed it from afar like an old friend, calling it by the nickname which might most truly be called its Christian name.

That is only one incident out of a life of such incidents; and I have selected it partly because it shows what is meant here by that shadow of gesture there is in all his words, the dramatic gesture of the south; and partly because its special reference to courtesy covers the next fact to be noted. The popular instinct of St. Francis, and his perpetual preoccupation with the idea of brotherhood, will be entirely misunderstood if it is understood in the sense of what is often called camaraderie; the back-slapping sort of brotherhood. Frequently from the enemies and too frequently from the friends of the democratic ideal, there has come a notion that this note is necessary to that ideal. It is assumed that equality means all men being equally uncivil, whereas it obviously ought to mean all men being equally civil. Such people have forgotten the very meaning and derivation of the word civility, if they do not see that to be uncivil is to be uncivic. But anyhow that was not the equality which Francis of Assisi encouraged; but an equality of the opposite kind; it was a camaraderie actually founded on courtesy.

Even in that fairy borderland of his mere fancies about flowers and animals and even inanimate things, he retained this permanent posture of a sort of deference. A friend of mine said that somebody was the sort of man who apologises to the cat. St. Francis really would have apologised to the cat. When he was about to preach in a wood full of the chatter of birds, he said, with a gentle gesture "Little sisters, if you have now had your say, it is time that I also should be heard." And all the birds were silent; as I for one can very easily believe. In deference to my special design of making matters intelligible to average modernity, I have treated separately the subject of the miraculous powers that St. Francis most certainly possessed. But even apart from any miraculous powers, men of that magnetic sort, with that intense interest in animals, often have an extraordinary power over them. St. Francis's power was always exercised with this elaborate politeness. Much of it was doubtless a sort of symbolic joke, a pious pantomime intended to convey the vital distinction in his divine mission, that he not only loved but reverenced God in all his creatures. In this sense he had the air not only of apologising to the cat or to the birds, but of apologising to a chair for sitting on it or to a table for sitting down at it. Anyone who had followed him through life merely to laugh at him, as a sort of lovable lunatic, might easily have had an impression as of a lunatic who bowed to every post or took off his hat to every tree. This was all a part of his instinct for imaginative gesture. He taught the world a large part of its lesson by a sort of divine dumb alphabet. But if there was this ceremonial element even in lighter or lesser matters, its significance became far more serious in the serious work of his life, which was an appeal to humanity, or rather to human beings.

I have said that St. Francis deliberately did not see the wood for the trees. It is even more true that he deliberately did not see the mob for the men. What distinguishes this very genuine democrat from any mere demagogue is that he never either deceived or was deceived by the illusion of mass-suggestion. Whatever his taste in monsters, he never saw before him a many-headed beast. He only saw the image of God multiplied but never monotonous. To him a man was always a man and did not disappear in a dense crowd any more than in a desert. He honoured all men; that is, he not only loved but respected them all. What gave him his extraordinary personal power was this; that from the Pope to the beggar, from the sultan of Syria in his pavilion to the ragged robbers crawling out of the wood, there was never a man who looked into those brown burning eyes without being certain that Francis Bernardone was really interested in *him*; in his own inner individual life from the cradle to the grave; that he himself was being valued and taken seriously, and not merely added to the spoils of some social policy or the names in some clerical document. Now for this particular moral and religious idea there is no external expression except courtesy. Exhortation does not express it, for it is not mere abstract enthusiasm; beneficence does not express it, for it is not mere pity. It can only be conveyed by a certain grand manner which may be called good manners. We may say if we like that St. Francis, in the bare and barren simplicity of his life, had clung to one rag of luxury; the manners of a court. But whereas in a court there is one king and a hundred courtiers, in this story there was one courtier, moving among a hundred kings. For he treated the whole mob of men as a mob of kings. And this was really and truly the only attitude that will appeal to that part of man to which he wished to appeal. It cannot be done by giving gold or even bread; for it is a proverb that any reveller may fling largesse in mere scorn. It cannot even be done by giving time and attention; for any number of philanthropists and benevolent bureaucrats do such work with a scorn far more cold and horrible in their hearts. No plans or proposals or efficient rearrangements will give back to a broken man his self-respect and sense of speaking with an equal. One gesture will do it.

With that gesture Francis of Assisi moved among men; and it was soon found to have something in it of magic and to act, in a double sense, like a charm. But it must always be conceived as a completely natural gesture; for indeed it was almost a gesture of apology. He must be imagined as moving thus swiftly through the world with a sort of impetuous politeness; almost like the movement of a man who stumbles on one knee half in haste and half in obeisance. The eager face under the brown hood was that of a man always going somewhere, as if he followed as well as watched the flight of the birds. And this sense of motion is indeed the meaning of the whole revolution that he made; for the work that has now to be described was of the nature of an earthquake or a volcano, an explosion that drove outwards with dynamic energy the forces stored up by ten centuries in the monastic fortress or arsenal and scattered all its riches recklessly to the ends of the earth. In a better sense than the antithesis commonly conveys, it is true to say that what St. Benedict had stored St. Francis scattered; but in the world of spiritual things what had been stored into the barns like grain was scattered over the world as seed. The servants of God who had been a besieged garrison became a marching army; the ways of the world were filled as with thunder with the trampling of their feet and far ahead of that ever swelling host went a man singing; as simply he had sung that morning in the winter woods, where he walked alone.

# VII

# THE THREE ORDERS

There is undoubtedly a sense in which two is company and three is none; there is also another sense in which three is company and four is none, as is proved by the procession of historic and fictitious figures moving three deep, the famous trios like the Three Musketeers or the Three Soldiers of Kipling. But there is yet another and a different sense in which four is company and three is none; if we use the word company in the vaguer sense of a crowd or a mass. With the fourth man enters the shadow of a mob; the group is no longer one of three individuals only conceived individually. That shadow of the fourth man fell across the little hermitage of the Portiuncula when a man named Egidio, apparently a poor workman, was invited by St. Francis to enter. He mingled without difficulty with the merchant and the canon who had already become the companions of Francis; but with his coming an invisible line was crossed; for it must have been felt by this time that the growth of that small group had become potentially infinite, or at least that its outline had become permanently indefinite. It may have been in the time of that transition that Francis had another of his dreams full of voices; but now the voices were a clamour of the tongues of all nations, Frenchmen and Italians and English and Spanish and Germans, telling of the glory of God each in his own tongue; a new Pentecost and a happier Babel.

Before describing the first steps he took to regularise the growing group, it is well to have a rough grasp of what he conceived that group to be. He did not call his followers monks; and it is not clear, at this time at least, that he even thought of them as monks. He called them by a name which is generally rendered in English as the Friars Minor; but we shall be much closer to the atmosphere of his own mind if we render it almost literally as The Little Brothers. Presumably he was already resolved, indeed, that they should take the three vows of poverty, chastity and obedience which had always been the mark of a monk. But it would seem that he was not so much afraid of the idea of a monk as of the idea of an abbot. He was afraid that the great spiritual magistracies which had given even to their holiest possessors at least a sort of impersonal and corporate pride, would import an element of pomposity that would spoil his extremely and almost extravagantly simple version of the life of humility. But the supreme difference between his discipline and the discipline of the old monastic system was concerned, of course, with the idea that the monks were to become migratory and almost nomadic instead of stationary. They were to mingle with the world; and to this the more old-fashioned monk would naturally reply by asking how they were to mingle with the world without becoming entangled with the world. It was a much more real question than a loose religiosity is likely to realise; but St. Francis had his answer to it, of his own individual sort; and the interest of the problem is in that highly individual answer.

The good Bishop of Assisi expressed a sort of horror at the hard life which the Little Brothers lived at the Portiuncula, without comforts, without possessions, eating anything they could get and sleeping anyhow on the ground. St. Francis answered him with that curious and almost stunning shrewdness which the unworldly can sometimes wield like a club of stone. He said, "If we had any possessions, we should need weapons and laws to defend them." That sentence is the clue to the whole policy that he pursued. It rested upon a real piece of logic; and about that he was never anything but logical. He was ready to own himself wrong about anything else; but he was quite certain he was right about this particular rule. He was only once seen angry; and that was when there was talk of an exception to the rule.

His argument was this: that the dedicated man might go anywhere among any kind of men, even the worst kind of men, so long as there was nothing by which they could hold him. If he had any ties or needs like ordinary men, he would become like ordinary men. St. Francis was the last man in the world to think any the worse of ordinary men for being ordinary. They had more affection and admiration from him than they are ever likely to have again. But for his own particular purpose of stirring up the world to a new spiritual enthusiasm, he saw with a logical clarity that was quite reverse of fanatical or sentimental, that friars must not become like ordinary men; that the salt must not lose its savour even to turn into human nature's daily food. And the difference between a friar and an ordinary man was really that a friar was freer than an ordinary man. It was necessary that he should be free from the cloister; but it was even more important that he should be free from the world. It is perfectly sound common sense to say that there is a sense in which the ordinary man cannot be free from the world; or rather ought not to be free from the world. The feudal world in particular was one labyrinthine system of dependence; but it was not only the feudal world that went to make up the medieval world nor the medieval world that went to make up the whole world; and the whole world is full of this fact. Family life as much as feudal life is in its nature a system of dependence. Modern trade unions as much as medieval guilds are interdependent among themselves even in order to be independent of others. In medieval as in modern life, even where these limitations do exist for the sake of liberty, they have in them a considerable element of luck. They are partly the result of circumstances; sometimes the almost unavoidable result of circumstances. So the twelfth century had been the age of vows; and there was something of relative freedom in that feudal gesture of the vow; for no man asks vows from slaves any more than from spades. Still, in practice, a man rode to war in support of the ancient house of the Column or behind the Great Dog of the Stairway largely because he had been born in a certain city or countryside. But no man need obey little Francis in the old brown coat unless he chose. Even in his relations with his chosen leader he was in one sense relatively free, compared with the world around him. He was obedient but not dependent. And he was as free as the wind, he was almost wildly free, in his relation to that world around him. The world around him was, as has been noted, a network of feudal and family and other forms of dependence. The whole idea of St. Francis was that the Little Brothers should be like little fishes who could go freely in and out of that net. They could do so precisely because they were small fishes and in that sense even slippery fishes. There was nothing that the world could hold them by; for the world catches us mostly by the fringes of our garments, the futile externals of our lives. One of the Franciscans says later, "A monk should own nothing but his harp"; meaning, I suppose, that he should value nothing but his song, the song with which it was his business as a minstrel to serenade every castle and cottage, the song of the joy of the Creator in his creation and the beauty of the brotherhood of men. In imagining the life of this sort of visionary vagabond, we may already get a glimpse also of the practical side of that asceticism which puzzles those who think themselves practical. A man had to be thin to pass always through the bars and out of the cage; he had to travel light in order to ride so fast and so far. It was the whole calculation, so to speak, of that innocent cunning, that the world was to be outflanked and outwitted by him, and be embarrassed about what to do with him.

You could not threaten to starve a man who was ever striving to fast. You could not ruin him and reduce him to beggary, for he was already a beggar. There was a very lukewarm satisfaction even in beating him with a stick, when he only indulged in little leaps and cries of joy because indignity was his only dignity. You could not put his head in a halter without the risk of putting it in a halo.

But one distinction between the old monks and the new friars counted especially in the matter of practicality and especially of promptitude. The old fraternities with their fixed habitations and enclosed existence had the limitations of ordinary householders. However simply they lived there must be a certain number of cells or a certain number of beds or at least a certain cubic space for a certain number of brothers; their numbers therefore depended on their land and building material. But since a man could become a Franciscan by merely promising to take his chance of eating berries in a lane or begging a crust from a kitchen, of sleeping under a hedge or sitting patiently on a doorstep, there was no economic reason why there should not be any number of such eccentric enthusiasts within any short period of time. It must also be remembered that the whole of this rapid development was full of a certain kind of democratic optimism that really was part of the personal character of St. Francis. His very asceticism was in one sense the height of optimism. He demanded a great ideal of human nature not because he despised it but rather because he trusted it. He was expecting a very great deal from the extraordinary men who followed him; but he was also expecting a good deal from the ordinary men to whom he sent them. He asked the laity for food as confidently as he asked the fraternity for fasting. But he counted on the hospitality of humanity because he really did regard every house as the house of a friend. He really did love and honour ordinary men and ordinary things; indeed we may say that he only sent out the extraordinary men to encourage men to be ordinary.

This paradox may be more exactly stated or explained when we come to deal with the very interesting matter of the Third Order, which was designed to assist ordinary men to be ordinary with an extraordinary exultation. The point at issue at present is the audacity and simplicity of the Franciscan plan for quartering its spiritual soldiery upon the population; not by force but by persuasion, and even by the persuasion of impotence. It was an act of confidence and therefore a compliment. It was completely successful. It was an example of something that clung about St. Francis always; a kind of tact that looked like luck because it was as simple and direct as a thunderbolt. There are many examples in his private relations of this sort of tactless tact; this surprise effected by striking at the heart of the matter. It is said that a young friar was suffering from a sort of sulks between morbidity and humility, common enough in youth and hero-worship, in which he had got it into his head that his hero hated or despised him. We can imagine how tactfully social diplomatists would steer clear of scenes and excitements, how cautiously psychologists would watch and handle such delicate cases. Francis suddenly walked up to the young man, who was of course secretive and silent as the grave, and said, "Be not troubled in your thoughts for you are dear to me, and even among the number of those who are most dear. You know that you are worthy of my friendship and society; therefore come to me, in confidence, whensoever you will, and from friendship learn faith." Exactly as he spoke to that morbid boy he spoke to all mankind. He always went to the point; he always seemed at once more right and more simple than the person he was speaking to. He seemed at once to be laying open his guard and yet lunging at the heart. Something in this attitude disarmed the world as it has never been disarmed again. He was better than other men; he was a benefactor of other men; and yet he was not hated. The world came into church by a newer and nearer door; and by friendship it learnt faith.

It was while the little knot of people at the Portiuncula was still small enough to gather in a small room that St. Francis resolved on his first important and even sensational stroke. It is said that there were only twelve Franciscans in the whole world when he decided to march, as it were, on Rome and found a Franciscan order. It would seem that this appeal to remote headquarters was not generally regarded as necessary; possibly something could have been done in a secondary way under the Bishop of Assisi and the local clergy. It would seem even more probable that people thought it somewhat unnecessary to trouble the supreme tribunal of Christendom about what a dozen chance men chose to call themselves. But Francis was obstinate and as it were blind on this point; and his brilliant blindness is exceedingly characteristic of him. A man satisfied with small things, or even in love with small things, he yet never felt quite as we do about the disproportion between small things and large. He never saw things to scale in our sense, but with a dizzy disproportion which makes the mind reel. Sometimes it seems merely out of drawing like a gaily coloured medieval map; and then again it seems to have escaped from everything like a short cut in the fourth dimension. He is said to have made a journey to interview the Emperor, throned among his armies under the eagle of the Holy Roman Empire, to intercede for the lives of certain little birds. He was quite capable of facing fifty emperors to intercede for one bird. He started out with two companions to convert the Mahomedan world. He started out with eleven companions to ask the Pope to make a new monastic world.

Innocent III, the great Pope, according to Bonaventura, was walking on the terrace of St. John Lateran, doubtless revolving the great political questions which troubled his reign, when there appeared abruptly before him a person in peasant costume whom he took to be some sort of shepherd. He appears to have got rid of the shepherd with all convenient speed; possibly he formed the opinion that the shepherd was mad. Anyhow he thought no more about it until, says the great Franciscan biographer, he dreamed that night a strange dream. He fancied that he saw the whole huge ancient temple of St. John Lateran, on whose high terraces he had walked so securely, leaning horribly and crooked against the sky as if all its domes and turrets were stooping before an earthquake. Then he looked again and saw that a human figure was holding it up like a living caryatid; and the figure was that of the ragged shepherd or peasant from whom he had turned away on the terrace. Whether this be a fact or figure it is a very true figure of the abrupt simplicity with which Francis won the attention and the favour of Rome. His first friend seems to have been the Cardinal Giovanni di San Paolo who pleaded for the Franciscan idea before a conclave of Cardinals summoned for the purpose. It is interesting to note that the doubts thrown upon it seem to have been chiefly doubts about whether the rule was not too hard for humanity, for the Catholic Church is always on the watch against excessive asceticism and its evils. Probably they meant, especially when they said it was unduly hard, that it was unduly dangerous. For a certain element that can only be called danger is what marks the innovation as compared with older institutions of the kind. In one sense indeed the friar was almost the opposite of the monk. The value of the old monasticism had been that there was not only an ethical but an economic repose. Out of that repose had come the works for which the world will never be sufficiently grateful, the preservation of the classics, the beginning of the Gothic, the schemes of science and philosophies, the illuminated manuscripts and the coloured glass. The whole point of a monk was that his economic affairs were settled for good; he knew where he would get his supper, though it was a very plain supper. But the whole point of a friar was that he did not know where he would get his supper. There was always a possibility that he might get no supper. There was an element of what would be called romance, as of the gipsy or adventurer. But there was also an element of potential tragedy, as of the tramp or the casual labourer. So the Cardinals of the thirteenth century were filled with compassion, seeing a few men entering of their own free will that estate to which the poor of the twentieth century are daily driven by cold coercion and moved on by the police.

Cardinal San Paolo seems to have argued more or less in this manner: it may be a hard life, but after all it is the life apparently described as ideal in the Gospel; make what compromises you think wise or humane about that ideal; but do not commit yourselves to saying that men shall *not* fulfil that ideal if they can. We shall see the importance of this argument when we come to the whole of that higher aspect of the life of St. Francis which may be called the Imitation of Christ. The upshot of the discussion was that the Pope gave his verbal approval to the project and promised a more definite endorsement, if the movement should grow to more considerable proportions. It is probable that Innocent, who was himself a man of no ordinary mentality, had very little doubt that it would do so; anyhow he was not left long in doubt before it did do so. The next passage in the history of the order is simply the story of more and more people flocking to its standard; and as has already been remarked, once it had begun to grow, it could in its nature grow much more quickly than any ordinary society requiring ordinary funds and public buildings. Even the return of the twelve pioneers from their papal audience seems to have been a sort of triumphal procession. In one place in particular, it is said, the whole population of a town, men, women and children, turned out, leaving their work and wealth and homes exactly as they stood and begging to be taken into the army of God on the spot. According to the story, it was on this occasion that St. Francis first foreshadowed his idea of the Third Order which enabled men to share in the movement without leaving the homes and habits of normal humanity. For the moment it is most important to regard this story as one example of the riot of conversion with which he was already filling all the roads of Italy. It was a world of wandering; friars perpetually coming and going in all the highways and byways, seeking to ensure that any man who met one of them by chance should have a spiritual adventure. The First Order of St. Francis had entered history.

This rough outline can only be rounded off here with some description of the Second and Third Orders, though they were founded later and at separate times. The former was an order for women and owed its existence, of course, to the beautiful friendship of St. Francis and St. Clare. There is no story about which even the most sympathetic critics of another creed have been more bewildered and misleading. For there is no story that more clearly turns on that simple test which I have taken as crucial throughout this criticism. I mean that what is the matter with these critics is that they will not believe that a heavenly love can be as real as an earthly love. The moment it is treated as real, like an earthly love, their whole riddle is easily resolved. A girl of seventeen, named Clare and belonging to one of the noble families of Assisi, was filled with an enthusiasm for the conventual life; and Francis helped her to escape from her home and to take up the conventual life. If we like to put it so, he helped her to elope into the cloister, defying her parents as he had defied his father. Indeed the scene had many of the elements of a regular romantic elopement; for she escaped through a hole in the wall, fled through a wood and was received at midnight by the light of torches. Even Mrs. Oliphant, in her fine and delicate study of St. Francis, calls it "an incident which we can hardly record with satisfaction."

Now about that incident I will here only say this. If it had really been a romantic elopement and the girl had become a bride instead of a nun, practically the whole modern world would have made her a heroine. If the action of the Friar towards Clare had been the action of the Friar towards Juliet, everybody would be sympathising with her exactly as they sympathise with Juliet. It is not conclusive to say that Clare was only seventeen. Juliet was only fourteen. Girls married and boys fought in battles at such early ages in medieval times; and a girl of seventeen in the thirteenth century was certainly old enough to know her own mind. There cannot be the shadow of a doubt, for any sane person considering subsequent events, that St. Clare did know her own mind. But the point for the moment is that modern romanticism entirely encourages such defiance of parents when it is done in the name of romantic love. For it knows that romantic love is a reality, but it does not know that divine love is a reality. There may have been something to be said for the parents of Clare; there may have been something to be said for Peter Bernardone. So there may have been a great deal to be said for the Montagues or the Capulets; but the modern world does not want it said; and does not say it. The fact is that as soon as we assume for a moment as a hypothesis, what St. Francis and St. Clare assumed all the time as an absolute, that there is a direct divine relation more glorious than any romance, the story of St. Clare's elopement is simply a romance with a happy ending; and St. Francis is the St. George or knight-errant who gave it a happy ending. And seeing that some millions of men and women have lived and died treating this relation as a reality, a man is not much of a philosopher if he cannot even treat it as a hypothesis.

For the rest, we may at least assume that no friend of what is called the emancipation of women will regret the revolt of St. Clare. She did most truly, in the modern jargon, live her own life, the life that she herself wanted to lead, as distinct from the life into which parental commands and conventional arrangements would have forced her. She became the foundress of a great feminine movement which still profoundly affects the world; and her place is with the powerful women of history. It is not clear that she would have been so great or so useful if she had made a runaway match, or even stopped at home and made a *mariage de convenance*. So much any sensible man may well say considering the matter merely from the outside; and I have no intention of attempting to consider it from the inside. If a man may well doubt whether he is worthy to write a word about St. Francis, he will certainly want words better than his own to speak of the friendship of St. Francis and St. Clare. I have often remarked that the mysteries of this story are best expressed symbolically in certain silent attitudes and actions. And I know no better symbol than that found by the felicity of popular legend, which says that one night the people of Assissi thought the trees and the holy house were on fire, and rushed up to extinguish the conflagration. But they found all quiet within, where St. Francis broke bread with St. Clare at one of their rare meetings, and talked of the love of God. It would be hard to find a more imaginative image for some sort of utterly pure and disembodied passion, than that red halo round the unconscious figures on the hill; a flame feeding on nothing and setting the very air on fire.

But if the Second Order was the memorial of such an unearthly love, the Third Order was as solid a memorial of a very solid sympathy with earthly loves and earthly lives. The whole of this feature in Catholic life, the lay orders in touch with clerical orders, is very little understood in Protestant countries and very little allowed for in Protestant history. The vision which has been so faintly suggested in these pages has never been confined to monks or even to friars. It has been an inspiration to innumerable crowds of ordinary married men and women; living lives like our own, only entirely different. That morning glory which St. Francis spread over earth and sky has lingered as a secret sunshine under a multitude of roofs and in a multitude of rooms. In societies like ours nothing is known of such a Franciscan following. Nothing is known of such obscure followers; and if possible less is known of the well-known followers. If we imagine passing us in the street a pageant of the Third Order of St. Francis, the famous figures would surprise us more than the strange ones. For us it would be like the unmasking of some mighty secret society. There rides St. Louis, the great king, lord of the higher justice whose scales hang crooked in favour of the poor. There is Dante crowned with laurel, the poet who in his life of passions sang the praises of the Lady Poverty, whose grey garment is lined with purple and all glorious within. All sorts of great names from the most recent and rationalistic centuries would stand revealed; the great Galvani, for instance, the father of all electricity, the magician who has made so many modern systems of stars and sounds. So various a following would alone be enough to prove that St. Francis had no lack of sympathy with normal men, if the whole of his own life did not prove it.

But in fact his life did prove it, and that possibly in a more subtle sense. There is, I fancy, some truth in the hint of one of his modern biographers, that even his natural passions were singularly normal and even noble, in the sense of turning towards things not unlawful in themselves but only unlawful for him. Nobody ever lived of whom we could less fitly use the word "regret" than Francis of Assisi. Though there was much that was romantic, there was nothing in the least sentimental about his mood. It was not melancholy enough for that. He was of far too swift and rushing a temper to be troubled with doubts and reconsiderations about the race he ran; though he had any amount of self-reproach about not running faster. But it is true, one suspects, that when he wrestled with the devil, as every man must to be worth calling a man, the whispers referred mostly to those healthy instincts that he would have approved for others; they bore no resemblance to that ghastly painted paganism which sent its demoniac courtesans to plague St. Anthony in the desert. If St. Francis had only pleased himself, it would have been with simpler pleasures. He was moved to love rather than lust, and by nothing wilder than wedding-bells. It is suggested in that strange story of how he defied the devil by making images in the snow, and crying out that these sufficed him for a wife and family. It is suggested in the saying he used when disclaiming any security from sin, "I may yet have children"; almost as if it was of the children rather than the woman that he dreamed. And this, if it be true, gives a final touch to the truth about his character. There was so much about him of the spirit of the morning, so much that was curiously young and clean, that even what was bad in him was good. As it was said of others that the light in their body was darkness, so it may be said of this luminous spirit that the very shadows in his soul were of light. Evil itself could not come to him save in the form of a forbidden good; and he could only be tempted by a sacrament.

# VIII

# THE MIRROR OF CHRIST

No man who has been given the freedom of the Faith is likely to fall into those hole-and-corner extravagances in which later degenerate Franciscans, or rather Fraticelli, sought to concentrate entirely on St. Francis as a second Christ, the creator of a new gospel. In fact any such notion makes nonsense of every motive in the man's life: for no man would reverently magnify what he was meant to rival, or only profess to follow what he existed to supplant. On the contrary, as will appear later, this little study would rather specially insist that it was really the papal sagacity that saved the great Franciscan movement for the whole world and the universal Church, and prevented it from petering out as that sort of stale and second-rate sect that is called a new religion. Everything that is written here must be understood not only as distinct from but diametrically opposed to the idolatry of the Fraticelli. The difference between Christ and St. Francis was the difference between the Creator and the creature; and certainly no creature was ever so conscious of that colossal contrast as St. Francis himself. But subject to this understanding, it is perfectly true and it is vitally important that Christ was the pattern on which St. Francis sought to fashion himself; and that at many points their human and historical lives were even curiously coincident; and above all, that compared to most of us at least St. Francis is a most sublime approximation to his Master, and, even in being an intermediary and a reflection, is a splendid and yet a merciful Mirror of Christ. And this truth suggests another, which I think has hardly been noticed; but which happens to be a highly forcible argument for the authority of Christ being continuous in the Catholic Church.

Cardinal Newman wrote in his liveliest controversial work a sentence that might be a model of what we mean by saying that his creed tends to lucidity and logical courage. In speaking of the ease with which truth may be made to look like its own shadow or sham, he said, "And if Antichrist is like Christ, Christ I suppose is like Antichrist." Mere religious sentiment might well be shocked at the end of the sentence; but nobody could object to it except the logician who said that Caesar and Pompey were very much alike, especially Pompey. It may give a much milder shock if I say here, what most of us have forgotten, that if St. Francis was like Christ, Christ was to that extent like St. Francis. And my present point is that it is really very enlightening to realise that Christ was like St. Francis. What I mean is this; that if men find certain riddles and hard sayings in the story of Galilee, and if they find the answers to those riddles in the story of Assisi, it really does show that a secret has been handed down in one religious tradition and no other. It shows that the casket that was locked in Palestine can be unlocked in Umbria; for the Church is the keeper of the keys.

Now in truth while it has always seemed natural to explain St. Francis in the light of Christ, it has not occurred to many people to explain Christ in the light of St. Francis. Perhaps the word "light" is not here the proper metaphor; but the same truth is admitted in the accepted metaphor of the mirror. St. Francis is the mirror of Christ rather as the moon is the mirror of the sun. The moon is much smaller than the sun, but it is also much nearer to us; and being less vivid it is more visible. Exactly in the same sense St. Francis is nearer to us, and being a mere man like ourselves is in that sense more imaginable. Being necessarily less of a mystery, he does not, for us, so much open his mouth in mysteries.

Yet as a matter of fact, many minor things that seem mysteries in the mouth of Christ would seem merely characteristic paradoxes in the mouth of St. Francis. It seems natural to re-read the more remote incidents with the help of the more recent ones. It is a truism to say that Christ lived before Christianity; and it follows that as an historical figure He is a figure in heathen history. I mean that the medium in which He moved was not the medium of Christendom but of the old pagan empire; and from that alone, not to mention the distance of time, it follows that His circumstances are more alien to us than those of an Italian monk such as we might meet even to-day. I suppose the most authoritative commentary can hardly be certain of the current or conventional weight of all His words or phrases; of which of them would then have seemed a common allusion and which a strange fancy. This archaic setting has left many of the sayings standing like hieroglyphics and subject to many and peculiar individual interpretations. Yet it is true of almost any of them that if we simply translate them into the Umbrian dialect of the first Franciscans, they would seem like any other part of the Franciscan story; doubtless in one sense fantastic, but quite familiar. All sorts of critical controversies have revolved round the passage which bids men consider the lilies of the field and copy them in taking no thought for the morrow. The sceptic has alternated between telling us to be true Christians and do it, and explaining that it is impossible to do. When he is a communist as well as an atheist, he is generally doubtful whether to blame us for preaching what is impracticable or for not instantly putting it into practice. I am not going to discuss here the point of ethics and economics; I merely remark that even those who are puzzled at the saying of Christ would hardly pause in accepting it as a saying of St. Francis. Nobody would be surprised to find that he had said, "I beseech you, little brothers, that you be as wise as Brother Daisy and Brother Dandelion; for never do they lie awake thinking of to-morrow, yet they have gold crowns like kings and emperors or like Charlemagne in all his glory." Even more bitterness and bewilderment has arisen about the command to turn the other cheek and to give the coat to the robber who has taken the cloak. It is widely held to imply the wickedness of war among nations; about which, in itself, not a word seems to have been said. Taken thus literally and universally, it much more clearly implies the wickedness of all law and government. Yet there are many prosperous peacemakers who are much more shocked at the idea of using the brute force of soldiers against a powerful foreigner than they are at using the brute force of policemen against a poor fellow-citizen. Here again I am content to point out that the paradox becomes perfectly human and probable if addressed by Francis to Franciscans. Nobody would be surprised to read that Brother Juniper did then run after the thief that had stolen his hood, beseeching him to take his gown also; for so St. Francis had commanded him. Nobody would be surprised if St. Francis told a young noble, about to be admitted to his company, that so far from pursuing a brigand to recover his shoes, he ought to pursue him to make him a present of his stockings. We may like or not the atmosphere these things imply; but we know what atmosphere they do imply. We recognise a certain note as natural and clear as the note of a bird; the note of St. Francis. There is in it something of gentle mockery of the very idea of possessions; something of a hope of disarming the enemy by generosity; something of a humorous sense of bewildering the worldly with the unexpected; something of the joy of carrying an enthusiastic conviction to a logical extreme. But anyhow we have no difficulty in recognising it, if we have read any of the literature of the Little Brothers and the movement that began in Assisi. It seems reasonable to infer that if it was this spirit that made such strange things possible in Umbria, it was the same spirit that made them possible in Palestine. If we hear the same unmistakable note and sense the same indescribable savour in two things at such a distance from each other, it seems natural to suppose that the case that is more remote from our experience was like the case that is closer in our experience. As the thing is explicable on the assumption that Francis was speaking to Franciscans, it is not an irrational explanation to suggest that Christ also was speaking to some dedicated band that had much the same function as Franciscans. In other words, it seems only natural to hold, as the Catholic Church has held, that these counsels of perfection were part of a particular vocation to astonish and awaken the world. But in any case it is important to note that when we do find these particular features, with their seemingly fantastic fitness, reappearing after more than a thousand years, we find them produced by the same religious system which claims continuity and authority from the scenes in which they first appeared. Any number of philosophies will repeat the platitudes of Christianity. But it is the ancient Church that can again startle the world with the paradoxes of Christianity. *Ubi Petrus ibi Franciscus.*[1]

But if we understand that it was truly under the inspiration of his divine Master that St. Francis did these merely quaint or eccentric acts of charity, we must understand that it was under the same inspiration that he did acts of self-denial and austerity. It is clear that these more or less playful parables of the love of men were conceived after a close study of the Sermon on the Mount. But it is evident that he made an even closer study of the silent sermon on that other mountain; the mountain that was called Golgotha. Here again he

[1] "Where Peter is, there is Francis."

was speaking the strict historical truth, when he said that in fasting or suffering humiliation he was but trying to do something of what Christ did; and here again it seems probable that as the same truth appears at the two ends of a chain of tradition, the tradition has preserved the truth. But the import of this fact at the moment affects the next phase in the personal history of the man himself.

For as it becomes clearer that his great communal scheme is an accomplished fact and past the peril of an early collapse, as it becomes evident that there already is such a thing as an Order of the Friars Minor, this more individual and intense ambition of St. Francis emerges more and more. So soon as he certainly has followers, he does not compare himself with his followers, towards whom he might appear as a master; he compares himself more and more with his Master, towards whom he appears only as a servant. This, it may be said in passing, is one of the moral and even practical conveniences of the ascetical privilege. Every other sort of superiority may be superciliousness. But the saint is never supercilious, for he is always by hypothesis in the presence of a superior. The objection to an aristocracy is that it is a priesthood without a god. But in any case the service to which St. Francis had committed himself was one which, about this time, he conceived more and more in terms of sacrifice and crucifixion. He was full of the sentiment that he had not suffered enough to be worthy even to be a distant follower of his suffering God. And this passage in his history may really be roughly summarised as the Search for Martyrdom.

This was the ultimate idea in the remarkable business of his expedition among the Saracens in Syria. There were indeed other elements in his conception, which are worthy of more intelligent understanding than they have often received. His idea, of course, was to bring the Crusades in a double sense to their end; that is, to reach their conclusion and to achieve their purpose. Only he wished to do it by conversion and not by conquest; that is, by intellectual and not material means. The modern mind is hard to please; and it generally calls the way of Godfrey ferocious and the way of Francis fanatical. That is, it calls any moral method unpractical, when it has just called any practical method immoral. But the idea of St. Francis was far from being a fanatical or necessarily even an unpractical idea; though perhaps he saw the problem as rather too simple, lacking the learning of his great inheritor Raymond Lully,[2] who understood more but has been quite as little understood. The way he approached the matter was indeed highly personal and peculiar; but that was true of almost everything he did. It was in one way a simple idea, as most of his ideas were simple ideas. But it was not a silly idea; there was a great deal to be said for it and it might have succeeded. It was, of course, simply the idea that it is better to create Christians than to destroy Moslems. If Islam had been converted, the world would have been immeasurably more united and happy; for one thing, three quarters of the wars of modern history would never have taken place. It was not absurd to suppose that this might be effected, without military force, by missionaries who were also martyrs. The Church had conquered Europe in that way and may yet conquer Asia or Africa in that way. But when all this is allowed for, there is still another sense in which St. Francis was not thinking of Martyrdom as a means to an end, but almost as an end in itself; in the sense that to him the supreme end was to come closer to the example of Christ.

[2] Raymond Lully (c. 1232–1316). Known as "Doctor Illuminatus" he was a Spanish Franciscan theologian, philosopher and author. Lully sought to re-establish the unification of truth in theology and philosophy in opposition to the "double-truth" theory of rationalists such as Boethius and Siger of Brabant.

Through all his plunging and restless days ran the refrain: I have not suffered enough; I have not sacrificed enough; I am not yet worthy even of the shadow of the crown of thorns. He wandered about the valleys of the world looking for the hill that has the outline of a skull.

A little while before his final departure for the East a vast and triumphant assembly of the whole order had been held near the Portiuncula; and called The Assembly of the Straw Huts, from the manner in which that mighty army encamped in the field. Tradition says that it was on this occasion that St. Francis met St. Dominic for the first and last time. It also says, what is probable enough, that the practical spirit of the Spaniard was almost appalled at the devout irresponsibility of the Italian, who had assembled such a crowd without organising a commissariat. Dominic the Spaniard was, like nearly every Spaniard, a man with the mind of a soldier. His charity took the practical form of provision and preparation. But, apart from the disputes about faith which such incidents open, he probably did not understand in this case the power of mere popularity produced by mere personality. In all his leaps in the dark, Francis had an extraordinary faculty of falling on his feet. The whole countryside came down like a landslide to provide food and drink for this sort of pious picnic. Peasants brought waggons of wine and game; great nobles walked about doing the work of footmen. It was a very real victory for the Franciscan spirit of a reckless faith not only in God but in man. Of course there is much doubt and dispute about the whole story and the whole relation of Francis and Dominic; and the story of the Assembly of the Straw Huts is told from the Franciscan side. But the alleged meeting is worth mentioning, precisely because it was immediately before St. Francis set forth on his bloodless crusade that he is said to have met St. Dominic, who has been so much criticised for lending himself to a more bloody one. There is no space in this little book to explain how St. Francis, as much as St. Dominic, would ultimately have defended the defence of Christian unity by arms. Indeed it would need a large book instead of a little book to develop that point alone from its first principles. For the modern mind is merely a blank about the philosophy of toleration; and the average agnostic of recent times has really had no notion of what he meant by religious liberty and equality. He took his own ethics as self-evident and enforced them; such as decency or the error of the Adamite heresy. Then he was horribly shocked if he heard of anybody else, Moslem or Christian, taking *his* ethics as self-evident and enforcing *them*; such as reverence or the error of the Atheist heresy. And then he wound up by taking all this lop-sided illogical deadlock, of the unconscious meeting the unfamiliar, and called it the liberality of his own mind. Medieval men thought that if a social system was founded on a certain idea it must fight for that idea, whether it was as simple as Islam or as carefully balanced as Catholicism. Modern men really think the same thing, as is clear when communists attack their ideas of property. Only they do not think it so clearly, because they have not really thought out their idea of property. But while it is probable that St. Francis would have reluctantly agreed with St. Dominic that war for the truth was right in the last resort, it is certain that St. Dominic did enthusiastically agree with St. Francis that it was far better to prevail by persuasion and enlightenment if it were possible. St. Dominic devoted himself much more to persuading than to persecuting; but there was a difference in the methods simply because there was a difference in the men. About everything St. Francis did there was something that was in a good sense childish, and, even in a good sense wilful. He threw himself into things abruptly, as if they had just occurred to him. He made a dash for his Mediterranean enterprise with something of the air of a schoolboy running away to sea.

In the first act of that attempt he characteristically distinguished himself by becoming the Patron Saint of Stowaways. He never thought of waiting for introductions or bargains or any of the considerable backing that he already had from rich and responsible people. He simply saw a boat and threw himself into it, as he threw himself into everything else. It has all that air of running a race which makes his whole life read like an escapade or even literally an escape. He lay like lumber among the cargo, with one companion whom he had swept with him in his rush; but the voyage was apparently unfortunate and erratic and ended in an enforced return to Italy. Apparently it was after this first false start that the great re-union took place at the Portiuncula, and between this and the final Syrian journey there was also an attempt to meet the Moslem menace by preaching to the Moors in Spain. In Spain indeed several of the first Franciscans had already succeeded gloriously in being martyred. But the great Francis still went about stretching out his arms for such torments and desiring that agony in vain. No one would have said more readily than he that he was probably less like Christ than those others who had already found their Calvary; but the thing remained with him like a secret; the strangest of the sorrows of man.

His later voyage was more successful, so far as arriving at the scene of operations was concerned. He arrived at the headquarters of the Crusade which was in front of the besieged city of Damietta, and went on in his rapid and solitary fashion to seek the headquarters of the Saracens. He succeeded in obtaining an interview with the Sultan; and it was at that interview that he evidently offered, and as some say proceeded, to fling himself into the fire as a divine ordeal, defying the Moslem religious teachers to do the same. It is quite certain that he would have done so at a moment's notice. Indeed throwing himself into the fire was hardly more desperate, in any case, than throwing himself among the weapons and tools of torture of a horde of fanatical Mahomedans and asking them to renounce Mahomet. It is said further that the Mahomedan muftis showed some coldness towards the proposed competition, and that one of them quietly withdrew while it was under discussion; which would also appear credible. But for whatever reason Francis evidently returned as freely as he came. There may be something in the story of the individual impression produced on the Sultan, which the narrator represents as a sort of secret conversion. There may be something in the suggestion that the holy man was unconsciously protected among half-barbarous orientals by the halo of sanctity that is supposed in such places to surround an idiot. There is probably as much or more in the more generous explanation of that graceful though capricious courtesy and compassion which mingled with wilder things in the stately Soldans of the type and tradition of Saladin. Finally, there is perhaps something in the suggestion that the tale of St. Francis might be told as a sort of ironic tragedy and comedy called The Man Who Could Not Get Killed. Men liked him too much for himself to let him die for his faith; and the man was received instead of the message. But all these are only converging guesses at a great effort that is hard to judge, because it broke off short like the beginnings of a great bridge that might have united East and West, and remains one of the great might-have-beens of history.

Meanwhile the great movement in Italy was making giant strides. Backed now by papal authority as well as popular enthusiasm, and creating a kind of comradeship among all classes, it had started a riot of reconstruction on all sides of religious and social life; and especially began to express itself in that enthusiasm for building which is the mark of all the resurrections of Western Europe. There had notably been established at Bologna a magnificent mission house of the Friars Minor; and a vast body of them and their sympathisers surrounded it with a chorus of acclamation. Their unanimity had a strange interruption. One man alone in that crowd was seen to turn and suddenly denounce the building as if it had been a Babylonian temple; demanding indignantly since when the Lady Poverty had thus been insulted with the luxury of palaces. It was Francis, a wild figure, returned from his Eastern Crusade; and it was the first and last time that he spoke in wrath to his children.

A word must be said later about this serious division of sentiment and policy, about which many Franciscans, and to some extent Francis himself, parted company with the more moderate policy which ultimately prevailed. At this point we need only note it as another shadow fallen upon his spirit after his disappointment in the desert; and as in some sense the prelude to the next phase of his career, which is the most isolated and the most mysterious. It is true that everything about this episode seems to be covered with some cloud of dispute, even including its date; some writers putting it much earlier in the narrative than this. But whether or no it was chronologically it was certainly logically the culmination of the story, and may best be indicated here. I say indicated for it must be a matter of little more than indication; the thing being a mystery both in the higher moral and the more trivial historical sense. Anyhow the conditions of the affair seem to have been these. Francis and a young companion, in the course of their common wandering, came past a great castle all lighted up with the festivities attending a son of the house receiving the honour of knighthood. This aristocratic mansion, which took its name from Monte Feltro, they entered in their beautiful and casual fashion and began to give their own sort of good news. There were some at least who listened to the saint "as if he had been an angel of God"; among them a gentleman named Orlando of Chiusi, who had great lands in Tuscany, and who proceeded to do St. Francis a singular and somewhat picturesque act of courtesy. He gave him a mountain; a thing somewhat unique among the gifts of the world. Presumably the Franciscan rule which forbade a man to accept money had made no detailed provision about accepting mountains. Nor indeed did St. Francis accept it save as he accepted everything, as a temporary convenience rather than a personal possession; but he turned it into a sort of refuge for the eremitical rather than the monastic life; he retired there when he wished for a life of prayer and fasting which he did not ask even his closest friends to follow. This was Alverno of the Apennines, and upon its peak there rests for ever a dark cloud that has a rim or halo of glory.

What it was exactly that happened there may never be known. The matter has been, I believe, a subject of dispute among the most devout students of the saintly life as well as between such students and others of the more secular sort. It may be that St. Francis never spoke to a soul on the subject; it would be highly characteristic, and it is certain in any case that he said very little; I think he is only alleged to have spoken of it to one man. Subject however to such truly sacred doubts, I will confess that to me personally this one solitary and indirect report that has come down to us reads very like the report of something real; of some of those things that are more real than what we call daily realities. Even something as it were double and bewildering about the image seems to carry the impression of an experience shaking the senses; as does the passage in Revelations about the supernatural creatures full of eyes. It would seem that St. Francis beheld the heavens above him occupied by a vast winged being like a seraph spread out like a cross. There seems some mystery about whether the winged figure was itself crucified as in the posture of crucifixion, or whether it merely enclosed in its frame of wings some colossal crucifix. But it seems clear that there was some question of the former impression; for St. Bonaventura distinctly says that St. Francis doubted how a seraph could be crucified, since those awful and ancient principalities were without the infirmity of the Passion. St. Bonaventura suggests that the seeming contradiction may have meant that St. Francis was to be crucified as a spirit since he could not be crucified as a man; but whatever the meaning of the vision, the general idea of it is very vivid and overwhelming. St. Francis saw above him, filling the whole heavens, some vast immemorial unthinkable power, ancient like the Ancient of Days, whose calm men had conceived under the forms of winged bulls or monstrous cherubim, and all that winged wonder was in pain like a wounded bird. This seraphic suffering, it is said, pierced his soul with a sword of grief and pity; it may be inferred that some sort of mounting agony accompanied the ecstasy. Finally after some fashion the apocalypse faded from the sky and the agony within subsided; and silence and the natural air filled the morning twilight and settled slowly in the purple chasms and cleft abysses of the Apennines.

The head of the solitary sank, amid all that relaxation and quiet in which time can drift by with the sense of something ended and complete; and as he stared downwards, he saw the marks of nails in his own hands.

# IX

# MIRACLES AND DEATH

The tremendous story of the Stigmata of St. Francis, which was the end of the last chapter, was in some sense the end of his life. In a logical sense, it would have been the end even if it had happened at the beginning. But truer traditions refer it to a later date and suggest that his remaining days on the earth had something about them of the lingering of a shadow. Whether St. Bonaventura was right in his hint that St. Francis saw in that seraphic vision something against like a vast mirror of his own soul, that could at least suffer like an angel though not like a god, or whether it expressed under an imagery more primitive and colossal than common Christian art the primary paradox of the death of God, it is evident from its traditional consequences that it was meant for a crown and for a seal. It seems to have been after seeing this vision that he began to go blind.

But the incident has another and much less important place in this rough and limited outline. It is the natural occasion for considering briefly and collectively all the facts or fables of another aspect of the life of St. Francis; an aspect, which is, I will not say more disputable, but certainly more disputed. I mean all that mass of testimony and tradition that concerns his miraculous powers and supernatural experiences, with which it would have been easy to stud and bejewel every page of the story; only that certain circumstances necessary to the conditions of this narration make it better to gather, somewhat hastily, all such jewels into a heap.

I have here adopted this course in order to make allowance for a prejudice. It is indeed to a great extent a prejudice of the past; a prejudice that is plainly disappearing in days of greater enlightenment, and especially of a greater range of scientific experiment and knowledge. But it is a prejudice that is still tenacious in many of an older generation and still traditional in many of the younger. I mean, of course, what used to be called the belief "that miracles do not happen," as I think Matthew Arnold expressed it, in expressing the standpoint of so many of our Victorian uncles and great-uncles. In other words it was the remains of that sceptical simplification by which some of the philosophers of the early eighteenth century had popularised the impression (for a very short time) that we had discovered the regulations of the cosmos like the works of a clock, of so very simple a clock that it was possible to distinguish almost at a glance what could or could not have happened in human experience. It should be remembered that these real sceptics, of the golden age of scepticism, were quite as scornful of the first fancies of science as of the lingering legends of religion. Voltaire, when he was told that a fossil fish had been found on the peaks of the Alps, laughed openly at the tale and said that some fasting monk or hermit had dropped his fish-bones there; possibly in order to effect another monkish fraud. Everybody knows by this time that science has had its revenge on scepticism. The border between the credible and the incredible has not only become once more as vague as in any barbaric twilight; but the credible is obviously increasing and the incredible shrinking. A man in Voltaire's time did not know what miracle he would next have to throw up. A man in our time does not know what miracle he will next have to swallow.

But long before these things had happened, in those days of my boyhood when I first saw the figure of St. Francis far away in the distance and drawing me even at that distance, in those Victorian days which did seriously separate the virtues from the miracles of the saints—even in those days I could not help feeling vaguely puzzled about how this method could be applied to history. Even then I did not quite understand, and even now I do not quite understand, on what principle one is to pick and choose in the chronicles of the past which seem to be all of a piece. All our knowledge of certain historical periods, and notably of the whole medieval period, rests on certain connected chronicles written by people who are some of them nameless and all of them dead, who cannot in any case be cross-examined and cannot in some cases be corroborated. I have never been quite clear about the nature of the right by which historians accepted masses of detail from them as definitely true, and suddenly denied their truthfulness when one detail was preternatural. I do not complain of their being sceptics; I am puzzled about why the sceptics are not more sceptical. I can understand their saying that these details would never have been included in a chronicle except by lunatics or liars; but in that case the only inference is that the chronicle was written by liars or lunatics. They will write for instance: "Monkish fanaticism found it easy to spread the report that miracles were already being worked at the tomb of Thomas Becket." Why should they not say equally well, "Monkish fanaticism found it easy to spread the slander that four knights from King Henry's court had assassinated Thomas Becket in the cathedral"? They would write something like this: "The credulity of the age readily believed that Joan of Arc had been inspired to point out the Dauphin although he was in disguise." Why should they not write on the same principle: "The credulity of the age was such as to suppose that an obscure peasant girl could get an audience at the court of the Dauphin"? And so, in the present case, when they tell us there is a wild story that St. Francis flung himself into the fire and emerged scathless, upon what precise principle are they forbidden to tell us of a wild story that St. Francis flung himself into the camp of the ferocious

Moslems and returned safe? I only ask for information; for I do not see the rationale of the thing myself. I will undertake to say there was not a word written of St. Francis by any contemporary who was himself incapable of believing and telling a miraculous story. Perhaps it is all monkish fables and there never was any St. Francis or any St. Thomas Becket or any Joan of Arc. This is undoubtedly a *reductio ad absurdum*; but it is a *reductio ad absurdum* of the view which thought all miracles absurd.

And in abstract logic this method of selection would lead to the wildest absurdities. An intrinsically incredible story could only mean that the authority was unworthy of credit. It could not mean that other parts of his story must be received with complete credulity. If somebody said he had met a man in yellow trousers, who proceeded to jump down his own throat, we should not exactly take our Bible oath or be burned at the stake for the statement that he wore yellow trousers. If somebody claimed to have gone up in a blue balloon and found that the moon was made of green cheese, we should not exactly take an affidavit that the balloon was blue any more than that the moon was green. And the really logical conclusion from throwing doubts on all tales like the miracles of St. Francis was to throw doubts on the existence of men like St. Francis. And there really was a modern moment, a sort of high-water mark of insane scepticism, when this sort of thing was really said or done. People used to go about saying that there was no such person as St. Patrick; which is every bit as much of a human and historical howler as saying there was no such person as St. Francis. There was a time, for instance, when the madness of mythological explanation had dissolved a large part of solid history under the universal and luxuriant warmth and radiance of the Sun-Myth. I believe that that particular sun has already set, but there have been any number of moons and meteors to take its place.

St. Francis, of course, would make a magnificent Sun-Myth. How could anybody miss the chance of being a Sun-Myth when he is actually best known by a song called "The Canticle of the Sun"? It is needless to point out that the fire in Syria was the dawn in the East and the bleeding wounds in Tuscany the sunset in the West. I could expound this theory at considerable length; only, as so often happens to such fine theorists, another and more promising theory occurs to me. I cannot think how everybody, including myself, can have overlooked the fact that the whole tale of St. Francis is of Totemistic origin. It is unquestionably a tale that simply swarms with totems. The Franciscan woods are as full of them as any Red Indian fable. Francis is made to call himself an ass, because in the original mythos Francis was merely the name given to the real four-footed donkey, afterwards vaguely evolved into a half-human god or hero. And that, no doubt, is why I used to feel that the Brother Wolf and Sister Bird of St. Francis were somehow like the Brer Fox and Sis Cow of Uncle Remus. Some say there is an innocent stage of infancy in which we do really believe that a cow talked or a fox made a tar baby. Anyhow there is an innocent period of intellectual growth in which we do sometimes really believe that St. Patrick was a Sun-Myth or St. Francis a Totem. But for the most of us both those phases of paradise are past.

As I shall suggest in a moment, there is one sense in which we can for practical purposes distinguish between probable and improbable things in such a story. It is not so much a question of cosmic criticism about the nature of the event as of literary criticism about the nature of the story. Some stories are told much more seriously than others. But apart from this, I shall not attempt here any definite differentiation between them. I shall not do so for a practical reason affecting the utility of the proceeding; I mean the fact that in a practical sense the whole of this matter is again in the melting pot, from which many things may emerge moulded into what rationalism would have called monsters. The fixed points of faith and philosophy do indeed remain always the same. Whether a man believes that fire in one case could fail to burn, depends on why he thinks it generally does burn. If it burns nine sticks out of ten because it is its nature or doom to do so, then it will burn the tenth stick as well. If it burns nine sticks because it is the will of God that it should, then it might be the will of God that the tenth should be unburned. Nobody can get behind that fundamental difference about the reason of things; and it is as rational for a theist to believe in miracles as for an atheist to disbelieve in them. In other words there is only one intelligent reason why a man does not believe in miracles and that is that he does believe in materialism. But these fixed points of faith and philosophy are things for a theoretical work and have no particular place here. And in the matter of history and biography, which have their place here, nothing is fixed at all. The world is in a welter of the possible and impossible, and nobody knows what will be the next scientific hypothesis to support some ancient superstition. Three-quarters of the miracles attributed to St. Francis would already be explained by psychologists, not indeed as a Catholic explains them, but as a materialist must necessarily refuse to explain them. There is one whole department of the miracles of St. Francis; the miracles of healing. What is the good of a superior sceptic throwing them away as unthinkable, at the moment when faith-healing is already a big booming Yankee business like Barnum's Show? There is another whole department analogous to the tales of Christ "perceiving men's thoughts." What is the use of censoring them and blacking them out because they are marked "miracles," when thought-reading is already a parlour game like musical chairs? There is another whole department, to be studied separately if such scientific study were possible, of the well-attested wonders worked from his relics and fragmentary possessions. What is the use of dismissing all that as inconceivable, when even these common psychical parlour tricks turn perpetually upon touching some familiar object or holding in the hand some personal possession? I do not believe, of course, that these tricks are of the same type as the good works of the saint; save perhaps in the sense of *Diabolus simius Dei.*[1] But it is not a question of what I believe and why, but of what the sceptic disbelieves and why. And the moral for the practical biographer and historian is that he must wait till things settle down a little more, before he claims to disbelieve anything.

This being so he can choose between two courses; and not without some hesitation, I have here chosen between them. The best and boldest course would be to tell the whole story in a straightforward way, miracles and all, as the original historians told it. And to this sane and simple course the new historians will probably have to return. But it must be remembered that this book is avowedly only an introduction to St. Francis or the study of St. Francis. Those who need an introduction are in their nature strangers. With them the object is to get them to listen to St. Francis at all; and in doing so it is perfectly legitimate so to arrange the order of the facts that the familiar come before the unfamiliar and those they can at once understand before those they have a difficulty in understanding. I should only be too thankful if this thin and scratchy sketch contains a line or two that attracts men to study St. Francis for themselves; and if they do study him for themselves, they will soon find that the supernatural part of the story seems quite as natural as the rest. But it was necessary that my outline should be a merely

[1] "The Devil an ape of God."

human one, since I was only presenting his claim on all humanity, including sceptical humanity. I therefore adopted the alternative course, of showing first that nobody but a born fool could fail to realise that Francis of Assisi was a very real historical human being; and then summarising briefly in this chapter the superhuman powers that were certainly a part of that history and humanity. It only remains to say a few words about some distinctions that may reasonably be observed in the matter by any man of any views; that he may not confuse the point and climax of the saint's life with the fancies or rumours that were really only the hinges of his reputation.

There is so immense a mass of legends and anecdotes about St. Francis of Assisi, and there are so many admirable compilations that cover nearly all of them, that I have been compelled within these narrow limits to pursue a somewhat narrow policy; that of following one line of explanation and only mentioning one anecdote here or there because it illustrates that explanation. If this is true about all the legends and stories, it is especially true about the miraculous legends and the supernatural stories. If we were to take some stories as they stand, we should receive a rather bewildered impression that the biography contains more supernatural events than natural ones. Now it is clean against Catholic tradition, co-incident in so many points with common sense, to suppose that this is really the proportion of these things in practical human life. Moreover, even considered as supernatural or preternatural stories, they obviously fall into certain different classes, not so much by our experience of miracles as by our experience of stories. Some of them have the character of fairy stories, in their form even more than their incident. They are obviously tales told by the fire to peasants or the children of peasants, under conditions in which nobody thinks he is propounding a religious doctrine to be received or rejected, but only rounding off a story in the most symmetrical way, according to that sort of decorative scheme or pattern that runs through all fairy stories. Others are obviously in their form most emphatically evidence; that is they are testimony that is truth or lies; and it will be very hard for any judge of human nature to think they are lies.

It is admitted that the story of the Stigmata is not a legend but can only be a lie. I mean that it is certainly not a late legendary accretion added afterwards to the fame of St. Francis; but is something that started almost immediately with his earliest biographers. It is practically necessary to suggest that it was a conspiracy; indeed there has been some disposition to put the fraud upon the unfortunate Elias, whom so many parties have been disposed to treat as a useful universal villain. It has been said, indeed, that these early biographers, St. Bonaventura and Celano and the Three Companions, though they declare that St. Francis received the mystical wounds, do not say that they themselves saw those wounds. I do not think this argument conclusive; because it only arises out of the very nature of the narrative. The Three Companions are not in any case making an affidavit; and therefore none of the admitted parts of their story are in the form of an affidavit. They are writing a chronicle of a comparatively impersonal and very objective description. They do not say, "I saw St. Francis's wounds"; they say, "St. Francis received wounds." But neither do they say, "I saw St. Francis go into the Portiuncula"; they say, "St. Francis went into the Portiuncula." But I still cannot understand why they should be trusted as eye-witnesses about the one fact and not trusted as eye-witnesses about the other. It is all of a piece; it would be a most abrupt and abnormal interruption in their way of telling the story if they suddenly began to curse and to swear, and give their names and addresses, and take their oath that they themselves saw and verified the physical facts in question. It seems to me, therefore, that this particular discussion goes back to the general question I have already mentioned; the question of why these chronicles should be credited at all, if they are credited with abounding in the incredible. But that again will probably be found to revert, in the last resort, to the mere fact that some men cannot believe in miracles because they are materialists. That is logical enough; but they are bound to deny the preternatural as much in the testimony of a modern scientific professor as in that of a medieval monkish chronicler. And there are plenty of professors for them to contradict by this time.

But whatever may be thought of such supernaturalism in the comparatively material and popular sense of supernatural acts, we shall miss the whole point of St. Francis, especially of St. Francis after Alverno, if we do not realise that he was living a supernatural life. And there is more and more of such supernaturalism in his life as he approaches towards his death. This element of the supernatural did not separate him from the natural; for it was the whole point of his position that it united him more perfectly to the natural. It did not make him dismal or dehumanised; for it was the whole meaning of his message that such mysticism makes a man cheerful and humane. But it was the whole point of his position, and it was the whole meaning of his message, that the power that did it was a supernatural power. If this simple distinction were not apparent from the whole of his life, it would be difficult for anyone to miss it in reading the account of his death.

In a sense he may be said to have wandered as a dying man, just as he had wandered as a living one. As it became more and more apparent that his health was failing, he seems to have been carried from place to place like a pageant of sickness or almost like a pageant of mortality. He went to Rieti, to Nursia, perhaps to Naples, certainly to Cortona by the lake of Perugia. But there is something profoundly pathetic, and full of great problems, in the fact that at last, as it would seem, his flame of life leapt up and his heart rejoiced when they saw afar off on the Assisian hill the solemn pillars of the Portiuncula. He who had become a vagabond for the sake of a vision, he who had denied himself all sense of place and possession, he whose whole gospel and glory it was to be homeless, received like a Parthian shot from nature, the sting of the sense of home. He also had his *maladie du clocher*, his sickness of the spire; though his spire was higher than ours. "Never," he cried with the sudden energy of strong spirits in death, "never give up this place. If you would go anywhere or make any pilgrimage, return always to your home; for this is the holy house of God." And the procession passed under the arches of his home; and he laid down on his bed and his brethren gathered round him for the last long vigil. It seems to me no moment for entering into the subsequent disputes about which successors he blessed or in what form and with what significance. In that one mighty moment he blessed us all.

After he had taken farewell of some of his nearest and especially some of his oldest friends, he was lifted at his own request off his own rude bed and laid on the bare ground; as some say clad only in a hair-shirt, as he had first gone forth into the wintry woods from the presence of his father. It was the final assertion of his great fixed idea; of praise and thanks springing to their most towering height out of nakedness and nothing. As he lay there we may be certain that his seared and blinded eyes saw nothing but their object and their origin. We may be sure that the soul, in its last inconceivable isolation, was face to face with nothing less than God Incarnate and Christ Crucified. But for the men standing around him there must have been other thoughts mingling with these; and many memories must have gathered like ghosts in the twilight, as that day wore on and that great darkness descended in which we all lost a friend.

For what lay dying there was not Dominic of the Dogs of God,[2] a leader in logical and controversial wars that could be reduced to a plan and handed on like a plan; a master of a machine of democratic discipline by which others could organise themselves. What was passing from the world was a person; a poet; an outlook on life like a light that was never after on sea or land; a thing not to be replaced or repeated while the earth endures. It has been said that there was only one Christian, who died on the cross; it is truer to say in this sense that there was only one Franciscan, whose name was Francis. Huge and happy as was the popular work he left behind him, there was something that he could not leave behind, any more than a landscape painter can leave his eyes in his will. It was an artist in life who was here called to be an artist in death; and he had a better right than Nero, his anti-type, to say *Qualis artifex pereo*.[3] For Nero's life was full of posing for the occasion like that of an actor; while the Umbrian's had a natural and continuous grace like that of an athlete. But St. Francis had better things to say and better things to think about, and his thoughts were caught upwards where we cannot follow them, in divine and dizzy heights to which death alone can lift us up.

Round about him stood the brethren in their brown habits, those that had loved him even if they afterwards disputed with each other. There was Bernard his first friend and Angelo who had served as his secretary and Elias his successor, whom tradition tried to turn into a sort of Judas, but who seems to have been little worse than an official in the wrong place. His tragedy was that he had a Franciscan habit without a Franciscan heart, or at any rate with a very

[2] The symbol for the Dominican order is the dog. A pun on *Domini canes*—hounds of the Lord.

[3] "As an actor do I die."

un-Franciscan head. But though he made a bad Franciscan, he might have made a decent Dominican. Anyhow, there is no reason to doubt that he loved Francis, for ruffians and savages did that. Anyhow he stood among the rest as the hours passed and the shadows lengthened in the house of the Portiuncula; and nobody need think so ill of him as to suppose that his thoughts were then in the tumultuous future, in the ambitions and controversies of his later years.

A man might fancy that the birds must have known when it happened; and made some motion in the evening sky. As they had once, according to the tale, scattered to the four winds of heaven in the pattern of a cross at his signal of dispersion, they might now have written in such dotted lines a more awful augury across the sky. Hidden in the woods perhaps were little cowering creatures never again to be so much noticed and understood; and it has been said that animals are sometimes conscious of things to which man their spiritual superior is for the moment blind. We do not know whether any shiver passed through all the thieves and the outcasts and the outlaws, to tell them what had happened to him who never knew the nature of scorn. But at least in the passages and porches of the Portiuncula there was a sudden stillness, where all the brown figures stood like bronze statues; for the stopping of the great heart that had not broken till it held the world.

# X

# THE TESTAMENT OF ST. FRANCIS

In one sense doubtless it is a sad irony that St. Francis, who all his life had desired all men to agree, should have died amid increasing disagreements. But we must not exaggerate this discord, as some have done, so as to turn it into a mere defeat of all his ideals. There are some who represent his work as having been merely ruined by the wickedness of the world, or what they always assume to be the even greater wickedness of the Church.

This little book is an essay on St. Francis and not on the Franciscan Order, still less on the Catholic Church or the Papacy or the policy pursued towards the extreme Franciscans or the Fraticelli. It is therefore only necessary to note in a very few words what was the general nature of the controversy that raged after the great saint's death, and to some extent troubled the last days of his life. The dominant detail was the interpretation of the vow of poverty, or the refusal of all possessions. Nobody so far as I know ever proposed to interfere with the vow of the individual friar that he would have no individual possessions. Nobody, that is, proposed to interfere with his negation of private property. But some Franciscans, invoking the authority of Francis on their side, went further than this and further I think than anybody else has ever gone. They proposed to abolish not only private property but property. That is, they refused to be corporately responsible for anything at all; for any buildings or stores or tools; they refused to own them collectively even when they used them collectively. It is perfectly true that many, especially among the first supporters of this view, were men of a splendid and selfless spirit, wholly devoted to the great saint's ideal. It is also perfectly true that the Pope and the authorities of the Church did not think this conception was a workable arrangement, and went so far in modifying it as to set aside certain clauses in the great saint's will. But it is not at all easy to see that it *was* a workable arrangement or even an arrangement at all; for it was really a refusal to arrange anything. Everybody knew of course that Franciscans were communists; but this was not so much being a communist as being an anarchist. Surely upon any argument somebody or something must be answerable for what happened to or in or concerning a number of historic edifices and ordinary goods and chattels. Many idealists of a socialistic sort, notably of the school of Mr. Shaw or Mr. Wells, have treated this dispute as if it were merely a case of the tyranny of wealthy and wicked pontiffs crushing the true Christianity of Christian Socialists. But in truth this extreme ideal was in a sense the very reverse of Socialist, or even social. Precisely the thing which these enthusiasts refused was that social ownership on which Socialism is built; what they primarily refused to do was what Socialists primarily exist to do; to own legally in their corporate capacity. Nor is it true that the tone of the Popes towards the enthusiasts was merely harsh and hostile. The Pope maintained for a long time a compromise which he had specially designed to meet their own conscientious objections; a compromise by which the Papacy itself held the property in a kind of trust for the owners who refused to touch it. The truth is that this incident shows two things which are common enough in Catholic history, but very little understood by the journalistic history of industrial civilisation. It shows that the Saints were sometimes great men when the Popes were small men. But it also shows that great men are sometimes wrong when small men are right. And it will be found, after all, very difficult for any candid and clear-headed outsider to deny that the Pope was right, when he insisted that the world was not made only for Franciscans.

For that was what was behind the quarrel. At the back of this particular practical question there was something much larger and more momentous, the stir and wind of which we can feel as we read the controversy. We might go so far as to put the ultimate truth thus. St. Francis was so great and original a man that he had something in him of what makes the founder of a religion. Many of his followers were more or less ready, in their hearts, to treat him as the founder of a religion. They were willing to let the Franciscan spirit escape from Christendom as the Christian spirit had escaped from Israel. They were willing to let it eclipse Christendom as the Christian spirit had eclipsed Israel. Francis, the fire that ran through the roads of Italy, was to be the beginning of a conflagration in which the old Christian civilisation was to be consumed. That was the point the Pope had to settle; whether Christendom should absorb Francis or Francis Christendom. And he decided rightly, apart from the duties of his place; for the Church could include all that was good in the Franciscans and the Franciscans could not include all that was good in the Church.

There is one consideration which, though sufficiently clear in the whole story, has not perhaps been sufficiently noted, especially by those who cannot see the case for a certain Catholic common sense larger even than Franciscan enthusiasm. Yet it arises out of the very merits of the man whom they so rightly admire. Francis of Assisi, as has been said again and again, was a poet; that is, he was a person who could express his personality. Now it is everywhere the mark of this sort of man that his very limitations make him larger. He is what he is, not only by what he has, but in some degree by what he has not. But the limits that make the lines of such a personal portrait cannot be made the limits of all humanity. St. Francis is a very strong example of this quality in the man of genius, that in him even what is negative is positive, because it is part of a character. An excellent example of what I mean may be found in his attitude towards learning and scholarship. He ignored and in some degree discouraged books and book-learning; and from his own point of view and that of his own work in the world he was absolutely right. The whole point of his message was to be so simple that the village idiot could understand it. The whole point of his point of view was that it looked out freshly upon a fresh world, that might have been made that morning. Save for the great primal things, the Creation and the Story of Eden, the first Christmas and the first Easter, the world had no history. But is it desired or desirable that the whole Catholic Church should have no history?

It is perhaps the chief suggestion of this book that St. Francis walked the world like the Pardon of God. I mean that his appearance marked the moment when men could be reconciled not only to God but to nature and, most difficult of all, to themselves. For it marked the moment when all the stale paganism that had poisoned the ancient world was at last worked out of the social system. He opened the gates of the Dark Ages as of a prison of purgatory, where men had cleansed themselves as hermits in the desert or heroes in the barbarian wars. It was in fact his whole function to tell men to start afresh and, in that sense, to tell them to forget. If they were to turn over a new leaf and begin a fresh page with the first large letters of the alphabet, simply drawn and brilliantly coloured in the early medieval manner, it was clearly a part of that particular childlike cheerfulness that they should paste down the old page that was all black and bloody with horrid things. For instance, I have already noted that there is not a trace in the poetry of this first Italian poet of all that pagan mythology which lingered long after paganism. The first Italian poet seems the only man in the world who has never even heard of Virgil. This was exactly right for the special sense in which he is the first Italian poet. It is quite right that he should call a nightingale a nightingale, and not have its song spoilt or saddened by the terrible tales of Itylus or Procne.[1] In short, it is really quite right and quite desirable that St. Francis should never have heard of Virgil. But do we really desire that Dante should never have heard of Virgil? Do we really desire that Dante should never have read any pagan mythology? It has been truly said that the use that Dante makes of such fables is altogether part of a deeper orthodoxy; that his huge heathen fragments, his gigantic figures of Minos or of Charon, only give a hint of some enormous natural religion behind all history and from the first foreshadowing the Faith. It is well to have the Sybil as well as David in the Dies Irae. That St. Francis would have burned all the leaves of all the books of the Sybil, in exchange for one fresh leaf from the nearest tree, is perfectly true; and perfectly proper to St. Francis. But it is good to have the Dies Irae as well as the Canticle of the Sun.

By this thesis, in short, the coming of St. Francis was like the birth of a child in a dark house, lifting its doom; a child that grows up unconscious of the tragedy and triumphs over it by his innocence. In him it is necessarily not only innocence but ignorance. It is the essence of the story that *he* should pluck at the green grass without knowing it grows over a murdered man or climb the apple-tree without knowing it was the gibbet of a suicide. It was such an amnesty and reconciliation that the freshness of the Franciscan spirit brought to all the world. But it does not follow that it ought to impose its ignorance on all the world. And I think it would

[1] Procne cooked her son Itylus and served him to her husband Tereus for dinner. Procne was changed into a swallow.

have tried to impose it on all the world. For some Franciscans it would have seemed right that Franciscan poetry should expel Benedictine prose. For the symbolic child it was quite rational. It was right enough that for such a child the world should be a large new nursery with blank white-washed walls, on which he could draw his own pictures in chalk in the childish fashion, crude in outline and gay in colour; the beginnings of all our art. It was right enough that to him such a nursery should seem the most magnificent mansion of the imagination of man. But in the Church of God are many mansions.

Every heresy has been an effort to narrow the Church. If the Franciscan movement had turned into a new religion, it would after all have been a narrow religion. In so far as it did turn here and there into a heresy, it was a narrow heresy. It did what heresy always does; it set the mood against the mind. The mood was indeed originally the good and glorious mood of the great St. Francis, but it was not the whole mind of God or even of man. And it is a fact that the mood itself degenerated, as the mood turned into a monomania. A sect that came to be called the Fraticelli declared themselves the true sons of St. Francis and broke away from the compromises of Rome in favour of what they would have called the complete programme of Assisi. In a very little while these loose Franciscans began to look as ferocious as Flagellants. They launched new and violent vetoes; they denounced marriage; that is, they denounced mankind. In the name of the most human of saints they declared war upon humanity. They did not perish particularly through being persecuted; many of them were eventually persuaded; and the unpersuadable rump of them that remained remained without producing anything in the least calculated to remind anybody of the real St. Francis. What was the matter with these people was that they were mystics; mystics and nothing else but mystics;

mystics and not Catholics; mystics and not Christians; mystics and not men. They rotted away because, in the most exact sense, they would not listen to reason. And St. Francis, however wild and romantic his gyrations might appear to many, always hung on to reason by one invisible and indestructible hair.

The great saint was sane; and with the very sound of the word sanity, as at a deeper chord struck upon a harp, we come back to something that was indeed deeper than everything about him that seemed an almost elvish eccentricity. He was not a mere eccentric because he was always turning towards the centre and heart of the maze; he took the queerest and most zigzag short cuts through the wood, but he was always going home. He was not only far too humble to be an heresiarch, but he was far too human to desire to be an extremist, in the sense of an exile at the ends of the earth. The sense of humour which salts all the stories of his escapades alone prevented him from ever hardening into the solemnity of sectarian sell-righteousness. He was by nature ready to admit that he was wrong; and if his followers had on some practical points to admit that he was wrong, they only admitted that he was wrong in order to prove that he was right. For it is they, his real followers, who have really proved that he was right and even in transcending some of his negations have triumphantly extended and interpreted his truth. The Franciscan order did not fossilise or break off short like something of which the true purpose has been frustrated by official tyranny or internal treason. It was this, the central and orthodox trunk of it, that afterwards bore fruit for the world. It counted among its sons Bonaventura the great mystic and Bernardino the popular preacher, who filled Italy with the very beatific buffooneries of a Jongleur de Dieu. It counted Raymond Lully with his strange learning and his large and daring plans for the conversion of the world; a man intensely individual exactly as St. Francis was intensely individual. It counted Roger Bacon, the first naturalist whose experiments with light and water had all the luminous quaintness that belongs to the beginnings of natural history; and whom even the most material scientists have hailed as a father of science. It is not merely true that these were great men who did great work for the world; it is also true that they were a certain kind of men keeping the spirit and savour of a certain kind of man, that we can recognise in them a taste and tang of audacity and simplicity, and know them for the sons of St. Francis.

For that is the full and final spirit in which we should turn to St. Francis; in the spirit of thanks for what he has done. He was above all things a great giver; and he cared chiefly for the best kind of giving which is called thanksgiving. If another great man wrote a grammar of assent, he may well be said to have written a grammar of acceptance; a grammar of gratitude. He understood down to its very depths the theory of thanks; and its depths are a bottomless abyss. He knew that the praise of God stands on its strongest ground when it stands on nothing. He knew that we can best measure the towering miracle of the mere fact of existence if we realise that but for some strange mercy we should not even exist. And something of that larger truth is repeated in a lesser form in our own relations with so mighty a maker of history. He also is a giver of things we could not have even thought of for ourselves; he also is too great for anything but gratitude. From him came a whole awakening of the world and a dawn in which all shapes and colours could be seen anew. The mighty men of genius who made the Christian civilisation that we know appear in history almost as his servants and imitators. Before Dante was, he had given poetry to Italy; before St. Louis ruled, he had risen as the tribune of the poor; and before Giotto had painted the pictures, he had enacted the scenes. That great painter who began the whole human inspiration of European painting had himself gone to St. Francis to be inspired. It is said that when St. Francis staged in his own simple fashion a Nativity Play of Bethlehem, with kings and angels in the stiff and gay medieval garments and the golden wigs that stood for haloes, a miracle was wrought full of the Franciscan glory. The Holy Child was a wooden doll or bambino, and it was said that he embraced it and that the image came to life in his arms. He assuredly was not thinking of lesser things; but we may at least say that one thing came to life in his arms; and that was the thing that we call the drama. Save for his intense individual love of song, he did not perhaps himself embody this spirit in any of these arts. He was the spirit that was embodied. He was the spiritual essence and substance that walked the world, before anyone had seen these things in visible forms derived from it: a wandering fire as if from nowhere, at which men more material could light both torches and tapers. He was the soul of medieval civilisation before it even found a body. Another and quite different stream of spiritual inspiration derives largely from him; all that reforming energy of medieval and modern times that goes to the burden of *Deus est Deus Pauperum.*[2] His abstract ardour for human beings was in a multitude of just medieval laws against the pride and cruelty of riches; it is to-day behind much that is loosely called Christian Socialist and can more correctly be called Catholic Democrat. Neither on the artistic nor the social side would anybody pretend that these things would not have existed without him; yet it is strictly true to say that we cannot now imagine them without him; since he has lived and changed the world.

[2] "God is the God of the poor."

And something of that sense of impotence which was more than half his power will descend on anyone who knows what that inspiration has been in history, and can only record it in a series of straggling and meagre sentences. He will know something of what St. Francis meant by the great and good debt that cannot be paid. He will feel at once the desire to have done infinitely more and the futility of having done anything. He will know what it is to stand under such a deluge of a dead man's marvels, and have nothing in return to establish against it; to have nothing to set up under the overhanging, overwhelming arches of such a temple of time and eternity, but this brief candle burnt out so quickly before his shrine.